STATISTICS WITH R FOR MACHINE LEARNING

Volume 1

Data Preparation and Splitting with R for Machine Learning

Mohsen Nady

ARCLER PRESS

www.arclerpress.com

Statistics with R for Machine Learning

Volume 1 Data Preparation and Splitting with R for Machine Learning

Mohsen Nady

Arcler Press
4164 Lakeshore Road
Burlington, ON L7L 1A4
Canada
www.arclerpress.com
Email: orders@arclereducation.com

ISBN: 978-1-77956-470-2 (Hardcover)

ABOUT THE AUTHOR

Mohsen Nady is a pharmacist with a M.D. in Microbiology and a Diploma in Industrial Pharmacy. Besides, Mohsen has more than 10 years of experience in Statistics and Data Analytics. Mohsen has applied his skills to different projects related to Genomics, Microbiology, Biostatistics, Six Sigma, Data Analytics, Data Visualization, Building Apps, Geography, Market Analysis, Business Analysis, Machine Learning, etc. Mohsen also published his thesis in a high-impact journal that attracted many citations, where all the statistical analyses were performed by him in addition to the methodological part. Furthermore, Mohsen has earned different certificates, from top universities (Harvard, Johns Hopkins, Denmark, etc) in Statistics, Data Analytics, Data Visualization, and Machine Learning that highlight his outstanding diverse skills.

TABLE OF CONTENTS

LIST OF TABLES

PREFACE

This book, *Statistics with R for Machine Learning*, covers the introductory steps of building machine learning models using the R programming language. Machine learning models are essential for identifying patterns in data or making predictions about future outcomes. Today, nearly all industries—including business, healthcare, finance, and retail—have been transformed by the machine learning revolution.

The book is organized into three chapters that outline the initial steps of creating machine learning models using R. Chapter 1 introduces key definitions and the main types of machine learning models. It uses small, cleaned datasets to explain the two primary types of models: regression and classification. Linear regression is presented as an example of a regression model for numerical outcomes, while decision trees are used as an example of a classification model for categorical outcomes. Data are not always clean and ready for machine learning. Therefore, Chapter 2 is fully dedicated to the data cleaning steps necessary to prepare datasets for modeling. It features two survey datasets that are cleaned extensively and later used in the next Chapter 3. In Chapters 3, various techniques for splitting data into training and testing subsets are discussed. Chapter 3 explores various approaches of data splitting and highlight their importance in evaluating model performance on unseen, future data.

I hope this book, with its example codes for building models in R, serves as a valuable resource for your first steps into the world of machine learning.

–Author

Chapter 1

Introduction

Contents

1.1. DATA USED IN THIS CHAPTER

1.1.1. Marketing Data

This data contains the impact of three advertising media (YouTube, Facebook, and newspaper) on sales. The column values are the advertising budget or sales in thousands of dollars. The advertising experiment has been repeated 200 times so we have 200 rows in this data. The data is part of the datarium package under the name "marketing." First, we load the datarium package using the library function then, we load the marketing data using the data function.

We also load the tidyverse package into our R session because it contains many useful packages for data analysis, and the flextable package to make the different code outputs into readable tables.

```
library(datarium)
data("marketing")
library(tidyverse)
library(flextable)
```

To see this data structure, we use the glimpse function.

```
glimpse(marketing)
## Rows: 200
## Columns: 4
## $ YouTube <dbl> 276.12, 53.40, 20.64, 181.80, 216.96, 10.44, 69.00, 144.24, …
## $ Facebook <dbl> 45.36, 47.16, 55.08, 49.56, 12.96, 58.68, 39.36, 23.52, 2.52…
## $ newspaper <dbl> 83.04, 54.12, 83.16, 70.20, 70.08, 90.00, 28.20, 13.92, 1.20…
## $ sales <dbl> 26.52, 12.48, 11.16, 22.20, 15.48, 8.64, 14.16, 15.84, 5.76,…
```

The glimpse function gives the number of rows, the number of columns, the column names with the prefix "$," the column classes between "<>" parentheses, and the first values of every column.

The data contains 200 rows (200 advertising experiments) and 4 columns:

1. **YouTube:** A double (dbl) or numeric column with decimals for advertising budget using YouTube. The first column values are 276.12, 53.40, 20.64, 181.80, etc.

2. **Facebook:** A double or numeric column with decimals for advertising budget using Facebook. The first column values are 45.36, 47.16, 55.08, 49.56, etc.
3. **Newspaper:** A double or numeric column with decimals for advertising budget using newspaper. The first column values are 83.04, 54.12, 83.16, 70.20, 70.08, etc.
4. **Sales:** A double or numeric column with decimals for sales in thousands of dollars. The first column values are 26.52, 12.48, 11.16, 22.20, 15.48, etc.

1.1.2. Edgar Anderson's Iris Data

The iris data gives the measurements in centimeters of sepal length, sepal width, petal length, and petal width for 50 flowers from each of the 3 species of iris. The species are *Iris setosa*, *versicolor*, and *virginica*. The data is part of the datasets package which is part of core R programming under the name "iris" so to load this data into our R session, we will only load this data using the data function. Then, to see its structure, we will use the glimpse function.

```
data("iris")
glimpse(iris)
## Rows: 150
## Columns: 5
## $ Sepal.Length <dbl> 5.1, 4.9, 4.7, 4.6, 5.0, 5.4, 4.6, 5.0,
4.4, 4.9, 5.4, 4.…
## $ Sepal.Width <dbl> 3.5, 3.0, 3.2, 3.1, 3.6, 3.9, 3.4, 3.4,
2.9, 3.1, 3.7, 3.…
## $ Petal.Length <dbl> 1.4, 1.4, 1.3, 1.5, 1.4, 1.7, 1.4, 1.5,
1.4, 1.5, 1.5, 1.…
## $ Petal.Width <dbl> 0.2, 0.2, 0.2, 0.2, 0.2, 0.4, 0.3, 0.2,
0.2, 0.1, 0.2, 0.…
## $ Species <fct> setosa, setosa, setosa, setosa, setosa,
setosa, setosa, s…
```

The data contains 150 rows (150 flowers) and 5 columns:

1. **Sepal.Length:** A numeric (dbl) column with decimals for the sepal length. The first column values are 5.1, 4.9, 4.7, 4.6, 5.0, etc.
2. **Sepal.Width:** A numeric column with decimals for the sepal width. The first column values are 3.5, 3.0, 3.2, 3.1, 3.6, 3.9, etc.

3. **Petal.Length:** A numeric column with decimals for the petal length. The first column values are 1.4, 1.4, 1.3, 1.5, 1.4, 1.7, 1.4, etc.
4. **Petal.Width:** A numeric column with decimals for the petal width. The first column values are 0.2, 0.2, 0.2, 0.2, 0.2, 0.4, etc.
5. **Species:** A factor (fct) or categorical column for the species. The species are *Iris setosa*, *versicolor*, and *virginica* as we said before. The first column values are setosa, setosa, setosa, setosa, setosa, setosa, etc.

1.2. DEFINITIONS

According to Arthur Samuel 1959, Machine learning is the field of study that gives computers the ability to learn without being explicitly programmed.

According to Tom Mitchell 1997, Machine learning is a computer program that learns from experience E on some task T with performance measure P if its performance P on task T improves with experience E.

In the marketing data, the computer program learns the sales according to the budget in the 3 advertising media (YouTube, Facebook, and newspaper), and based on that learns how to better predict future sales.

In the iris data, the computer program learns the species according to the value of the 4 columns (sepal length, sepal width, petal length, and petal width), and based on that learns how to better predict the species of any observed new flower.

1.3. TYPES OF MACHINE LEARNING MODELS

Most machine learning models fall into one of two categories: supervised or unsupervised models depending on the data type we have.

1.3.1. Supervised Learning

Where each observation of our data contains predictor measurements and a response measurement. We fit a supervised model that relates the response or outcome to the predictors, with one of 2 goals:

- *Prediction* or accurately predicting the response for future observations.
- *Inference* or understanding of the relationship between the response and the predictors.

Supervised models can be classified into two main groups:

- *Regression models* when we have a continuous or numerical outcome.
- *Classification models* when we have a categorical outcome.

1.3.1.1. Regression Models

For example, in the marketing data, we want to predict sales based on the budget in of three advertising media (YouTube, Facebook, and newspaper). We fit a multiple linear model "mod" using the lm function with the arguments:

- formula = sales ~ YouTube+Facebook + newspaper which means we want to predict the sales column using the values in the YouTube, Facebook, and newspaper columns.
- data = marketing which is the data frame containing the outcome column (sales) and the predictor columns (YouTube, Facebook, and newspaper).

```
mod<-lm(formula = sales ~ YouTube+Facebook + newspaper,
data = marketing)
```

Then, we create a new data frame (marketing_pred) by adding a new column (pred) to the marketing data using the function mutate with the argument pred = predict(mod) to add the "pred" column that contains the results of the predict function on the "mod" model.

Then, we use the glimpse function on the marketing_pred to see its structure.

```
marketing_pred<-marketing %>% mutate(pred = predict(mod))
glimpse(marketing_pred)
## Rows: 200
## Columns: 5
## $ YouTube <dbl> 276.12, 53.40, 20.64, 181.80, 216.96, 10.44,
69.00, 144.24, …
## $ Facebook <dbl> 45.36, 47.16, 55.08, 49.56, 12.96, 58.68,
39.36, 23.52, 2.52…
## $ newspaper <dbl> 83.04, 54.12, 83.16, 70.20, 70.08, 90.00,
28.20, 13.92, 1.20…
## $ sales <dbl> 26.52, 12.48, 11.16, 22.20, 15.48, 8.64, 14.16,
15.84, 5.76,…
## $ pred <dbl> 24.628769, 14.805426, 14.769205, 21.117395,
15.826406, 14.97…
```

The data contains 200 rows and 5 columns instead of 4. The new "pred" column is a numeric column with decimals.

1.3.1.2. Assess the Regression Model Performance

We use the Root Mean Squared Error (RMSE) which measures the model prediction error.

The formula for calculating RMSE is:

where; *pred* is the predicted outcome value; *actual* is the actual outcome value; *n* is the number of observations or rows in the data; is the sum all squared differences between the predicted and actual values from i = 1 or first row till n or last row.

- The residual error = predicted value – actual value.
- The lower RMSE, the better our model. RMSE has the same scale as the outcome column.

To calculate the RMSE of the "mod" model, we use the following functions:

- The select function to select the important 2 columns, the sales column containing the actual sales values and the pred column containing the predicted sales values.
- The head function to see the first six values of actual and predicted sales values.
- The flextable function converts the resulting data frame to a readable table. We use the argument cwidth = 1.5 to make the columns a bit wider.
- The theme_box function to add lines to all cells of the resulting table.
- The set_caption function with the caption argument to add a caption to the table.

```
marketing_pred %>% select(sales, pred) %>% head() %>%
flextable(cwidth = 1.5) %>% theme_box() %>%
set_caption(caption = "The first six values of the actual sales (sales) and predicted sales (pred) from the regression model")
```

Table 1.1. The First Six Values of the Actual Sales (Sales) and Predicted Sales (Pred) from the Regression Model

sales	pred
26.52	24.62877
12.48	14.80543
11.16	14.76920

22.20	21.11740
15.48	15.82641
8.64	14.97402

We see that:

- The 1st actual sales value was 26.52, while the predicted value was 24.62877.
- The 2nd actual sales value was 12.48, while the predicted value was 14.80543.
- The 3rd actual sales value was 11.16, while the predicted value was 14.76920.
- The 4th actual sales value was 22.20, while the predicted value was 21.11740.
- The 5th actual sales value was 15.48, while the predicted value was 15.82641.
- The 6th actual sales value was 8.64, while the predicted value was 14.97402.

Again, we use the mutate function to add 2 new columns:

- The "resid_err" column contains the residual error by subtracting the actual value from the predicted value.
- The "row_no" column contains the row number by using the row_number function. Remember that we have 200 rows in the marketing data.

Finally, we use the head, flextable, theme_box, set_caption functions as before.

```
marketing_pred %>% select(sales, pred) %>%
mutate(resid_err = pred-sales, row_no = row_number()) %>%
head() %>%
flextable(cwidth = 1.5) %>% theme_box() %>%
set_caption(caption = "The first six values of the actual sales (sales), predicted sales (pred), residual error (resid_err) of the 1st 6 rows in the marketing data")
```

Table 1.2. The First Six Values of the Actual Sales (Sales), Predicted Sales (Pred), Residual Error (resid_err) of the 1st 6 Rows in the Marketing Data

sales	pred	resid_err	row_no
26.52	24.62877	−1.8912307	1
12.48	14.80543	2.3254258	2

11.16	14.76920	3.6092049	3
22.20	21.11740	–1.0826046	4
15.48	15.82641	0.3464062	5
8.64	14.97402	6.3340172	6

We see that:

- The residual error is negative in the 1st and 4th rows because the predicted value is smaller than the actual value.
- The residual error is positive in the 2nd, 3rd, 5th, and 6th rows because the predicted value is larger than the actual value.

To see the top 6 highest absolute residual errors, we use the following functions after the mutate function:

- The abs function with the resid_err argument to extract the absolute value from each residual error.
- The arrange and desc functions surrounding the abs function arrange the absolute values of the residual errors in descending order.
- The head function to extract the top 6 highest absolute values.

```
marketing_pred %>% select(sales, pred) %>%
mutate(resid_err = pred-sales, row_no = row_number()) %>%
arrange(desc(abs(resid_err))) %>%
head() %>%
flextable(cwidth = 1.5) %>% theme_box() %>%
set_caption(caption = "The top highest six absolute residual error values in the marketing data")
```

Table 1.3. The Top Highest Six Absolute Residual Error Values in the Marketing Data

sales	pred	resid_err	row_no
1.92	12.51322	10.593225	131
8.64	14.97402	6.334017	6
14.16	19.21320	5.053197	179
15.36	20.40819	5.048191	36
7.92	12.69261	4.772609	127
14.40	18.73205	4.332046	26

We see that:

- Row number 131 has the highest error of 10.593225 because the predicted value is 12.51322 and the actual value is 1.92 only.

- Row number 6 has the 2nd highest error of 6.334017 because the predicted value is 14.97402 and the actual value is 8.64 only.
- Row number 179 has the 3rd highest error of 5.053197 because the predicted value is 19.21320 and the actual value is 14.16 and so on.

To see the lowest absolute errors, we delete the desc function from the above functions.

```
marketing_pred %>% select(sales, pred) %>%
mutate(resid_err = pred-sales, row_no = row_number()) %>%
arrange(abs(resid_err)) %>%
head() %>%
flextable(cwidth = 1.5) %>% theme_box() %>%
set_caption(caption = "The top lowest six absolute residual error values in the marketing data")
```

Table 1.4. The Top Lowest Six Absolute Residual Error Values in the Marketing Data

sales	pred	resid_err	row_no
9.12	9.129231	0.009230854	173
18.00	17.987417	–0.012582854	27
15.36	15.343105	–0.016895020	198
18.24	18.217689	–0.022310532	86
17.88	17.936138	0.056138469	163
24.96	25.021502	0.061502382	138

We see that:

- No predicted value perfectly equals the actual sales value with a residual error of 0.
- Row number 173 has the lowest error of 0.009230854 because the predicted value is 9.129231 and the actual value is 9.12 only.
- Row number 27 has the 2nd lowest absolute error of –0.012582854 because the predicted value is 17.987417 and the actual value is 18.00, and so on.

Then, we use the mutate function again to create the squared error column "sq_err" by raising the residual error to the power of 2.

```
marketing_pred %>% select(sales, pred) %>%
mutate(resid_err = pred-sales, row_no = row_number()) %>%
```

```
mutate(sq_err = resid_err^2) %>%
head() %>%
flextable(cwidth = 1.5) %>% theme_box() %>%
set_caption(caption = "The first six values of the actual sales, predicted sales, residual error, and squared error of the 1st 6 rows in the marketing data")
```

Table 1.5. The First Six Values of the Actual Sales, Predicted Sales, Residual Error, and Squared Error of the 1st 6 Rows in the Marketing Data

sales	pred	resid_err	row_no	sq_err
26.52	24.62877	−1.8912307	1	3.5767536
12.48	14.80543	2.3254258	2	5.4076051
11.16	14.76920	3.6092049	3	13.0263603
22.20	21.11740	−1.0826046	4	1.1720327
15.48	15.82641	0.3464062	5	0.1199973
8.64	14.97402	6.3340172	6	40.1197734

Then, we can use the summarize function to create a column "mean_sq_err" that contains the mean of the squared error by using the mean function.

```
marketing_pred %>% select(sales, pred) %>%
mutate(resid_err = pred-sales, row_no = row_number()) %>%
mutate(sq_err = resid_err^2) %>%
summarise(mean_sq_err = mean(sq_err))
## mean_sq_err
## 1 4.009142
```

The mean squared error = 4.009142.

Alternatively, we can use the summarize function to create a column "root_mean_sq_err" that contains the root of the mean squared error (RMSE) by using the sqrt and mean functions.

```
marketing_pred %>% select(sales, pred) %>%
mutate(resid_err = pred-sales, row_no = row_number()) %>%
mutate(sq_err = resid_err^2) %>%
summarise(root_mean_sq_err = sqrt(mean(sq_err)))
## root_mean_sq_err
## 1 2.002284
```

RMSE for this model = 2.002284.

Another way for calculating RMSE is using the rmse function from the modelr package with the arguments:

- model = mod which is the multiple linear model.
- data = marketing which is the data used to create that model and contains the predictor columns (YouTube, Facebook, newspaper) and the outcome column (sales).

Because we are using functions from the modelr package, so we must load it first using the library function.

```
library(modelr)
rmse(model = mod, data = marketing)
## [1] 2.002284
```

The RMSE value is the same as that calculated before and equals 2.002284. So, the mean prediction error from this model is about 2000 dollars (the same unit of the sales outcome).

1.3.1.3. Plot the Regression Model Results

We can plot the actual sales on the x-axis and the predicted sales on the y-axis by using the functions:

- The ggplot function with the arguments, aes(x = sales, y = pred), to plot actual sales on the x-axis and the predicted sales on the y-axis.
- The geom_point function to plot a scatter plot.
- The geom_abline function plots a diagonal perfect line that corresponds to the same value of actual sales and predicted sales. We use the arguments, linetype = "dashed" so the line is dashed, size = 1 to increase the line size, and color = "red" to make the line in red color.
- The labs function with the arguments, title to add a plot title, x to add an x-axis title, and y to add a y-axis title.
- The theme_light to add a light theme and remove the grey background and the black background lines from the default ggplot.
- The theme function with the plot.title argument and using the element_text function with the argument hjust = 0.5 to place the plot title at the top center of the plot.

All these functions were applied in sequence using the "%>%" operator on the marketing_pred data and then using the "+" operator after the ggplot function.

```
marketing_pred %>% ggplot(aes(x = sales, y = pred))+ geom_point()+
geom_abline(linetype = "dashed", size = 1,
color = "red")+
labs(title = "Scatter plot of actual and predicted sales from a
linear model \n with a diagonal perfect line",
x = "Actual sales", y = "Predicted sales")+
theme_light()+
theme(plot.title = element_text(hjust = 0.5))
```

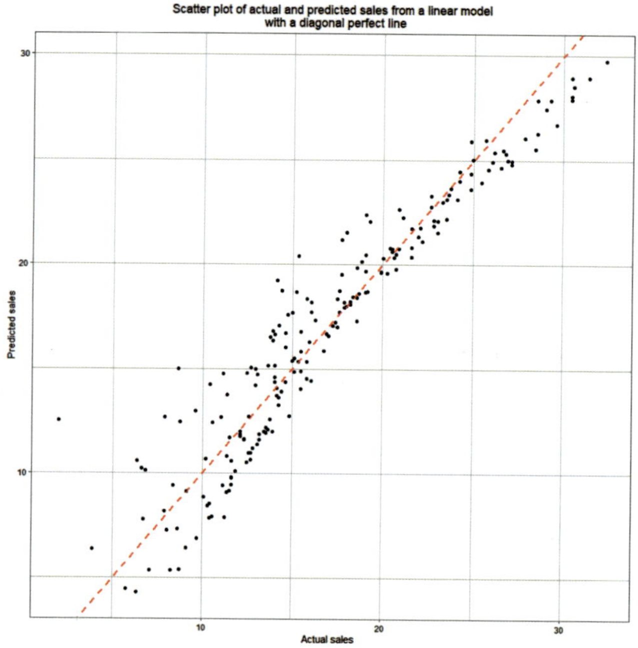

We have 2 types of points:

- Points above the perfect diagonal line indicate that the predicted value is larger than the actual value.
- Points below the perfect diagonal line indicate that the predicted value is smaller than the actual value.

1.3.1.4. Classification Models

For example, in the iris data, we want to predict the flower species based on the values of the sepal length, sepal width, petal length, and petal width.

We fit a decision tree model "mod_tree" using the rpart function, from the rpart package, with the arguments:

- formula = Species ~ Sepal.Length+Sepal.Width+Petal.Length+Petal.Width which means we want to predict the species using the values in the sepal length, sepal width, petal length, and petal width columns.
- data = iris which is the data frame containing the outcome column (Species) and the predictor columns (sepal length, sepal width, petal length, and petal width).

Because we are using functions from the rpart package, so we must load it first using the library function.

```
library(rpart)
mod_tree<-rpart(formula = Species ~ Sepal.Length+Sepal.
Width+Petal.Length+Petal.Width,
data = iris)
```

Then, we create a new data frame (iris_pred) by adding a new column (pred) to the iris data using the function mutate with the argument pred = predict(mod_tree) to add the "pred" column that contains the results of predict function on the "mod_tree" model. We use the argument type = "class" to get the predicted species class for each row of our data.

Finally, we use the glimpse function on the iris_pred to see its structure.

```
iris_pred<-iris %>% mutate(pred = predict(mod_tree, type =
"class"))
glimpse(iris_pred)
## Rows: 150
## Columns: 6
## $ Sepal.Length <dbl> 5.1, 4.9, 4.7, 4.6, 5.0, 5.4, 4.6, 5.0,
4.4, 4.9, 5.4, 4.…
## $ Sepal.Width <dbl> 3.5, 3.0, 3.2, 3.1, 3.6, 3.9, 3.4, 3.4,
2.9, 3.1, 3.7, 3.…
## $ Petal.Length <dbl> 1.4, 1.4, 1.3, 1.5, 1.4, 1.7, 1.4, 1.5,
1.4, 1.5, 1.5, 1.…
## $ Petal.Width <dbl> 0.2, 0.2, 0.2, 0.2, 0.2, 0.4, 0.3, 0.2,
0.2, 0.1, 0.2, 0.…
## $ Species <fct> setosa, setosa, setosa, setosa, setosa,
setosa, setosa, s…
## $ pred <fct> setosa, setosa, setosa, setosa, setosa, setosa,
setosa, s…
```

The data contains 150 rows and 6 columns instead of 5. The new "pred" column is a factor column with 3 species *setosa*, *versicolor*, and *virginica* as the Species column.

1.3.1.5. Assess the Classification Model Performance

The performance of any classification model is assessed through its accuracy. The accuracy is the proportion of true predictions to all rows or observations in the data.

We can use the count function on the iris_pred data frame with Species and pred arguments to see how many actual species classes are predicted correctly.

```
iris_pred %>%
count(Species, pred) %>% flextable(cwidth = 1.5) %>% theme_box()
%>%
set_caption(caption = "The actual species and predicted species
using mod_tree model")
```

Table 1.6. The Actual Species and Predicted Species Using mod_tree Model

Species	pred	n
setosa	setosa	50
versicolor	versicolor	49
versicolor	virginica	1
virginica	versicolor	5
virginica	virginica	45

We see that:

- There are 50 setosa flowers (Species value of "setosa") that are predicted correctly as setosa (pred value of "setosa").
- There are 49 versicolor flowers (Species value of "versicolor") that are predicted correctly as versicolor (pred value of "versicolor").
- There is 1 versicolor flower (Species value of "versicolor") that is predicted incorrectly as virginica (pred value of "virginica").
- There are 5 virginica flowers (Species value of "virginica") that are predicted incorrectly as versicolor (pred value of "versicolor").
- There are 45 virginica flowers (Species value of "virginica") that are predicted correctly as virginica (pred value of "virginica").
- The accuracy of the tree model is the proportion of data points that are predicted correctly = (50 + 49 + 45)/(50 + 49 + 1 + 5 + 45)= (50 + 49 + 45)/150 = 0.96 or 96%.

1.3.1.6. Plot the Classification Model Results

To plot the classification model results, we use the confusion matrix. The confusion matrix is just a cross-tabulation of actual and predicted classes we see before using the count function.

We will use the conf_mat function, from the yardstick package, to create the confusion matrix using the Species and pred columns.

The conf_mat function requires the following arguments:

- truth = Species which is the column containing the actual or true species of our flowers.
- estimate = pred which is the column containing the predicted species.

Because we use a function from the yardstick package so we must load it first into our R session using the library function.

```
library(yardstick)
iris_pred %>%
conf_mat(truth = Species, estimate = pred)
## Truth
## Prediction setosa versicolor virginica
## setosa 50 0 0
## versicolor 0 49 5
## virginica 0 1 45
```

We get the same numbers as above:

- The true species are in columns and the predicted species are in rows.
- There are 50 setosa flowers that are predicted correctly as setosa.
- There are 49 versicolor flowers that are predicted correctly as versicolor.
- There is 1 versicolor flower that is predicted incorrectly as virginica.
- There are 5 virginica flowers that are predicted incorrectly as versicolor.
- There are 45 virginica flowers that are predicted correctly as virginica.

The confusion matrix can be plotted as a heatmap using the autoplot function with type = "heatmap" argument. Then, we use the labs and theme function as before,

```
iris_pred %>% conf_mat(truth = Species, estimate = pred) %>%
autoplot(type = "heatmap")+
labs(title = "The confusion matrix of applying the decision tree model on the iris data")+
theme(plot.title = element_text(hjust = 0.5))
```

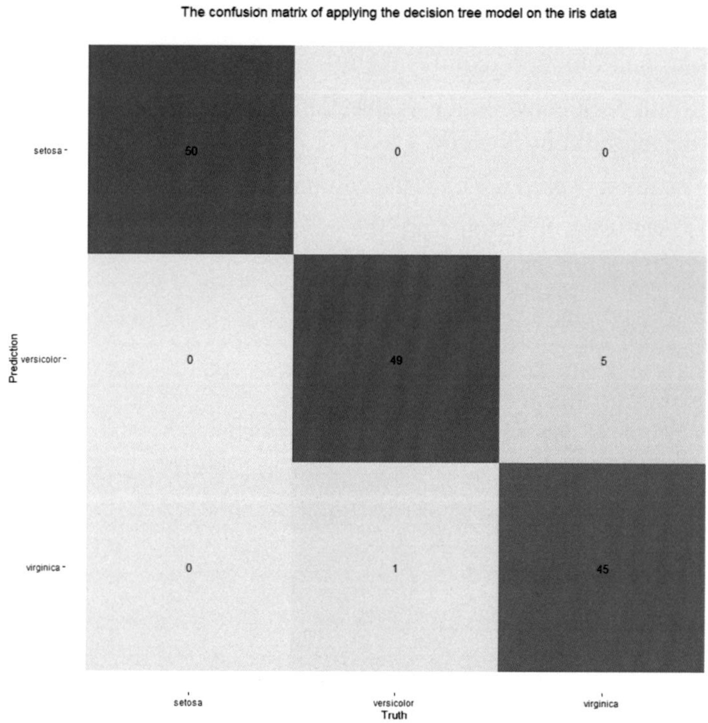

1.3.2. Unsupervised Learning

Unsupervised learning is a more challenging situation in which each observation of our data contains predictor measurements and no response measurements.

This situation is called unsupervised because we lack a response variable that can supervise our analysis.

The most famous unsupervised learning methods include:

- *Principal component analysis* in which we summarize the most important information as fewer principal components that contained most of the variation of many predictors.
- *Cluster analysis* in which we group the observations or rows with similar predictor measurements according to specific criteria.

In this book, we focus on supervised models only.

1.4. GENERAL STEPS OF SUPERVISED MACHINE LEARNING MODELS

The general steps of supervised models are:

1. Clean the raw data, for example, correcting strange values or checking missing. This step will be discussed in Chapter 2 of this book.
2. Splitting data to train and test data. There are many approaches for splitting and also for creating different resamples (versions) of training data. This step will be discussed in Chapters 3,4, and 5 of this book.
3. Univariate and bivariate analysis. Univariate analysis explores every column in the data separately using summary statistics and plots, while bivariate analysis examines the relation between every predictor and the outcome of interest using summary statistics and plots.
4. Clean the data with some preprocessing steps. The preprocessing steps can include imputing missing values, transformation, dummification, etc.
5. Model fitting.
6. Model comparison.

Chapter 2

Clean the Raw Data

Contents

2.1. DATA USED IN THIS CHAPTER

2.1.1. General Social Survey Data

The general social survey data frame is part of the forcats package (which is part of the tidyverse package) under the name "gss_cat." The gss_cat data contains a sample of categorical and numerical variables from the General Social Survey of about 21,000 participants.

To load this data into our R session, we will load the tidyverse package using the library function then, we load this data using the data function.

We also load the flextable package to convert the different code outputs into readable tables.

```
library(tidyverse)
data("gss_cat")
library(flextable)
```

2.1.2. The Behavioral Risk Factor Surveillance System (BRFSS) Survey Data

The data is a subset of the 2009 survey from BRFSS, an ongoing data collection program designed to measure behavioral risk factors for the adult population (18 years of age or older) living in households.

The data is part of the naniar package under the name "riskfactors" so to load this data, we load the naniar package first using the library function, then we load this data using the data function.

```
library(naniar)
data("riskfactors")
```

2.2. DATA STRUCTURE

2.2.1. Data Structure of General Social Survey Data

We can see the data structure of general social survey data by using the glimpse function.

```
glimpse(gss_cat)
## Rows: 21,483
## Columns: 9
```

```
## $ year <int> 2000, 2000, 2000, 2000, 2000, 2000, 2000, 2000, 2000, 2000, 20…
## $ marital <fct> Never married, Divorced, Widowed, Never married, Divorced, Mar…
## $ age <int> 26, 48, 67, 39, 25, 25, 36, 44, 44, 47, 53, 52, 52, 51, 52, 40…
## $ race <fct> White, White, White, White, White, White, White, White, White,…
## $ rincome <fct> $8000 to 9999, $8000 to 9999, Not applicable, Not applicable, …
## $ partyid <fct> "Ind,near rep", "Not str republican", "Independent", "Ind,near…
## $ relig <fct> Protestant, Protestant, Protestant, Orthodox-christian, None, …
## $ denom <fct> "Southern baptist", "Baptist-dk which", "No denomination", "No…
## $ tvhours <int> 12, NA, 2, 4, 1, NA, 3, NA, 0, 3, 2, NA, 1, NA, 1, 7, NA, 3, 3…
```

The data contains 21,483 rows (respondents) and 9 columns:

1. **Year:** An integer (int) column containing the year of the survey.
2. **Marital:** A factor (fct) or categorical column containing the respondent's marital status.
3. **Age:** An integer column containing the respondent's age.
4. **Race:** A factor or categorical column containing the participant's race.
5. **Rincome:** A factor or categorical column containing the respondent's reported income category.
6. **Partyid:** A factor or categorical column containing the respondent's party affiliation.
7. **Relig:** A factor or categorical column containing the participant's religion.
8. **Denom:** A factor or categorical column containing the participant's denomination.
9. **Tvhours:** An integer column containing the participant's hours per day watching TV.

2.2.2. Data Structure of BRFSS Survey Data

We use the glimpse function too.

```
glimpse(riskfactors)
## Rows: 245
## Columns: 34
## $ state <fct> 26, 40, 72, 42, 32, 19, 45, 56, 18, 8, 55, 48, 26, 12…
## $ sex <fct> Female, Female, Female, Male, Female, Male, Male, Fem…
## $ age <int> 49, 48, 55, 42, 66, 66, 37, 62, 38, 42, 41, 64, 58, 8…
## $ weight_lbs <int> 190, 170, 163, 230, 135, 165, 150, 170, 146, 260, 192…
## $ height_inch <int> 64, 68, 64, 74, 62, 70, 68, 70, 70, 73, 72, 66, 62, N…
## $ bmi <dbl> 32.68, 25.90, 28.04, 29.59, 24.74, 23.72, 22.86, 24.4…
## $ marital <fct> Married, Divorced, Married, Married, Widowed, Married…
## $ pregnant <fct> NA, NA, NA, NA, NA, NA, NA, NA, NA, No, NA, NA, NA, N…
## $ children <int> 0, 0, 0, 1, 0, 0, 3, 0, 2, 3, 2, 0, 0, 0, 0, 0, 0, 0,…
## $ education <fct> 6, 5, 4, 6, 5, 5, 6, 6, 4, 5, 6, 4, 4, 3, 4, 4, 4, 6,…
## $ employment <fct> 2, 1, 5, 1, 1, 7, 2, 7, 1, 3, 1, 1, 1, 5, 1, 1, 2, 1,…
## $ income <fct> 35-50k, 35-50k, <10k, >75k, 50-75k, 35-50k, >75k, <10…
## $ veteran <fct> 5, 5, 5, 5, 5, 3, 5, 5, 5, 5, 5, 3, 5, 5, 5, 5, 5, 5,…
## $ hispanic <fct> No, No, Yes, No, No, No, No, No, No, No, No, No, No, …
## $ health_general <fct> Good, Fair, Fair, Excellent, Excellent, Excellent, Ve…
## $ health_physical <int> 3, 4, 0, 0, 0, 0, 0, 30, 30, 0, 0, 0, 5, 0, 0, 3, 3, …
```

```
## $ health_mental <int> 15, 30, 0, 0, 0, 0, 0, 30, 30, 20, 0,
2, 0, 0, 30, 0,…
## $ health_poor <int> 2, 3, NA, NA, NA, NA, NA, 30, 14, 4, NA,
0, 3, NA, 0,…
## $ health_cover <fct> Yes, Yes, Yes, Yes, Yes, Yes, Yes, No,
Yes, Yes, Yes,…
## $ provide_care <fct> No, No, No, No, No, No, Yes, No, No, No,
No, No, No, …
## $ activity_limited <fct> Yes, No, No, No, No, No, No, No, Yes,
NA, No, No, No,…
## $ drink_any <fct> No, No, No, Yes, No, No, Yes, No, No, NA,
Yes, Yes, Y…
## $ drink_days <int> NA, NA, NA, 15, NA, NA, 2, NA, NA, NA, 4,
3, 1, NA, N…
## $ drink_average <int> NA, NA, NA, NA, NA, NA, 2, NA, NA, NA,
2, 5, 1, NA, N…
## $ smoke_100 <fct> No, No, No, No, Yes, No, No, Yes, Yes, Yes,
No, Yes, …
## $ smoke_days <fct> NA, NA, NA, NA, Everyday, NA, NA, Not@All,
Everyday, …
## $ smoke_stop <fct> NA, NA, NA, NA, Yes, NA, NA, NA, Yes, NA,
NA, NA, NA,…
## $ smoke_last <fct> NA, NA, NA, NA, NA, NA, NA, 7, NA, 5, NA,
7, 7, NA, 6…
## $ diet_fruit <int> 1095, 52, 36, NA, -7, 24, 52, 156, 24, NA,
365, 104, …
## $ diet_salad <int> 261, 209, 156, NA, 261, 52, 156, 24, 84,
NA, 156, 52,…
## $ diet_potato <int> 104, 52, 52, NA, 209, 104, 24, 52, 144,
NA, 52, 104, …
## $ diet_carrot <int> 156, 0, 24, NA, 261, 52, 24, 104, 24, NA,
156, 0, 104…
## $ diet_vegetable <int> 521, 52, 24, NA, 365, 365, 730, 365,
0, NA, 1095, 24,…
## $ diet_juice <int> 12, 0, 24, NA, 104, 365, 104, 0, 0, NA,
261, 12, 104,…
```

The data is composed of 245 rows (respondents) and 34 columns:

1. **State:** A factor with 52 categories for the 52 states. The labels and states corresponding to the labels are as follows: 1:Alabama,

2:Alaska, 4:Arizona, 5:Arkansas, 6:California,8:Colorado, 9:Connecticut, 10:Delaware, 11:District of Columbia,12:Florida, 13:Georgia, 15:Hawaii, 16:Idaho, 17:Illinois,18:Indiana, 19:Iowa, 20:Kansas, 21:Kentucky, 22:Louisiana,23:Maine, 24:Maryland, 25:Massachusetts, 26:Michigan,27:Minnesota, 28:Mississippi, 2:Missouri, 30:Montana,31:Nebraska, 32:Nevada, 33:New Hampshire, 34:New Jersey, 35:NewMexico, 36:New York, 37:North Carolina, 38:North Dakota, 39:Ohio,40:Oklahoma, 41:Oregon, 42:Pennsylvania, 44:Rhode Island, 45:SouthCarolina, 46:South Dakota, 47:Tennessee, 48:Texas, 49:Utah, 50:Vermont, 51:Virginia, 53:Washington, 54:West Virginia,55:Wisconsin, 56:Wyoming, 66:Guam, 72:Puerto Rico, 78:Virgin Islands

2. **Sex:** A factor column containing the participant's sex with categories Male and Female.
3. **Age:** An integer column for the respondent's age.
4. **weight_lbs:** An integer column for the participant's weight without shoes in pounds.
5. **height_inch:** An integer column for the participant's height without shoes in inches.
6. **bmi:** A double or numeric column for the participant's Body Mass Index (BMI). BMI is computed by weight in Kilogram /(height in Meters X height in Meters). BMI will be a missing value if any of the participant's weight or height is missing.
7. **Marital:** A factor or categorical column for the participant's marital status.
8. **Pregnant:** A factor or categorical column for the participant's current pregnancy with two categories Yes and No.
9. **Children:** An integer column for the number of children less than 18 years of age in the participant's household.
10. **Education:** A factor or categorical column for the participant's education level with levels 1, 2, 3, 4, 5, 6.

- The interpretation of education levels is 1: Never attended school or only kindergarten; 2: Grades 1 through 8 (Elementary); 3: Grades 9 through 11 (Some high school); 4: Grade 12 or GED (High school graduate); 5: College 1 year to 3 years (Some college or technical school); 6: College 4 years or more (College graduate).

11. **Employment:** A factor or categorical column for the participant's employment status with levels 1, 2, 3, 4, 5,6, 7, 8.

- The labels mean: 1: Employed for wages; 2: Self-employed; 3: Out of work for more than 1 year; 4: Out of work for less than 1 year; 5: A homemaker; 6: A student; 7:Retired; 8: Unable to work.

12. **Income:** A factor or categorical column for the participant's annual household income from all sources with levels or categories <10k, 10–15k, 15–20k, 20–25k, 25–35k, 35–50k, 50–75k, >75k, Dontknow, or Refused.
13. **Veteran:** A factor or categorical column for the participant's response to the question "Have you ever served on active duty in the United States Armed Forces, either in the regular military or in a National Guard or military reserve unit?"

- The veteran factor column is with levels 1, 2, 3, 4, 5, and the labels meaning: 1: Yes, now on active duty; 2: Yes, on active duty during the last 12 months, but not now; 3: Yes, on active duty in the past, but not during the last 12 months; 4: No, training for Reserves or National Guard only; 5: No, never served in the military.

14. **hispanic:** A factor or categorical column for the participant's response to the question "Are you Hispanic or Latino?" with levels or categories, Yes or No.
15. **health_general:** A factor or categorical column for the participant's response to the question "In general your health is" with levels: Excellent, VeryGood, Good, Fair, Poor, or Refused.
16. **health_physical:** An integer column for the number of days during the last 30 days that the respondent's physical health was not good. –7 is for "Don't know/Not sure," and –9 is for "Refused."
17. **health_mental:** An integer column for the number of days during the last 30 days that the respondent's mental health was not good. –7 is for "Don't know/Not sure," and –9 is for "Refused."
18. **health_poor:** An integer column for the number of days during the last 30 days that poor physical or mental health keeps the respondent from doing usual activities, such as self-care, work, or recreation. –7 is for "Don't know/Not sure," and –9 is for "Refused."
19. **health_cover:** A factor column for the question of whether having any kind of health care coverage, including health insurance, prepaid plans, or government plans. The answer has two levels: Yes and No.
20. **provide_care:** A factor column for the question of whether providing any care or assistance to a friend or family member during the past month, with levels Yes and No.

21. **activity_limited:** A factor column for the question of whether being limited in any way in any activities because of physical, mental, or emotional problems, with levels Yes and No.

22. **drink_any:** A factor column for the question of whether having had at least one drink of any alcoholic beverage such as beer, wine, a malt beverage, or liquor during the past 30 days, with levels of Yes and No.

23. **drink_days:** An integer column for the number of days during the past 30 days that the respondent had at least one drink of any alcoholic beverage. –7 is for "Don't know/Not sure," and –9 is for "Refused."

24. **drink_average:** An integer column for the number of drinks on the average the respondent had on the days when he/she drank, during the past 30 days. –7 is for "Don't know/Not sure," and –9 is for "Refused."

25. **smoke_100:** A factor column for whether having smoked at least 100 cigarettes in the entire life, with levels of Yes and No.

26. **smoke_days:** A factor column for the frequency of days now smoking, with levels: Everyday, Somedays, and NotAtAll(not at all).

27. **smoke_stop:** A factor column for whether having stopped smoking for one day or longer during the past 12 months because the respondent was trying to quit smoking, with levels of Yes and No.

28. **smoke_last:** A factor column with levels: 3, 4, 5, 6, 7, and 8 corresponding to the question: how long has it been since last smoking cigarettes regularly? The labels mean: 3: Within the past 6 months (3 months but less than 6 months ago); 4: Within the past year (6 months but less than 1 year ago); 5: Within the past 5 years (1 year but less than 5 years ago); 6: Within the past 10 years (5 years but less than 10 years ago); 7: 10 years or more; 8: Never smoked regularly.

29. **diet_fruit:** An integer column for the number of fruits the respondent eats every year, not counting juice. –7 is for "Don't know/Not sure," and –9 is for "Refused."

30. **diet_salad:** An integer column for the number of servings of green salad the respondent eats every year. –7 is for "Don't know/Not sure," and –9 is for "Refused."

31. **diet_potato:** An integer column for the number of servings of potatoes, not including french fries, fried potatoes, or potato chips, that the respondent eats every year. –7 is for "Don't know/Not sure," and –9 is for "Refused."
32. **diet_carrot:** An integer column for the number of carrots the respondent eats every year. –7 is for "Don't know/Not sure," and –9 is for "Refused."
33. **diet_vegetable:** An integer column for the number of servings of vegetables the respondent eats every year, not counting carrots, potatoes, or salad. –7 is for "Don't know/Not sure," and –9 is for "Refused."
34. **diet_juice:** An integer column for the number of fruit juices such as orange, grapefruit, or tomato that the respondent drinks every year. –7 is for "Don't know/Not sure," and –9 is for "Refused."

2.3. CHECK DUPLICATES

2.3.1. Duplicates of General Social Survey Data

The get_dupes function from the janitor package can get rows of identical values for the specified columns.

We use the mutate function to add a new column (row_id) using the row_number function as we did before in chapter 1. The row numbers will be from 1 to 21483.

Then, to get all duplicated rows from the general social survey data, we use the get_dupes with the arguments (-row_id) to remove the row_id column before checking duplicates. If we keep the row_id column, we will not get any duplicates since every row has a different number from 1 to 21483. Then, we convert the result to a table as before.

Because we are using a function from the janitor package so we must load it first using the library function.

```
library(janitor)
gss_cat %>% mutate(row_id = row_number()) %>%
get_dupes(-row_id) %>% flextable() %>% theme_box() %>%
set_caption(caption = "The duplicated rows in the general social
survey data")
```

Table 2.1. The Duplicated Rows in the General Social Survey Data

year	marital	age	race	rincome	partyid	relig	denom	tvhours	dupe_count	row_id
2,000	Never married	19	White	$1000 to 2999	Not str republican	Catholic	Not applicable	–	2	167
2,000	Never married	19	White	$1000 to 2999	Not str republican	Catholic	Not applicable	–	2	1,667
2,000	Never married	30	White	$25000 or more	Not str republican	Catholic	Not applicable	1	2	790
2,000	Never married	30	White	$25000 or more	Not str republican	Catholic	Not applicable	1	2	1,547
2,000	Never married	39	Other	$25000 or more	Not str democrat	Catholic	Not applicable	–	2	433
2,000	Never married	39	Other	$25000 or more	Not str democrat	Catholic	Not applicable	–	2	605
2,000	Widowed	80	White	Not applicable	Strong democrat	Protestant	Southern baptist	3	2	1,990
2,000	Widowed	80	White	Not applicable	Strong democrat	Protestant	Southern baptist	3	2	2,493
2,000	Married	29	White	$25000 or more	Independent	Catholic	Not applicable	2	2	1,313
2,000	Married	29	White	$25000 or more	Independent	Catholic	Not applicable	2	2	2,042
2,000	Married	36	Other	$25000 or more	Not str democrat	Catholic	Not applicable	2	2	569
2,000	Married	36	Other	$25000 or more	Not str democrat	Catholic	Not applicable	2	2	1,047
2,000	Married	39	White	$10000–14999	Not str democrat	Catholic	Not applicable	3	2	1,030
2,000	Married	39	White	$10000–14999	Not str democrat	Catholic	Not applicable	3	2	2,114
2,000	Married	47	White	$25000 or more	Not str republican	Catholic	Not applicable	–	2	1,677
2,000	Married	47	White	$25000 or more	Not str republican	Catholic	Not applicable	–	2	2,003
2,000	Married	48	White	$25000 or more	Ind,near dem	Catholic	Not applicable	1	2	21
2,000	Married	48	White	$25000 or more	Ind,near dem	Catholic	Not applicable	1	2	160
2,002	Never married	20	White	Not applicable	Independent	None	Not applicable	–	2	4,254
2,002	Never married	20	White	Not applicable	Independent	None	Not applicable	–	2	5,097

2,002	Never married	22	White	$25000 or more	Not str republi-can	Catholic	Not ap-plicable	–	2	3,809
2,002	Never married	22	White	$25000 or more	Not str republi-can	Catholic	Not ap-plicable	–	2	5,267
2,002	Never married	24	White	Not appli-cable	Indepen-dent	None	Not ap-plicable	–	2	3,496
2,002	Never married	24	White	Not appli-cable	Indepen-dent	None	Not ap-plicable	–	2	4,333
2,002	Never married	27	White	$25000 or more	Not str democrat	Catholic	Not ap-plicable	2	2	4,260
2,002	Never married	27	White	$25000 or more	Not str democrat	Catholic	Not ap-plicable	2	2	5,104
2,002	Never married	27	White	$20000–24999	Strong democrat	None	Not ap-plicable	–	2	3,174
2,002	Never married	27	White	$20000–24999	Strong democrat	None	Not ap-plicable	–	2	3,675
2,002	Never married	28	White	$25000 or more	Not str democrat	Catholic	Not ap-plicable	–	2	3,340
2,002	Never married	28	White	$25000 or more	Not str democrat	Catholic	Not ap-plicable	–	2	4,354
2,002	Never married	31	White	$25000 or more	Strong democrat	Catholic	Not ap-plicable	–	2	4,401
2,002	Never married	31	White	$25000 or more	Strong democrat	Catholic	Not ap-plicable	–	2	4,730
2,002	Never married	54	White	$25000 or more	Strong democrat	Other	Not ap-plicable	–	2	3,841
2,002	Never married	54	White	$25000 or more	Strong democrat	Other	Not ap-plicable	–	2	4,733
2,002	Wid-owed	82	White	Not appli-cable	Not str republi-can	None	Not ap-plicable	–	2	4,089
2,002	Wid-owed	82	White	Not appli-cable	Not str republi-can	None	Not ap-plicable	–	2	4,326
2,002	Married	31	White	$20000–24999	Not str democrat	Catholic	Not ap-plicable	–	2	4,423
2,002	Married	31	White	$20000–24999	Not str democrat	Catholic	Not ap-plicable	–	2	5,014
2,002	Married	32	White	$25000 or more	Not str democrat	Catholic	Not ap-plicable	–	2	3,346
2,002	Married	32	White	$25000 or more	Not str democrat	Catholic	Not ap-plicable	–	2	3,359
2,002	Married	33	White	$25000 or more	Not str republi-can	Catholic	Not ap-plicable	–	2	3,375
2,002	Married	33	White	$25000 or more	Not str republi-can	Catholic	Not ap-plicable	–	2	5,138

2,002	Married	34	White	$10000–14999	Independent	None	Not applicable	–	2	3,539
2,002	Married	34	White	$10000–14999	Independent	None	Not applicable	–	2	4,378
2,002	Married	35	White	$25000 or more	Independent	Catholic	Not applicable	–	2	3,944
2,002	Married	35	White	$25000 or more	Independent	Catholic	Not applicable	–	2	4,794
2,002	Married	36	White	$25000 or more	Strong republican	Catholic	Not applicable	–	2	5,086
2,002	Married	36	White	$25000 or more	Strong republican	Catholic	Not applicable	–	2	5,526
2,002	Married	36	White	$25000 or more	Not str republican	Protestant	Other	–	2	4,113
2,002	Married	36	White	$25000 or more	Not str republican	Protestant	Other	–	2	4,658
2,002	Married	39	White	$25000 or more	Independent	Christian	Not applicable	–	2	3,735
2,002	Married	39	White	$25000 or more	Independent	Christian	Not applicable	–	2	4,390
2,002	Married	39	White	$25000 or more	Not str democrat	None	Not applicable	–	2	2,977
2,002	Married	39	White	$25000 or more	Not str democrat	None	Not applicable	–	2	4,465
2,002	Married	40	Black	$25000 or more	Not str democrat	Protestant	Baptist-dk which	–	2	3,057
2,002	Married	40	Black	$25000 or more	Not str democrat	Protestant	Baptist-dk which	–	2	4,430
2,002	Married	40	White	Not applicable	Not str republican	Catholic	Not applicable	–	2	3,822
2,002	Married	40	White	Not applicable	Not str republican	Catholic	Not applicable	–	2	5,383
2,002	Married	40	White	Not applicable	Independent	Catholic	Not applicable	–	2	3,325
2,002	Married	40	White	Not applicable	Independent	Catholic	Not applicable	–	2	3,350
2,002	Married	41	White	$25000 or more	Not str democrat	Catholic	Not applicable	–	2	3,969
2,002	Married	41	White	$25000 or more	Not str democrat	Catholic	Not applicable	–	2	5,429
2,002	Married	43	White	Not applicable	Independent	Catholic	Not applicable	–	2	3,031
2,002	Married	43	White	Not applicable	Independent	Catholic	Not applicable	–	2	3,309

2,002	Married	43	White	Not applicable	Ind,near dem	Catholic	Not applicable	–	2	3,674
2,002	Married	43	White	Not applicable	Ind,near dem	Catholic	Not applicable	–	2	4,427
2,002	Married	44	White	$25000 or more	Not str republican	Catholic	Not applicable	–	2	3,183
2,002	Married	44	White	$25000 or more	Not str republican	Catholic	Not applicable	–	2	5,395
2,002	Married	44	White	$25000 or more	Ind,near dem	Catholic	Not applicable	–	2	3,626
2,002	Married	44	White	$25000 or more	Ind,near dem	Catholic	Not applicable	–	2	4,699
2,002	Married	44	White	$25000 or more	Strong democrat	Catholic	Not applicable	–	2	3,532
2,002	Married	44	White	$25000 or more	Strong democrat	Catholic	Not applicable	–	2	3,542
2,002	Married	45	White	$25000 or more	Not str republican	Protestant	Other	–	2	3,128
2,002	Married	45	White	$25000 or more	Not str republican	Protestant	Other	–	2	5,419
2,002	Married	45	White	$25000 or more	Independent	Catholic	Not applicable	–	2	3,482
2,002	Married	45	White	$25000 or more	Independent	Catholic	Not applicable	–	2	3,999
2,002	Married	46	White	$25000 or more	Not str democrat	Catholic	Not applicable	1	2	4,807
2,002	Married	46	White	$25000 or more	Not str democrat	Catholic	Not applicable	1	2	4,963
2,002	Married	47	White	$25000 or more	Independent	Protestant	Other	–	2	3,553
2,002	Married	47	White	$25000 or more	Independent	Protestant	Other	–	2	5,264
2,002	Married	47	White	$25000 or more	Ind,near dem	Christian	Not applicable	–	2	3,904
2,002	Married	47	White	$25000 or more	Ind,near dem	Christian	Not applicable	–	2	5,397
2,002	Married	48	White	$25000 or more	Strong republican	Catholic	Not applicable	–	2	3,396
2,002	Married	48	White	$25000 or more	Strong republican	Catholic	Not applicable	–	2	3,411
2,002	Married	48	White	$25000 or more	Not str republican	Protestant	United methodist	1	2	3,703
2,002	Married	48	White	$25000 or more	Not str republican	Protestant	United methodist	1	2	5,081

2,002	Married	48	White	$25000 or more	Not str republi-can	Protestant	South-ern baptist	–	2	2,829
2,002	Married	48	White	$25000 or more	Not str republi-can	Protestant	South-ern baptist	–	2	4,063
2,002	Married	49	White	$25000 or more	Indepen-dent	None	Not ap-plicable	–	2	3,650
2,002	Married	49	White	$25000 or more	Indepen-dent	None	Not ap-plicable	–	2	4,981
2,002	Married	50	White	$25000 or more	Not str republi-can	Catholic	Not ap-plicable	–	4	2,995
2,002	Married	50	White	$25000 or more	Not str republi-can	Catholic	Not ap-plicable	–	4	3,355
2,002	Married	50	White	$25000 or more	Not str republi-can	Catholic	Not ap-plicable	–	4	3,975
2,002	Married	50	White	$25000 or more	Not str republi-can	Catholic	Not ap-plicable	–	4	4,615
2,002	Married	50	White	$25000 or more	Strong democrat	None	Not ap-plicable	–	2	4,765
2,002	Married	50	White	$25000 or more	Strong democrat	None	Not ap-plicable	–	2	5,360
2,002	Married	51	White	$25000 or more	Strong republi-can	Protestant	No denomi-nation	–	2	3,505
2,002	Married	51	White	$25000 or more	Strong republi-can	Protestant	No denomi-nation	–	2	5,554
2,002	Married	58	White	$25000 or more	Strong democrat	Catholic	Not ap-plicable	–	2	3,091
2,002	Married	58	White	$25000 or more	Strong democrat	Catholic	Not ap-plicable	–	2	4,413
2,002	Married	59	White	$15000–19999	Not str democrat	Catholic	Not ap-plicable	–	2	3,945
2,002	Married	59	White	$15000–19999	Not str democrat	Catholic	Not ap-plicable	–	2	5,271
2,002	Married	61	White	Not appli-cable	Strong democrat	Catholic	Not ap-plicable	–	2	3,455
2,002	Married	61	White	Not appli-cable	Strong democrat	Catholic	Not ap-plicable	–	2	4,467
2,002	Married	65	White	Not appli-cable	Not str republi-can	Protestant	United method-ist	–	3	3,820
2,002	Married	65	White	Not appli-cable	Not str republi-can	Protestant	United method-ist	–	3	4,301
2,002	Married	65	White	Not appli-cable	Not str republi-can	Protestant	United method-ist	–	3	5,518

2,002	Married	69	White	Not applicable	Ind,near rep	Protestant	Southern baptist	2	2	2,869
2,002	Married	69	White	Not applicable	Ind,near rep	Protestant	Southern baptist	2	2	3,724
2,002	Married	75	White	Not applicable	Not str democrat	Protestant	Southern baptist	–	2	5,316
2,002	Married	75	White	Not applicable	Not str democrat	Protestant	Southern baptist	–	2	5,346
2,002	Married	81	White	Not applicable	Strong democrat	Catholic	Not applicable	–	2	2,973
2,002	Married	81	White	Not applicable	Strong democrat	Catholic	Not applicable	–	2	4,018
2,004	Never married	18	White	Not applicable	Not str republican	None	Not applicable	–	2	6,032
2,004	Never married	18	White	Not applicable	Not str republican	None	Not applicable	–	2	7,893
2,004	Never married	21	White	Not applicable	Not str republican	None	Not applicable	–	2	7,351
2,004	Never married	21	White	Not applicable	Not str republican	None	Not applicable	–	2	7,396
2,004	Never married	26	White	Not applicable	Ind,near dem	Jewish	Not applicable	–	2	5,610
2,004	Never married	26	White	Not applicable	Ind,near dem	Jewish	Not applicable	–	2	6,428
2,004	Never married	28	White	$25000 or more	Not str democrat	Catholic	Not applicable	–	2	5,731
2,004	Never married	28	White	$25000 or more	Not str democrat	Catholic	Not applicable	–	2	6,009
2,004	Never married	30	White	$25000 or more	Not str democrat	Protestant	Other	–	2	7,274
2,004	Never married	30	White	$25000 or more	Not str democrat	Protestant	Other	–	2	7,357
2,004	Divorced	43	White	$25000 or more	Strong republican	Protestant	Southern baptist	–	2	6,311
2,004	Divorced	43	White	$25000 or more	Strong republican	Protestant	Southern baptist	–	2	7,957
2,004	Divorced	60	White	$25000 or more	Not str democrat	Catholic	Not applicable	–	2	5,694
2,004	Divorced	60	White	$25000 or more	Not str democrat	Catholic	Not applicable	–	2	6,710
2,004	Widowed	73	White	Not applicable	Not str democrat	Protestant	Other	–	2	6,537

2,004	Wid-owed	73	White	Not appli-cable	Not str democrat	Protestant	Other	–	2	7,905
2,004	Wid-owed	78	White	Not appli-cable	Not str republi-can	Catholic	Not ap-plicable	3	2	6,940
2,004	Wid-owed	78	White	Not appli-cable	Not str republi-can	Catholic	Not ap-plicable	3	2	7,469
2,004	Wid-owed	79	White	Not appli-cable	Strong republi-can	Protestant	United method-ist	–	2	5,773
2,004	Wid-owed	79	White	Not appli-cable	Strong republi-can	Protestant	United method-ist	–	2	7,754
2,004	Wid-owed	82	White	Not appli-cable	Strong democrat	Catholic	Not ap-plicable	–	2	5,922
2,004	Wid-owed	82	White	Not appli-cable	Strong democrat	Catholic	Not ap-plicable	–	2	6,641
2,004	Married	31	White	Refused	Indepen-dent	Catholic	Not ap-plicable	–	2	6,227
2,004	Married	31	White	Refused	Indepen-dent	Catholic	Not ap-plicable	–	2	6,794
2,004	Married	32	White	$25000 or more	Ind,near rep	Catholic	Not ap-plicable	–	2	5,737
2,004	Married	32	White	$25000 or more	Ind,near rep	Catholic	Not ap-plicable	–	2	5,942
2,004	Married	33	White	$25000 or more	Strong republi-can	Protestant	United method-ist	–	2	5,741
2,004	Married	33	White	$25000 or more	Strong republi-can	Protestant	United method-ist	–	2	6,341
2,004	Married	33	White	$25000 or more	Not str republi-can	Protestant	Baptist-dk which	2	2	7,993
2,004	Married	33	White	$25000 or more	Not str republi-can	Protestant	Baptist-dk which	2	2	8,279
2,004	Married	34	White	$25000 or more	Ind,near rep	Protestant	Other	–	2	6,330
2,004	Married	34	White	$25000 or more	Ind,near rep	Protestant	Other	–	2	8,257
2,004	Married	34	White	$25000 or more	Not str democrat	Catholic	Not ap-plicable	1	2	6,367
2,004	Married	34	White	$25000 or more	Not str democrat	Catholic	Not ap-plicable	1	2	6,791
2,004	Married	35	White	$25000 or more	Strong republi-can	Catholic	Not ap-plicable	–	2	5,704
2,004	Married	35	White	$25000 or more	Strong republi-can	Catholic	Not ap-plicable	–	2	6,903

2,004	Married	36	White	$25000 or more	Strong republican	Catholic	Not applicable	–	2	6,453
2,004	Married	36	White	$25000 or more	Strong republican	Catholic	Not applicable	–	2	6,838
2,004	Married	38	White	$25000 or more	Not str republican	Catholic	Not applicable	–	3	5,949
2,004	Married	38	White	$25000 or more	Not str republican	Catholic	Not applicable	–	3	6,016
2,004	Married	38	White	$25000 or more	Not str republican	Catholic	Not applicable	–	3	6,947
2,004	Married	39	White	$25000 or more	Strong republican	Catholic	Not applicable	–	2	6,256
2,004	Married	39	White	$25000 or more	Strong republican	Catholic	Not applicable	–	2	6,684
2,004	Married	40	White	$25000 or more	Not str republican	Catholic	Not applicable	–	2	5,644
2,004	Married	40	White	$25000 or more	Not str republican	Catholic	Not applicable	–	2	7,611
2,004	Married	42	White	Not applicable	Independent	Catholic	Not applicable	2	2	6,986
2,004	Married	42	White	Not applicable	Independent	Catholic	Not applicable	2	2	7,825
2,004	Married	44	Other	$25000 or more	Independent	None	Not applicable	–	2	5,924
2,004	Married	44	Other	$25000 or more	Independent	None	Not applicable	–	2	7,460
2,004	Married	44	White	Not applicable	Strong republican	Catholic	Not applicable	–	2	6,111
2,004	Married	44	White	Not applicable	Strong republican	Catholic	Not applicable	–	2	6,833
2,004	Married	45	Black	Not applicable	Strong democrat	Protestant	Baptist-dk which	–	2	6,059
2,004	Married	45	Black	Not applicable	Strong democrat	Protestant	Baptist-dk which	–	2	6,071
2,004	Married	45	White	Not applicable	Independent	Catholic	Not applicable	–	2	5,874
2,004	Married	45	White	Not applicable	Independent	Catholic	Not applicable	–	2	7,677

2,004	Married	46	White	$25000 or more	Ind,near dem	Protestant	Luther-an-dk which	–	2	7,715
2,004	Married	46	White	$25000 or more	Ind,near dem	Protestant	Luther-an-dk which	–	2	7,878
2,004	Married	46	White	$25000 or more	Not str democrat	Catholic	Not ap-plicable	–	2	6,365
2,004	Married	46	White	$25000 or more	Not str democrat	Catholic	Not ap-plicable	–	2	8,200
2,004	Married	47	White	$25000 or more	Not str republi-can	Catholic	Not ap-plicable	–	2	6,949
2,004	Married	47	White	$25000 or more	Not str republi-can	Catholic	Not ap-plicable	–	2	7,301
2,004	Married	47	White	$25000 or more	Strong democrat	None	Not ap-plicable	–	3	6,499
2,004	Married	47	White	$25000 or more	Strong democrat	None	Not ap-plicable	–	3	7,104
2,004	Married	47	White	$25000 or more	Strong democrat	None	Not ap-plicable	–	3	7,643
2,004	Married	48	White	$25000 or more	Indepen-dent	Catholic	Not ap-plicable	–	2	5,899
2,004	Married	48	White	$25000 or more	Indepen-dent	Catholic	Not ap-plicable	–	2	6,258
2,004	Married	49	White	$25000 or more	Strong republi-can	Protestant	Other	–	2	5,835
2,004	Married	49	White	$25000 or more	Strong republi-can	Protestant	Other	–	2	7,291
2,004	Married	49	White	$25000 or more	Ind,near dem	Protestant	Luther-an-mo synod	–	2	7,631
2,004	Married	49	White	$25000 or more	Ind,near dem	Protestant	Luther-an-mo synod	–	2	8,267
2,004	Married	49	White	Not appli-cable	Not str republi-can	None	Not ap-plicable	–	2	6,586
2,004	Married	49	White	Not appli-cable	Not str republi-can	None	Not ap-plicable	–	2	8,193
2,004	Married	52	White	$25000 or more	Strong republi-can	Catholic	Not ap-plicable	1	2	6,864
2,004	Married	52	White	$25000 or more	Strong republi-can	Catholic	Not ap-plicable	1	2	6,951
2,004	Married	55	White	$25000 or more	Strong republi-can	Catholic	Not ap-plicable	–	3	6,359

2,004	Married	55	White	$25000 or more	Strong republi-can	Catholic	Not ap-plicable	–	3	6,810
2,004	Married	55	White	$25000 or more	Strong republi-can	Catholic	Not ap-plicable	–	3	7,533
2,004	Married	55	White	$25000 or more	Not str democrat	Catholic	Not ap-plicable	–	2	6,548
2,004	Married	55	White	$25000 or more	Not str democrat	Catholic	Not ap-plicable	–	2	8,304
2,004	Married	55	White	$25000 or more	Strong democrat	None	Not ap-plicable	–	2	6,460
2,004	Married	55	White	$25000 or more	Strong democrat	None	Not ap-plicable	–	2	7,099
2,004	Married	56	White	$25000 or more	Strong republi-can	Protestant	Other	–	2	8,029
2,004	Married	56	White	$25000 or more	Strong republi-can	Protestant	Other	–	2	8,053
2,004	Married	56	White	$25000 or more	Indepen-dent	Catholic	Not ap-plicable	–	2	6,535
2,004	Married	56	White	$25000 or more	Indepen-dent	Catholic	Not ap-plicable	–	2	8,356
2,004	Married	67	White	Not appli-cable	Strong republi-can	Catholic	Not ap-plicable	2	2	5,877
2,004	Married	67	White	Not appli-cable	Strong republi-can	Catholic	Not ap-plicable	2	2	6,339
2,004	Married	70	White	Not appli-cable	Strong democrat	Catholic	Not ap-plicable	–	2	5,769
2,004	Married	70	White	Not appli-cable	Strong democrat	Catholic	Not ap-plicable	–	2	7,700
2,004	Married	75	White	Not appli-cable	Strong republi-can	Protestant	Other	–	2	7,881
2,004	Married	75	White	Not appli-cable	Strong republi-can	Protestant	Other	–	2	8,252
2,004	Married	75	White	Not appli-cable	Ind,near rep	Protestant	Other	–	2	7,439
2,004	Married	75	White	Not appli-cable	Ind,near rep	Protestant	Other	–	2	7,519
2,004	Married	80	White	Not appli-cable	Not str republi-can	Catholic	Not ap-plicable	–	2	7,107
2,004	Married	80	White	Not appli-cable	Not str republi-can	Catholic	Not ap-plicable	–	2	7,570
2,006	Never married	21	Other	Not appli-cable	Not str democrat	Catholic	Not ap-plicable	–	2	9,709

2,006	Never married	21	Other	Not applicable	Not str democrat	Catholic	Not applicable	–	2	12,697
2,006	Never married	21	White	Not applicable	Independent	None	Not applicable	–	2	9,034
2,006	Never married	21	White	Not applicable	Independent	None	Not applicable	–	2	10,171
2,006	Never married	23	White	Not applicable	Not str republican	None	Not applicable	–	2	10,566
2,006	Never married	23	White	Not applicable	Not str republican	None	Not applicable	–	2	12,865
2,006	Never married	24	Black	Not applicable	Strong democrat	Protestant	Baptist-dk which	–	2	12,104
2,006	Never married	24	Black	Not applicable	Strong democrat	Protestant	Baptist-dk which	–	2	12,379
2,006	Never married	24	White	Not applicable	Independent	None	Not applicable	–	2	10,228
2,006	Never married	24	White	Not applicable	Independent	None	Not applicable	–	2	11,957
2,006	Never married	25	White	$15000–19999	Strong democrat	None	Not applicable	3	2	9,092
2,006	Never married	25	White	$15000–19999	Strong democrat	None	Not applicable	3	2	10,220
2,006	Never married	27	Black	Not applicable	Not str democrat	Protestant	Southern baptist	–	2	11,822
2,006	Never married	27	Black	Not applicable	Not str democrat	Protestant	Southern baptist	–	2	12,631
2,006	Never married	30	White	$25000 or more	Not str democrat	None	Not applicable	–	2	9,966
2,006	Never married	30	White	$25000 or more	Not str democrat	None	Not applicable	–	2	10,161
2,006	Never married	31	White	$25000 or more	Independent	Catholic	Not applicable	–	2	9,577
2,006	Never married	31	White	$25000 or more	Independent	Catholic	Not applicable	–	2	11,325
2,006	Never married	35	Black	$25000 or more	Strong democrat	Protestant	Other	–	2	9,283
2,006	Never married	35	Black	$25000 or more	Strong democrat	Protestant	Other	–	2	9,307
2,006	Never married	35	White	$25000 or more	Strong democrat	None	Not applicable	–	2	9,897
2,006	Never married	35	White	$25000 or more	Strong democrat	None	Not applicable	–	2	9,985
2,006	Never married	37	Other	Not applicable	Not str democrat	Catholic	Not applicable	–	2	9,209

2,006	Never married	37	Other	Not applicable	Not str democrat	Catholic	Not applicable	–	2	9,432
2,006	Never married	38	White	$15000–19999	Independent	Catholic	Not applicable	–	2	9,107
2,006	Never married	38	White	$15000–19999	Independent	Catholic	Not applicable	–	2	12,424
2,006	Never married	39	Black	$25000 or more	Not str democrat	Protestant	No denomination	–	2	9,084
2,006	Never married	39	Black	$25000 or more	Not str democrat	Protestant	No denomination	–	2	9,720
2,006	Never married	45	White	$25000 or more	Ind,near dem	None	Not applicable	–	2	9,493
2,006	Never married	45	White	$25000 or more	Ind,near dem	None	Not applicable	–	2	11,085
2,006	Divorced	42	White	$25000 or more	Not str republican	Protestant	Baptist-dk which	–	2	9,229
2,006	Divorced	42	White	$25000 or more	Not str republican	Protestant	Baptist-dk which	–	2	10,368
2,006	Divorced	44	White	$25000 or more	Independent	Catholic	Not applicable	–	2	10,144
2,006	Divorced	44	White	$25000 or more	Independent	Catholic	Not applicable	–	2	11,840
2,006	Divorced	47	White	$25000 or more	Not str republican	Protestant	Other	–	2	10,444
2,006	Divorced	47	White	$25000 or more	Not str republican	Protestant	Other	–	2	10,476
2,006	Divorced	48	White	$25000 or more	Independent	None	Not applicable	–	2	11,354
2,006	Divorced	48	White	$25000 or more	Independent	None	Not applicable	–	2	11,619
2,006	Divorced	51	White	$25000 or more	Ind,near dem	Protestant	Southern baptist	–	2	12,218
2,006	Divorced	51	White	$25000 or more	Ind,near dem	Protestant	Southern baptist	–	2	12,566
2,006	Divorced	52	White	Not applicable	Not str republican	None	Not applicable	3	2	10,237
2,006	Divorced	52	White	Not applicable	Not str republican	None	Not applicable	3	2	10,428
2,006	Divorced	64	White	Not applicable	Strong republican	Protestant	Episcopal	–	2	8,933

2,006	Divorced	64	White	Not applicable	Strong republican	Protestant	Episcopal	–	2	10,851
2,006	Divorced	64	White	Not applicable	Ind,near rep	Protestant	Southern baptist	–	2	11,061
2,006	Divorced	64	White	Not applicable	Ind,near rep	Protestant	Southern baptist	–	2	11,213
2,006	Widowed	75	White	Not applicable	Independent	Protestant	Other	–	2	10,724
2,006	Widowed	75	White	Not applicable	Independent	Protestant	Other	–	2	11,396
2,006	Widowed	76	White	Not applicable	Independent	Protestant	Methodist-dk which	–	2	9,936
2,006	Widowed	76	White	Not applicable	Independent	Protestant	Methodist-dk which	–	2	11,285
2,006	Widowed	77	White	Not applicable	Not str democrat	Protestant	Other	–	2	12,454
2,006	Widowed	77	White	Not applicable	Not str democrat	Protestant	Other	–	2	12,455
2,006	Widowed	80	White	Not applicable	Strong republican	Catholic	Not applicable	–	2	9,063
2,006	Widowed	80	White	Not applicable	Strong republican	Catholic	Not applicable	–	2	10,662
2,006	Widowed	82	White	Not applicable	Strong democrat	Catholic	Not applicable	–	3	10,195
2,006	Widowed	82	White	Not applicable	Strong democrat	Catholic	Not applicable	–	3	10,250
2,006	Widowed	82	White	Not applicable	Strong democrat	Catholic	Not applicable	–	3	10,664
2,006	Widowed	89	White	Not applicable	Not str democrat	Protestant	United methodist	–	2	11,472
2,006	Widowed	89	White	Not applicable	Not str democrat	Protestant	United methodist	–	2	12,418
2,006	Married	27	White	$25000 or more	Ind,near rep	Catholic	Not applicable	–	2	10,599
2,006	Married	27	White	$25000 or more	Ind,near rep	Catholic	Not applicable	–	2	11,160
2,006	Married	28	Other	$25000 or more	Strong democrat	Catholic	Not applicable	–	2	8,476
2,006	Married	28	Other	$25000 or more	Strong democrat	Catholic	Not applicable	–	2	10,575
2,006	Married	28	White	$25000 or more	Not str republican	Catholic	Not applicable	–	2	8,535

2,006	Married	28	White	$25000 or more	Not str republi-can	Catholic	Not ap-plicable	–	2	10,874
2,006	Married	28	White	$25000 or more	Strong democrat	Catholic	Not ap-plicable	–	2	8,805
2,006	Married	28	White	$25000 or more	Strong democrat	Catholic	Not ap-plicable	–	2	10,904
2,006	Married	29	White	$25000 or more	Strong republi-can	Protestant	Other	–	2	9,727
2,006	Married	29	White	$25000 or more	Strong republi-can	Protestant	Other	–	2	11,599
2,006	Married	29	White	$25000 or more	Not str republi-can	Catholic	Not ap-plicable	–	2	8,541
2,006	Married	29	White	$25000 or more	Not str republi-can	Catholic	Not ap-plicable	–	2	11,643
2,006	Married	29	White	$25000 or more	Not str republi-can	Protestant	No denomi-nation	–	2	9,788
2,006	Married	29	White	$25000 or more	Not str republi-can	Protestant	No denomi-nation	–	2	11,042
2,006	Married	30	White	$25000 or more	Strong republi-can	Catholic	Not ap-plicable	–	2	10,445
2,006	Married	30	White	$25000 or more	Strong republi-can	Catholic	Not ap-plicable	–	2	10,560
2,006	Married	30	White	$25000 or more	Not str democrat	Protestant	No denomi-nation	–	2	9,794
2,006	Married	30	White	$25000 or more	Not str democrat	Protestant	No denomi-nation	–	2	12,098
2,006	Married	31	White	$25000 or more	Not str republi-can	Catholic	Not ap-plicable	–	2	8,585
2,006	Married	31	White	$25000 or more	Not str republi-can	Catholic	Not ap-plicable	–	2	11,157
2,006	Married	31	White	$15000–19999	Strong democrat	Catholic	Not ap-plicable	–	2	8,447
2,006	Married	31	White	$15000–19999	Strong democrat	Catholic	Not ap-plicable	–	2	10,325
2,006	Married	31	White	Not appli-cable	Strong republi-can	Protestant	Other	2	2	12,510
2,006	Married	31	White	Not appli-cable	Strong republi-can	Protestant	Other	2	2	12,849

2,006	Married	33	Other	Don't know	Indepen-dent	Catholic	Not ap-plicable	–	2	11,145
2,006	Married	33	Other	Don't know	Indepen-dent	Catholic	Not ap-plicable	–	2	11,882
2,006	Married	33	White	$25000 or more	Indepen-dent	Catholic	Not ap-plicable	–	2	8,863
2,006	Married	33	White	$25000 or more	Indepen-dent	Catholic	Not ap-plicable	–	2	10,385
2,006	Married	34	White	$25000 or more	Not str republi-can	None	Not ap-plicable	2	2	10,928
2,006	Married	34	White	$25000 or more	Not str republi-can	None	Not ap-plicable	2	2	11,450
2,006	Married	35	White	Refused	Indepen-dent	Catholic	Not ap-plicable	–	2	9,119
2,006	Married	35	White	Refused	Indepen-dent	Catholic	Not ap-plicable	–	2	11,997
2,006	Married	35	White	$25000 or more	Ind,near rep	Catholic	Not ap-plicable	–	2	8,547
2,006	Married	35	White	$25000 or more	Ind,near rep	Catholic	Not ap-plicable	–	2	11,657
2,006	Married	35	White	$25000 or more	Ind,near dem	Protestant	Luther-an-dk which	4	2	10,387
2,006	Married	35	White	$25000 or more	Ind,near dem	Protestant	Luther-an-dk which	4	2	11,818
2,006	Married	37	White	$25000 or more	Not str republi-can	Catholic	Not ap-plicable	3	2	10,526
2,006	Married	37	White	$25000 or more	Not str republi-can	Catholic	Not ap-plicable	3	2	12,745
2,006	Married	37	White	$25000 or more	Ind,near rep	Catholic	Not ap-plicable	–	2	11,382
2,006	Married	37	White	$25000 or more	Ind,near rep	Catholic	Not ap-plicable	–	2	12,249
2,006	Married	37	White	$25000 or more	Indepen-dent	Catholic	Not ap-plicable	–	2	8,432
2,006	Married	37	White	$25000 or more	Indepen-dent	Catholic	Not ap-plicable	–	2	11,520
2,006	Married	37	White	$25000 or more	Strong democrat	None	Not ap-plicable	–	2	8,958
2,006	Married	37	White	$25000 or more	Strong democrat	None	Not ap-plicable	–	2	10,395
2,006	Married	37	White	$20000–24999	Indepen-dent	Protestant	Other	–	2	11,838
2,006	Married	37	White	$20000–24999	Indepen-dent	Protestant	Other	–	2	12,442

2,006	Married	38	White	$25000 or more	Not str republi-can	None	Not ap-plicable	–	2	10,857
2,006	Married	38	White	$25000 or more	Not str republi-can	None	Not ap-plicable	–	2	11,646
2,006	Married	40	White	$25000 or more	Ind,near dem	None	Not ap-plicable	–	2	9,539
2,006	Married	40	White	$25000 or more	Ind,near dem	None	Not ap-plicable	–	2	9,783
2,006	Married	41	Black	$25000 or more	Strong democrat	Protestant	South-ern baptist	3	2	12,275
2,006	Married	41	Black	$25000 or more	Strong democrat	Protestant	South-ern baptist	3	2	12,393
2,006	Married	43	White	$25000 or more	Strong republi-can	Protestant	United method-ist	–	2	10,713
2,006	Married	43	White	$25000 or more	Strong republi-can	Protestant	United method-ist	–	2	10,758
2,006	Married	43	White	$25000 or more	Indepen-dent	None	Not ap-plicable	–	2	10,364
2,006	Married	43	White	$25000 or more	Indepen-dent	None	Not ap-plicable	–	2	12,532
2,006	Married	43	White	$25000 or more	Not str democrat	Catholic	Not ap-plicable	–	2	10,905
2,006	Married	43	White	$25000 or more	Not str democrat	Catholic	Not ap-plicable	–	2	12,370
2,006	Married	44	White	$25000 or more	Not str republi-can	Protestant	Episco-pal	–	2	9,380
2,006	Married	44	White	$25000 or more	Not str republi-can	Protestant	Episco-pal	–	2	10,470
2,006	Married	44	White	$25000 or more	Indepen-dent	Protestant	United method-ist	–	2	10,217
2,006	Married	44	White	$25000 or more	Indepen-dent	Protestant	United method-ist	–	2	11,839
2,006	Married	45	White	$25000 or more	Not str democrat	Catholic	Not ap-plicable	3	2	8,822
2,006	Married	45	White	$25000 or more	Not str democrat	Catholic	Not ap-plicable	3	2	10,673
2,006	Married	46	White	$25000 or more	Strong republi-can	Protestant	South-ern baptist	–	2	9,729
2,006	Married	46	White	$25000 or more	Strong republi-can	Protestant	South-ern baptist	–	2	9,755

2,006	Married	46	White	$25000 or more	Indepen-dent	None	Not ap-plicable	–	2	11,491
2,006	Married	46	White	$25000 or more	Indepen-dent	None	Not ap-plicable	–	2	11,968
2,006	Married	46	White	$25000 or more	Not str democrat	Catholic	Not ap-plicable	–	2	8,858
2,006	Married	46	White	$25000 or more	Not str democrat	Catholic	Not ap-plicable	–	2	8,927
2,006	Married	47	Other	Don't know	Indepen-dent	Catholic	Not ap-plicable	–	2	9,474
2,006	Married	47	Other	Don't know	Indepen-dent	Catholic	Not ap-plicable	–	2	11,104
2,006	Married	47	White	Refused	Strong republi-can	Catholic	Not ap-plicable	–	2	11,205
2,006	Married	47	White	Refused	Strong republi-can	Catholic	Not ap-plicable	–	2	11,650
2,006	Married	47	White	$25000 or more	Not str republi-can	Catholic	Not ap-plicable	–	2	10,358
2,006	Married	47	White	$25000 or more	Not str republi-can	Catholic	Not ap-plicable	–	2	12,235
2,006	Married	47	White	$25000 or more	Strong democrat	Protestant	United method-ist	2	2	10,515
2,006	Married	47	White	$25000 or more	Strong democrat	Protestant	United method-ist	2	2	11,771
2,006	Married	48	White	$25000 or more	Not str republi-can	Catholic	Not ap-plicable	–	2	10,143
2,006	Married	48	White	$25000 or more	Not str republi-can	Catholic	Not ap-plicable	–	2	10,458
2,006	Married	49	White	$25000 or more	Strong republi-can	Protestant	United method-ist	–	2	9,356
2,006	Married	49	White	$25000 or more	Strong republi-can	Protestant	United method-ist	–	2	9,571
2,006	Married	49	White	Not appli-cable	Indepen-dent	Catholic	Not ap-plicable	–	2	8,510
2,006	Married	49	White	Not appli-cable	Indepen-dent	Catholic	Not ap-plicable	–	2	8,855
2,006	Married	50	White	$25000 or more	Not str republi-can	Catholic	Not ap-plicable	–	2	12,744
2,006	Married	50	White	$25000 or more	Not str republi-can	Catholic	Not ap-plicable	–	2	12,864

2,006	Married	53	White	$25000 or more	Strong republi-can	Protestant	Other	2	2	8,542
2,006	Married	53	White	$25000 or more	Strong republi-can	Protestant	Other	2	2	12,839
2,006	Married	53	White	$25000 or more	Indepen-dent	Catholic	Not ap-plicable	–	2	8,486
2,006	Married	53	White	$25000 or more	Indepen-dent	Catholic	Not ap-plicable	–	2	9,661
2,006	Married	53	White	$25000 or more	Not str democrat	Protestant	Other	–	2	11,056
2,006	Married	53	White	$25000 or more	Not str democrat	Protestant	Other	–	2	11,724
2,006	Married	54	White	$25000 or more	Not str republi-can	None	Not ap-plicable	–	2	9,945
2,006	Married	54	White	$25000 or more	Not str republi-can	None	Not ap-plicable	–	2	12,740
2,006	Married	54	White	$25000 or more	Strong democrat	None	Not ap-plicable	–	2	9,536
2,006	Married	54	White	$25000 or more	Strong democrat	None	Not ap-plicable	–	2	10,493
2,006	Married	54	White	$25000 or more	Strong democrat	Protestant	South-ern baptist	–	2	10,794
2,006	Married	54	White	$25000 or more	Strong democrat	Protestant	South-ern baptist	–	2	11,941
2,006	Married	55	White	$25000 or more	Not str democrat	Catholic	Not ap-plicable	–	3	8,809
2,006	Married	55	White	$25000 or more	Not str democrat	Catholic	Not ap-plicable	–	3	9,019
2,006	Married	55	White	$25000 or more	Not str democrat	Catholic	Not ap-plicable	–	3	11,008
2,006	Married	56	White	$25000 or more	Indepen-dent	Catholic	Not ap-plicable	–	2	12,244
2,006	Married	56	White	$25000 or more	Indepen-dent	Catholic	Not ap-plicable	–	2	12,777
2,006	Married	57	White	Refused	Ind,near rep	Catholic	Not ap-plicable	2	2	10,459
2,006	Married	57	White	Refused	Ind,near rep	Catholic	Not ap-plicable	2	2	11,743
2,006	Married	58	White	Refused	Not str republi-can	Catholic	Not ap-plicable	–	2	8,568
2,006	Married	58	White	Refused	Not str republi-can	Catholic	Not ap-plicable	–	2	9,805
2,006	Married	58	White	$25000 or more	Ind,near dem	Protestant	Other	–	2	10,937

2,006	Married	58	White	$25000 or more	Ind,near dem	Protestant	Other	–	2	11,653
2,006	Married	59	White	$25000 or more	Strong republican	None	Not applicable	–	2	11,340
2,006	Married	59	White	$25000 or more	Strong republican	None	Not applicable	–	2	12,594
2,006	Married	59	White	$25000 or more	Independent	Protestant	Other	–	2	11,791
2,006	Married	59	White	$25000 or more	Independent	Protestant	Other	–	2	12,430
2,006	Married	60	White	Not applicable	Strong republican	Protestant	Presbyterian-dk wh	–	2	10,457
2,006	Married	60	White	Not applicable	Strong republican	Protestant	Presbyterian-dk wh	–	2	11,783
2,006	Married	61	White	$25000 or more	Not str democrat	Catholic	Not applicable	–	2	10,296
2,006	Married	61	White	$25000 or more	Not str democrat	Catholic	Not applicable	–	2	10,843
2,006	Married	62	White	$25000 or more	Strong democrat	None	Not applicable	–	2	10,202
2,006	Married	62	White	$25000 or more	Strong democrat	None	Not applicable	–	2	11,584
2,006	Married	63	White	$25000 or more	Not str republican	Catholic	Not applicable	–	2	9,090
2,006	Married	63	White	$25000 or more	Not str republican	Catholic	Not applicable	–	2	12,558
2,006	Married	65	White	Not applicable	Strong republican	Catholic	Not applicable	–	2	10,370
2,006	Married	65	White	Not applicable	Strong republican	Catholic	Not applicable	–	2	11,658
2,006	Married	67	White	Not applicable	Ind,near rep	Catholic	Not applicable	–	2	9,694
2,006	Married	67	White	Not applicable	Ind,near rep	Catholic	Not applicable	–	2	11,645
2,006	Married	68	White	Not applicable	Strong republican	Catholic	Not applicable	–	2	9,834
2,006	Married	68	White	Not applicable	Strong republican	Catholic	Not applicable	–	2	10,847
2,006	Married	69	White	Not applicable	Not str democrat	Catholic	Not applicable	–	2	9,698
2,006	Married	69	White	Not applicable	Not str democrat	Catholic	Not applicable	–	2	10,314

2,006	Married	72	White	Not applicable	Not str democrat	Protestant	Other	–	2	12,498
2,006	Married	72	White	Not applicable	Not str democrat	Protestant	Other	–	2	12,569
2,008	Never married	19	White	Not applicable	Not str republican	None	Not applicable	–	2	14,253
2,008	Never married	19	White	Not applicable	Not str republican	None	Not applicable	–	2	14,878
2,008	Never married	27	White	Not applicable	Ind,near dem	None	Not applicable	–	2	13,021
2,008	Never married	27	White	Not applicable	Ind,near dem	None	Not applicable	–	2	13,191
2,008	Never married	43	White	$25000 or more	Strong democrat	Protestant	Episcopal	–	2	13,695
2,008	Never married	43	White	$25000 or more	Strong democrat	Protestant	Episcopal	–	2	14,158
2,008	Divorced	65	White	Not applicable	Ind,near dem	None	Not applicable	2	2	13,672
2,008	Divorced	65	White	Not applicable	Ind,near dem	None	Not applicable	2	2	14,071
2,008	Widowed	79	White	Not applicable	Not str democrat	Protestant	United methodist	–	2	13,745
2,008	Widowed	79	White	Not applicable	Not str democrat	Protestant	United methodist	–	2	14,539
2,008	Widowed	89	White	Not applicable	Not str democrat	Catholic	Not applicable	8	2	13,550
2,008	Widowed	89	White	Not applicable	Not str democrat	Catholic	Not applicable	8	2	14,554
2,008	Widowed	89	White	Not applicable	Strong democrat	Protestant	United methodist	–	2	13,954
2,008	Widowed	89	White	Not applicable	Strong democrat	Protestant	United methodist	–	2	14,899
2,008	Married	34	White	Not applicable	Independent	Catholic	Not applicable	4	2	13,057
2,008	Married	34	White	Not applicable	Independent	Catholic	Not applicable	4	2	13,112
2,008	Married	39	White	$25000 or more	Not str republican	Catholic	Not applicable	1	2	13,182
2,008	Married	39	White	$25000 or more	Not str republican	Catholic	Not applicable	1	2	14,439
2,008	Married	46	White	$25000 or more	Ind,near dem	None	Not applicable	1	2	13,184
2,008	Married	46	White	$25000 or more	Ind,near dem	None	Not applicable	1	2	14,765

2,008	Married	51	White	$25000 or more	Not str republican	Protestant	Other	6	2	14,018
2,008	Married	51	White	$25000 or more	Not str republican	Protestant	Other	6	2	14,585
2,008	Married	56	White	$25000 or more	Not str republican	Protestant	United methodist	–	2	13,372
2,008	Married	56	White	$25000 or more	Not str republican	Protestant	United methodist	–	2	14,471
2,008	Married	75	White	Not applicable	Ind,near dem	Catholic	Not applicable	4	2	13,989
2,008	Married	75	White	Not applicable	Ind,near dem	Catholic	Not applicable	4	2	14,392
2,008	Married	76	White	Not applicable	Strong republican	Protestant	Other	4	2	13,945
2,008	Married	76	White	Not applicable	Strong republican	Protestant	Other	4	2	14,782
2,008	Married	76	White	Not applicable	Strong democrat	Protestant	Other	–	2	13,950
2,008	Married	76	White	Not applicable	Strong democrat	Protestant	Other	–	2	14,097
2,010	Never married	26	White	$20000–24999	Independent	Catholic	Not applicable	3	2	16,694
2,010	Never married	26	White	$20000–24999	Independent	Catholic	Not applicable	3	2	16,819
2,010	Never married	27	White	$25000 or more	Not str democrat	None	Not applicable	1	2	16,044
2,010	Never married	27	White	$25000 or more	Not str democrat	None	Not applicable	1	2	16,442
2,010	Divorced	37	White	$25000 or more	Independent	Catholic	Not applicable	–	2	15,315
2,010	Divorced	37	White	$25000 or more	Independent	Catholic	Not applicable	–	2	15,600
2,010	Divorced	57	White	$25000 or more	Ind,near dem	None	Not applicable	–	2	15,867
2,010	Divorced	57	White	$25000 or more	Ind,near dem	None	Not applicable	–	2	16,529
2,010	Divorced	60	White	$25000 or more	Strong democrat	None	Not applicable	–	2	15,162
2,010	Divorced	60	White	$25000 or more	Strong democrat	None	Not applicable	–	2	15,196
2,010	Married	30	White	$25000 or more	Not str democrat	Christian	No denomination	–	2	16,184
2,010	Married	30	White	$25000 or more	Not str democrat	Christian	No denomination	–	2	16,398

2,010	Married	43	White	Refused	Independent	None	Not applicable	2	2	14,963
2,010	Married	43	White	Refused	Independent	None	Not applicable	2	2	15,628
2,010	Married	43	White	$25000 or more	Strong republican	Catholic	Not applicable	–	2	15,200
2,010	Married	43	White	$25000 or more	Strong republican	Catholic	Not applicable	–	2	16,553
2,010	Married	44	White	$25000 or more	Strong republican	Catholic	Not applicable	–	2	14,993
2,010	Married	44	White	$25000 or more	Strong republican	Catholic	Not applicable	–	2	16,181
2,010	Married	49	White	$25000 or more	Not str republican	Protestant	Other	–	2	15,937
2,010	Married	49	White	$25000 or more	Not str republican	Protestant	Other	–	2	16,761
2,010	Married	50	White	$25000 or more	Strong republican	Catholic	Not applicable	1	2	15,661
2,010	Married	50	White	$25000 or more	Strong republican	Catholic	Not applicable	1	2	16,595
2,012	Never married	22	White	Not applicable	Ind,near dem	Catholic	Not applicable	1	2	16,972
2,012	Never married	22	White	Not applicable	Ind,near dem	Catholic	Not applicable	1	2	18,438
2,012	Never married	39	Other	Not applicable	Not str democrat	Catholic	Not applicable	–	2	16,993
2,012	Never married	39	Other	Not applicable	Not str democrat	Catholic	Not applicable	–	2	17,430
2,012	Widowed	80	White	Not applicable	Independent	Catholic	Not applicable	2	2	17,580
2,012	Widowed	80	White	Not applicable	Independent	Catholic	Not applicable	2	2	18,320
2,012	Married	26	White	Not applicable	Independent	Catholic	Not applicable	–	2	17,491
2,012	Married	26	White	Not applicable	Independent	Catholic	Not applicable	–	2	18,588
2,012	Married	36	White	$25000 or more	Strong democrat	None	Not applicable	–	2	17,187
2,012	Married	36	White	$25000 or more	Strong democrat	None	Not applicable	–	2	17,434
2,012	Married	42	White	$25000 or more	Ind,near dem	Catholic	Not applicable	3	2	17,006
2,012	Married	42	White	$25000 or more	Ind,near dem	Catholic	Not applicable	3	2	17,202

2,012	Married	50	White	$25000 or more	Not str democrat	Catholic	Not applicable	–	2	17,182
2,012	Married	50	White	$25000 or more	Not str democrat	Catholic	Not applicable	–	2	17,747
2,012	Married	51	White	$25000 or more	Strong republican	Catholic	Not applicable	2	2	17,407
2,012	Married	51	White	$25000 or more	Strong republican	Catholic	Not applicable	2	2	17,429
2,012	Married	62	White	Not applicable	Strong republican	Catholic	Not applicable	–	2	17,102
2,012	Married	62	White	Not applicable	Strong republican	Catholic	Not applicable	–	2	17,274
2,014	Never married	20	Black	$3000 to 3999	Ind,near dem	None	Not applicable	–	2	19,123
2,014	Never married	20	Black	$3000 to 3999	Ind,near dem	None	Not applicable	–	2	19,704
2,014	Never married	20	White	$4000 to 4999	Not str republican	Protestant	Other	–	2	20,218
2,014	Never married	20	White	$4000 to 4999	Not str republican	Protestant	Other	–	2	20,933
2,014	Never married	22	White	Not applicable	Independent	None	Not applicable	–	2	19,153
2,014	Never married	22	White	Not applicable	Independent	None	Not applicable	–	2	20,175
2,014	Never married	26	White	$20000–24999	Independent	None	Not applicable	–	2	19,640
2,014	Never married	26	White	$20000–24999	Independent	None	Not applicable	–	2	19,847
2,014	Never married	28	Other	Not applicable	Independent	None	Not applicable	–	2	19,853
2,014	Never married	28	Other	Not applicable	Independent	None	Not applicable	–	2	20,958
2,014	Never married	42	White	$25000 or more	Ind,near dem	None	Not applicable	4	2	19,919
2,014	Never married	42	White	$25000 or more	Ind,near dem	None	Not applicable	4	2	19,938
2,014	Divorced	56	White	$25000 or more	Not str democrat	Catholic	Not applicable	1	2	19,794
2,014	Divorced	56	White	$25000 or more	Not str democrat	Catholic	Not applicable	1	2	19,877
2,014	Divorced	60	White	$25000 or more	Not str democrat	Catholic	Not applicable	–	2	20,357
2,014	Divorced	60	White	$25000 or more	Not str democrat	Catholic	Not applicable	–	2	20,453

2,014	Wid-owed	70	Other	Not appli-cable	Not str democrat	Catholic	Not ap-plicable	–	2	20,166
2,014	Wid-owed	70	Other	Not appli-cable	Not str democrat	Catholic	Not ap-plicable	–	2	21,048
2,014	Married	29	White	Not appli-cable	Not str republi-can	Protestant	Other	2	2	20,975
2,014	Married	29	White	Not appli-cable	Not str republi-can	Protestant	Other	2	2	21,101
2,014	Married	38	Other	Not appli-cable	Indepen-dent	None	Not ap-plicable	–	2	19,821
2,014	Married	38	Other	Not appli-cable	Indepen-dent	None	Not ap-plicable	–	2	21,286
2,014	Married	41	White	$25000 or more	Not str democrat	Catholic	Not ap-plicable	2	2	19,084
2,014	Married	41	White	$25000 or more	Not str democrat	Catholic	Not ap-plicable	2	2	19,279
2,014	Married	44	White	$25000 or more	Ind,near dem	Catholic	Not ap-plicable	–	2	19,486
2,014	Married	44	White	$25000 or more	Ind,near dem	Catholic	Not ap-plicable	–	2	19,785
2,014	Married	47	White	$25000 or more	Not str democrat	None	Not ap-plicable	–	2	19,435
2,014	Married	47	White	$25000 or more	Not str democrat	None	Not ap-plicable	–	2	19,711
2,014	Married	52	White	$25000 or more	Ind,near dem	Catholic	Not ap-plicable	–	2	19,348
2,014	Married	52	White	$25000 or more	Ind,near dem	Catholic	Not ap-plicable	–	2	20,596
2,014	Married	52	White	Not appli-cable	Not str democrat	Christian	No denomi-nation	–	2	21,193
2,014	Married	52	White	Not appli-cable	Not str democrat	Christian	No denomi-nation	–	2	21,320
2,014	Married	53	White	$25000 or more	Not str republi-can	Catholic	Not ap-plicable	3	2	19,591
2,014	Married	53	White	$25000 or more	Not str republi-can	Catholic	Not ap-plicable	3	2	19,882
2,014	Married	54	White	$25000 or more	Ind,near dem	None	Not ap-plicable	–	2	19,449
2,014	Married	54	White	$25000 or more	Ind,near dem	None	Not ap-plicable	–	2	19,786
2,014	Married	54	White	$25000 or more	Ind,near dem	Catholic	Not ap-plicable	–	2	19,433
2,014	Married	54	White	$25000 or more	Ind,near dem	Catholic	Not ap-plicable	–	2	20,747

2,014	Married	54	White	$25000 or more	Not str democrat	None	Not applicable	2	2	21,343
2,014	Married	54	White	$25000 or more	Not str democrat	None	Not applicable	2	2	21,348
2,014	Married	57	White	$25000 or more	Strong democrat	Protestant	Other	3	2	20,493
2,014	Married	57	White	$25000 or more	Strong democrat	Protestant	Other	3	2	20,503
2,014	Married	58	White	$25000 or more	Ind,near dem	Catholic	Not applicable	–	3	20,263
2,014	Married	58	White	$25000 or more	Ind,near dem	Catholic	Not applicable	–	3	20,324
2,014	Married	58	White	$25000 or more	Ind,near dem	Catholic	Not applicable	–	3	21,355
2,014	Married	60	White	$25000 or more	Not str republican	Protestant	No denomination	–	2	19,905
2,014	Married	60	White	$25000 or more	Not str republican	Protestant	No denomination	–	2	20,932
2,014	Married	71	White	Not applicable	Not str democrat	Catholic	Not applicable	–	2	19,831
2,014	Married	71	White	Not applicable	Not str democrat	Catholic	Not applicable	–	2	20,715

We see that:

- There are many duplicated rows.
- The data has 2 additional columns "dupe_count" containing the count of the duplicated rows, and "row_id" containing the row numbers.
- The first row, with row_id or row number = 167, has 2000 for the year column, Never married for the marital column, 19 for the age column, White for the race column, $1000 to 2999 for the rincome column, Not str republican for the partyid column, Catholic for the relig column, Not applicable for the denom column, and missing value for tv hours.
- The 2nd row, with row_id or row number = 1667, has the same values as the first row so dupe_count has a count of 2 for both rows.
- The 3rd row, with row_id or row number = 790, has 2000 for the year column, Never married for the marital column, 30 for the age column, White for the race column, $25000 or more for the rincome column, Not str republican for the partyid column, Catholic for the relig column, Not applicable for the denom column, and 1 for tv hours.
- The 4th row, with row_id or row number = 1547, has the same values as the 3rd row so dupe_count has a count of 2 for both rows, and so on.

2.3.2. Removing Duplicated Rows of General Social Survey Data

If we are sure that the duplicated rows correspond to the same persons and not to different persons, we can use the distinct function with all column names of the gss_cat data to keep the unique combinations of these columns only.

The resulting data frame is called gss_cat2 and we use the glimpse function to see its structure.

```
gss_cat2<-gss_cat %>% distinct(year, marital, age, race, rincome,
partyid,relig,denom,tvhours)
glimpse(gss_cat2)
## Rows: 21,220
## Columns: 9
## $ year <int> 2000, 2000, 2000, 2000, 2000, 2000, 2000, 2000,
2000, 2000, 20…
## $ marital <fct> Never married, Divorced, Widowed, Never
married, Divorced, Mar…
## $ age <int> 26, 48, 67, 39, 25, 25, 36, 44, 44, 47, 53, 52,
52, 51, 52, 40…
## $ race <fct> White, White, White, White, White, White, White,
White, White,…
## $ rincome <fct> $8000 to 9999, $8000 to 9999, Not applicable,
Not applicable, …
## $ partyid <fct> "Ind,near rep", "Not str republican",
"Independent", "Ind,near…
## $ relig <fct> Protestant, Protestant, Protestant, Orthodox-
christian, None, …
## $ denom <fct> "Southern baptist", "Baptist-dk which", "No
denomination", "No…
## $ tvhours <int> 12, NA, 2, 4, 1, NA, 3, NA, 0, 3, 2, NA, 1,
NA, 1, 7, NA, 3, 3…
```

The data now contains 21220 rows and 9 columns. We can use the get_dupes function again to check that our data does not contain any duplicates now.

```
gss_cat2 %>% mutate(row_id = row_number()) %>%
get_dupes(-row_id)
## # A tibble: 0 × 11
```

```
## # i 11 variables: year <int>, marital <fct>, age <int>, race
<fct>,
## # rincome <fct>, partyid <fct>, relig <fct>, denom <fct>,
tvhours <int>,
## # dupe_count <int>, row_id <int>
```

The result is a tibble or data frame with 0 rows and 11 columns, so no rows are duplicated now.

2.3.3. Duplicates of BRFSS Survey Data

Similarly, We use the get_dupes function after the BRFSS data using the "%>%" operator.

```
riskfactors %>% get_dupes()
## # A tibble: 0 × 35
## # i 35 variables: state <fct>, sex <fct>, age <int>, weight_
lbs <int>,
## # height_inch <int>, bmi <dbl>, marital <fct>, pregnant <fct>,
## # children <int>, education <fct>, employment <fct>, income
<fct>,
## # veteran <fct>, hispanic <fct>, health_general <fct>, health_
physical <int>,
## # health_mental <int>, health_poor <int>, health_cover <fct>,
## # provide_care <fct>, activity_limited <fct>, drink_any <fct>,
## # drink_days <int>, drink_average <int>, smoke_100 <fct>,
smoke_days <fct>, …
```

We see that we have no duplicated rows in this data so we move to the next step which is checking missing.

2.4. CHECK MISSING

2.4.1. Check missing of the General Social Survey Data

The miss_var_summary function, from the naniar package, provides the number and percentage of missing in each column of our data, gss_cat2. We will use the gss_cat2 data because this data does not contain the duplicated rows in the previous step.

By default, the miss_var_summary function orders the columns from the most missing to the least missing. We will convert the result to a table as before.

```
gss_cat2 %>% miss_var_summary() %>% flextable() %>% theme_box()
%>%
set_caption(caption = "Count and percentage of missing in all
columns of the general social survey data")
```

Table 2.2. Count and Percentage of missing in All Columns of the General Social Survey Data

variable	n_miss	pct_miss
tvhours	9,933	46.8096136
age	76	0.3581527
year	0	0.0000000
marital	0	0.0000000
race	0	0.0000000
rincome	0	0.0000000
partyid	0	0.0000000
relig	0	0.0000000
denom	0	0.0000000

We see that:

- We have 3 columns: the variable for column names, n_miss for count of missing, and pct_miss for percentage of missing in each column.
- The tvhours column contains the largest number of missing (9933) with a percentage = 9933/21220 = 0.468 or 46.8 %. We divide by 21220 because this is the number of rows in the gss_cat2 data.
- The age column contains the 2nd largest number of missing (76) with a percentage = 76/21220 = 0.00358 or 0.358 %.
- All other columns have no missing.

2.4.2. Visualizing missing of the General Social Survey Data

The gg_miss_var function, from the naniar package too, plots the number of missing in each variable or column.

By default, the gg_miss_var function orders the columns to show which columns have the most missing data.

To further customize the plot, we use:

- The labs function to add a plot title.
- The theme function with the plot.title argument and using the element_text function with the argument hjust = 0.5 to place the plot title at the top center of the plot.

- The function gg_miss_var is applied to gss_cat2 data using the "%>%" operator, while to add other functions to gg_miss_var function, we use the "+" operator. This is because the result of gg_miss_var is a ggplot object that is built in layers with additional layers added using functions and the "+" operator.

```
gss_cat2 %>% gg_miss_var()+
labs(title = "Number of missing in columns of the general social
survey data")+
theme(plot.title = element_text(hjust = 0.5))
```

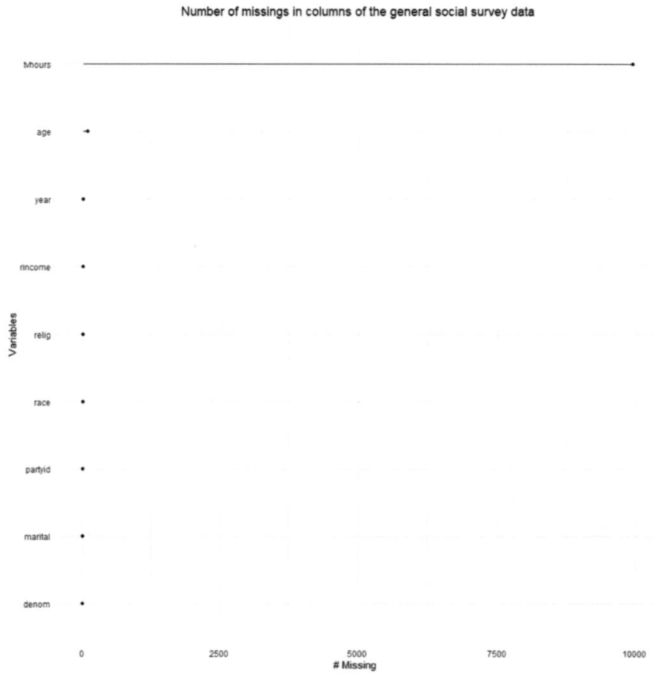

We see that most missing are in the tvhours column followed by the age column.

The same function can be used to plot the percentage of missing in each column by using the show_pct = TRUE argument.

```
gss_cat2 %>% gg_miss_var(show_pct = TRUE)+
labs(title = "Percentage of missing in columns of the general
social survey data")+
theme(plot.title = element_text(hjust = 0.5))
```

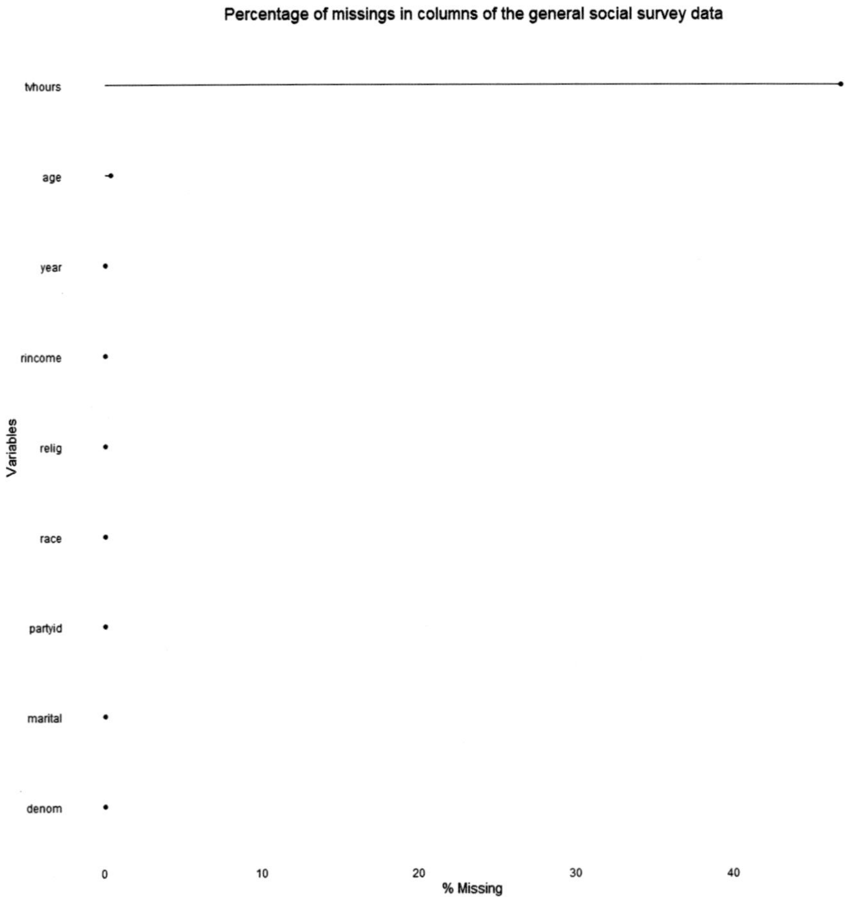

We see that the highest percentage of missing are in the tvhours column followed by the age column.

The vis_miss function provides a plot of the missing locations across all columns and rows of our data. The function also colors the cells according to missing. The black cell indicates a missing cell and the grey cell indicates a present cell.

```
gss_cat2 %>% vis_miss()+
labs(title = "Percentage and Location of missing in columns of the general social survey data")+
theme(plot.title = element_text(hjust = 0.5))
```

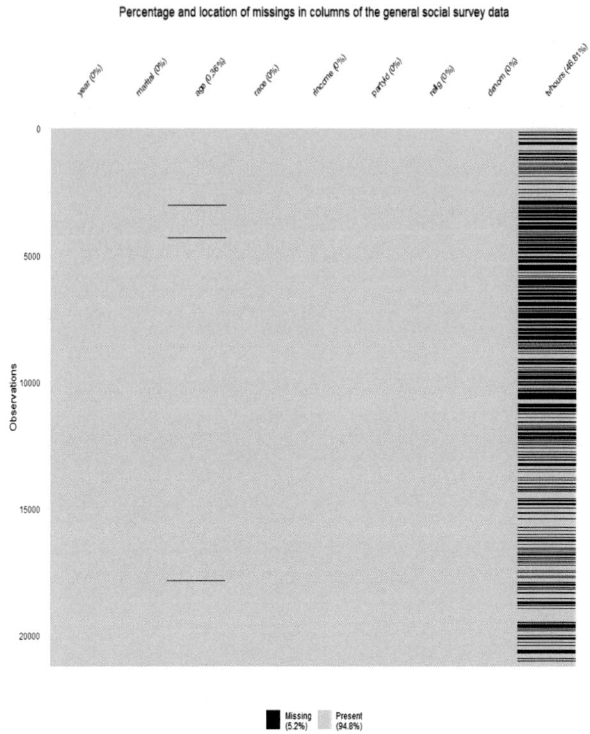

We see that:

- The plot provides information on the overall percentage of missing values in the legend and each column.
- We have 21220 rows X 9 columns = 190980 cells, and we have 9933 missing in the tvhours column, and 76 missing in the age column with a total of 10009 missing. So the percentage of missing in the whole data = 10009/190980 = 0.052 or 5.2%.
- Only the age and tvhours columns have missing with a percentage of 0.36 and 46.81 respectively.
- Other columns have a percentage of 0% or no missing.

2.4.3. Removing missing from the General Social Survey Data

We can remove the missing values by using the drop_na function that will keep only complete rows with no missing in any column. Because any row with missing will be deleted we are likely losing many rows and information from our data. Alternatively, we can impute the missing values using many techniques that will be described in our next book about machine learning.

We create another data frame "gss_cat3" by applying the drop_na function on the gss_cat2 data. Then, we use the glimpse function to see the data structure.

```
gss_cat3<-gss_cat2 %>% drop_na()
glimpse(gss_cat3)
## Rows: 11,249
## Columns: 9
## $ year <int> 2000, 2000, 2000, 2000, 2000, 2000, 2000, 2000, 2000, 2000, 20…
## $ marital <fct> Never married, Widowed, Never married, Divorced, Never married…
## $ age <int> 26, 67, 39, 25, 36, 44, 47, 53, 52, 52, 40, 44, 40, 48, 49, 19…
## $ race <fct> White, White, White, White, White, White, White, White, White,…
## $ rincome <fct> $8000 to 9999, Not applicable, Not applicable, Not applicable,…
## $ partyid <fct> "Ind,near rep", "Independent", "Ind,near rep", "Not str democr…
## $ relig <fct> Protestant, Protestant, Orthodox-christian, None, Christian, P…
## $ denom <fct> "Southern baptist", "No denomination", "Not applicable", "Not …
## $ tvhours <int> 12, 2, 4, 1, 3, 0, 3, 2, 1, 1, 7, 3, 3, 1, 2, 2, 1, 3, 4, 7, 3…
```

The data becomes 11249 rows (instead of 21220) and 9 columns.

We can quickly check the missing in this new data using the vis_miss function.

```
gss_cat3 %>% vis_miss()+
labs(title = "Percentage and location of missing in columns of the general social survey data after missing removal")+
theme(plot.title = element_text(hjust = 0.5))
```

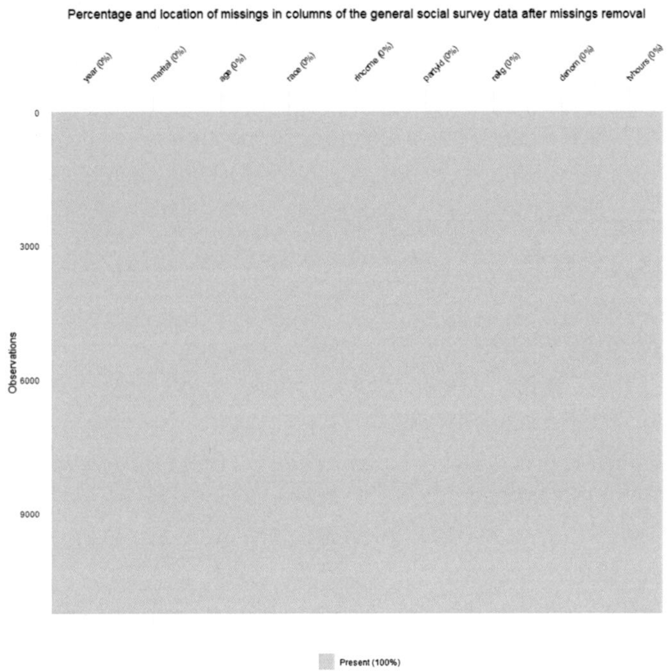

We have no missing anymore.

2.4.4. Check missing of the BRFSS Data

We will use the miss_var_summary function directly on the risk factors data because this data does not contain the duplicated rows in the previous step.

We will convert the result to a table as before.

```
riskfactors %>% miss_var_summary() %>% flextable() %>% theme_
box() %>%
set_caption(caption = "Count and percentage of missing in all
columns of the BRFSS data")
```

Table 2.3. Count and Percentage of missing in All Columns of the BRFSS Data

variable	n_miss	pct_miss
pregnant	215	87.7551020
smoke_stop	212	86.5306122
smoke_last	161	65.7142857
drink_average	135	55.1020408
drink_days	134	54.6938776

smoke_days	128	52.2448980
health_poor	113	46.1224490
bmi	11	4.4897959
weight_lbs	10	4.0816327
diet_fruit	8	3.2653061
diet_salad	8	3.2653061
diet_potato	8	3.2653061
diet_carrot	8	3.2653061
diet_vegetable	8	3.2653061
diet_juice	8	3.2653061
veteran	3	1.2244898
provide_care	3	1.2244898
activity_limited	3	1.2244898
height_inch	2	0.8163265
hispanic	2	0.8163265
drink_any	2	0.8163265
smoke_100	2	0.8163265
marital	1	0.4081633
education	1	0.4081633
state	0	0.0000000
sex	0	0.0000000
age	0	0.0000000
children	0	0.0000000
employment	0	0.0000000
income	0	0.0000000
health_general	0	0.0000000
health_physical	0	0.0000000
health_mental	0	0.0000000
health_cover	0	0.0000000

We see that:

- Again, we have 3 columns: the variable for column names, n_miss for count of missing, and pct_miss for percentage of missing in each column.
- The pregnant column contains the largest number of missing (215) with a percentage = 215/245 = 0.877 or 87.7 %. We divide by 245 because this is the number of rows in our data.

- The smoke_stop column contains the 2nd largest number of missing (212) with a percentage = 212/245 = 0.865 or 86.5 %.
- The smoke_last column contains the 3rd largest number of missing (161) with a percentage = 161/245 = 0.657 or 65.7 %, and so on.
- Some other columns have no missing like state, sex, age, children, etc.

2.4.5. Visualizing missing of the BRFSS Data

We use the gg_miss_var function as described previously to plot the number of missing in each column of the BRFSS data.

```
riskfactors %>% gg_miss_var()+
labs(title = "Number of missing in columns of the BRFSS data")+
theme(plot.title = element_text(hjust = 0.5))
```

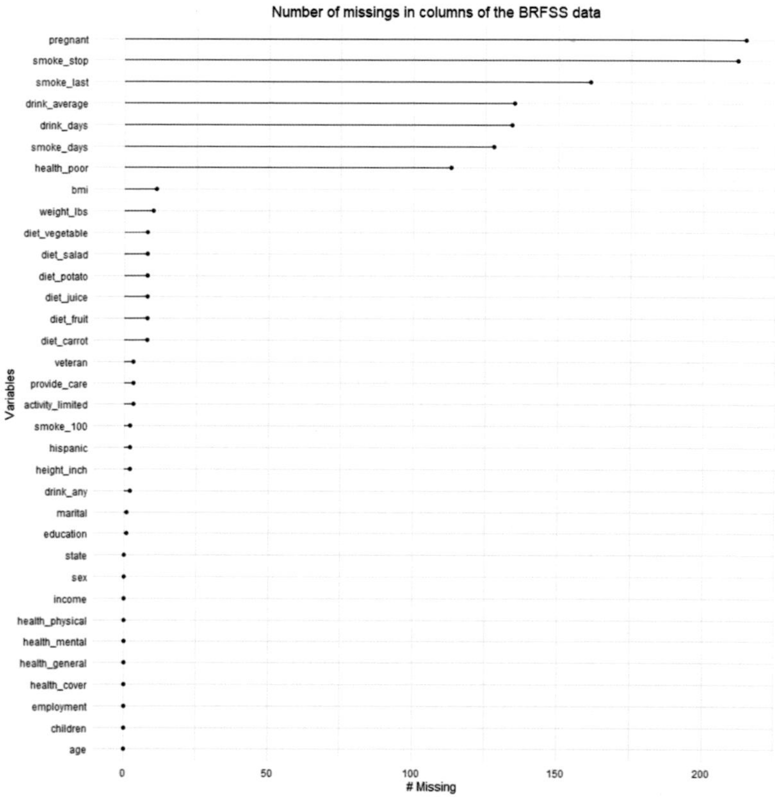

We see that most missing are in the pregnant column followed by smoke_ stop, smoke_last, drink_average, etc columns.

The same function can be used to plot the percentage of missing in each column by using the show_pct = TRUE argument.

```
riskfactors %>% gg_miss_var(show_pct = TRUE)+
labs(title = "Percentage of missing in columns of the BRFSS data")+
theme(plot.title = element_text(hjust = 0.5))
```

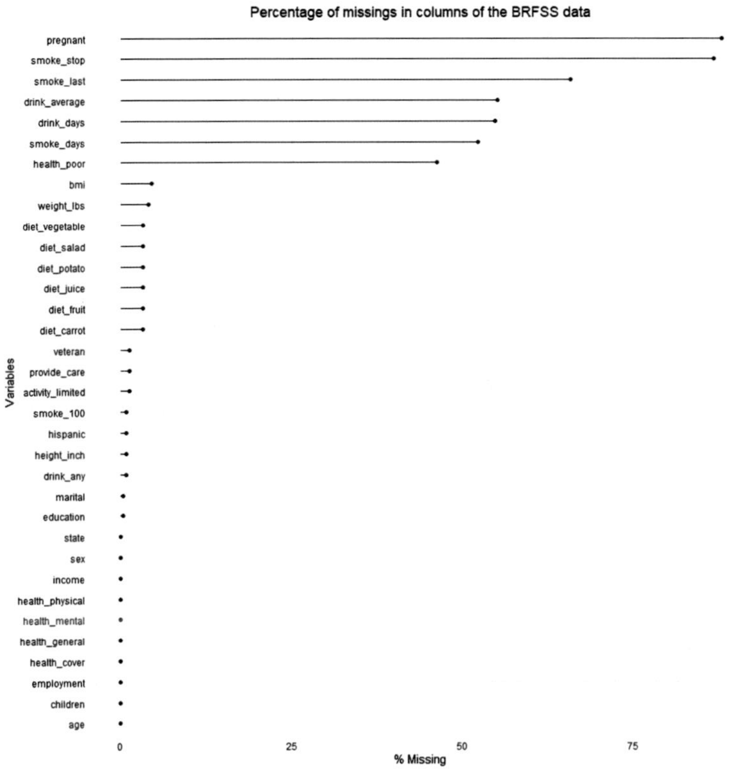

We see that the highest percentage of missing are in the pregnant column followed by smoke_stop, smoke_last, drink_average, etc columns.

We can also use the vis_miss function to provide a plot of the missing locations across all columns and rows of our data.

```
riskfactors %>% vis_miss()+
labs(title = "Percentage and location of missing in columns of the BRFSS data")+
theme(plot.title = element_text(hjust = 0.5))
```

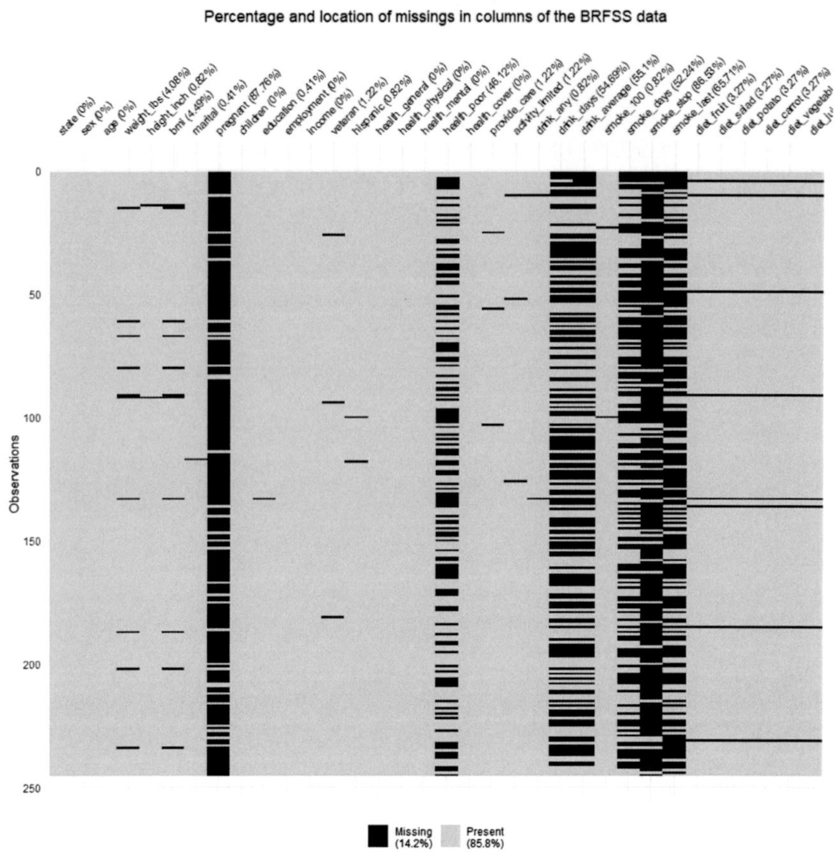

We see that:

- The plot provides information on the overall percentage of missing values in the legend and each column.
- The percentage of missing in the whole data = 14.2%.
- Each column has its percentage of missing. For example, the state and sex columns have 0% missing or no missing, while the weight_lbs and height_inch have a percentage of missing of 4.08% and 0.82% respectively.

2.4.6. Removing missing from the BRFSS Data

Similarly, we can remove the missing values by using the drop_na function that will keep only complete rows with no missing in any column.

We create another data frame "riskfactors2" by applying the drop_na function on the riskfactors data. Then, we use the glimpse function to see the data structure.

```
riskfactors2<-riskfactors %>% drop_na()
glimpse(riskfactors2)
## Rows: 0
## Columns: 34
## $ state <fct>
## $ sex <fct>
## $ age <int>
## $ weight_lbs <int>
## $ height_inch <int>
## $ bmi <dbl>
## $ marital <fct>
## $ pregnant <fct>
## $ children <int>
## $ education <fct>
## $ employment <fct>
## $ income <fct>
## $ veteran <fct>
## $ hispanic <fct>
## $ health_general <fct>
## $ health_physical <int>
## $ health_mental <int>
## $ health_poor <int>
## $ health_cover <fct>
## $ provide_care <fct>
## $ activity_limited <fct>
## $ drink_any <fct>
## $ drink_days <int>
## $ drink_average <int>
## $ smoke_100 <fct>
## $ smoke_days <fct>
## $ smoke_stop <fct>
## $ smoke_last <fct>
## $ diet_fruit <int>
## $ diet_salad <int>
## $ diet_potato <int>
```

```
## $ diet_carrot <int>
## $ diet_vegetable <int>
## $ diet_juice <int>
```

The data becomes 0 rows (instead of 245) and 34 columns. This makes the data useless since we do not have any row value in any column. So, we must go to the other options of imputation.

2.5. STRANGE VALUES

We will look at the unique values within each column and replace the strange values as necessary.

Although this step will take a lot of time, it is necessary to ensure that the column values are real and not fake or missing values.

2.5.1. The General Social Survey Data

2.5.1.1. The Year Column

We use the count function with the year argument to get the unique values of the year column.

```
gss_cat2 %>% count(year) %>% flextable() %>% theme_box() %>%
set_caption(caption = "The unique values of the year column in the general social survey data")
```

Table 2.4. The Unique Values of the Year Column in the General Social Survey Data

year	n
2,000	2,808
2,002	2,716
2,004	2,763
2,006	4,414
2,008	2,008
2,010	2,033
2,012	1,965
2,014	2,513

The values of the year column are ok and no strange values are present.

2.5.1.2. The Marital Column

```
gss_cat2 %>% count(marital) %>% flextable() %>% theme_box() %>%
set_caption(caption = "The unique values of the marital column
in the general social survey data")
```

Table 2.5. The Unique Values of the Marital Column in the General Social Survey Data

marital	n
No answer	17
Never married	5,372
Separated	743
Divorced	3,367
Widowed	1,789
Married	9,932

The "No answer" value is not a real marital status value and should be converted to NA or missing.

2.5.1.3. The Age Column

```
gss_cat2 %>% count(age) %>% flextable() %>% theme_box() %>%
set_caption(caption = "The unique values of the age column in the
general social survey data")
```

Table 2.6. The Unique Values of the Age Column in the General Social Survey Data

age	n
18	90
19	247
20	248
21	275
22	295
23	360
24	341
25	395
26	396

27	379
28	381
29	371
30	427
31	400
32	443
33	420
34	420
35	410
36	423
37	431
38	421
39	407
40	447
41	431
42	401
43	439
44	422
45	398
46	415
47	423
48	417
49	410
50	423
51	386
52	396
53	392
54	380
55	359
56	379
57	318
58	321
59	320
60	333
61	305
62	308

63	291
64	251
65	255
66	231
67	269
68	204
69	199
70	211
71	205
72	188
73	151
74	180
75	174
76	168
77	136
78	149
79	133
80	123
81	118
82	101
83	99
84	100
85	75
86	74
87	54
88	57
89	145
	76

The age values are ok and range from 18 to 89. No strange values are present in the age column.

2.5.1.4. The Race Column

```
gss_cat2 %>% count(race) %>% flextable() %>% theme_box() %>%
set_caption(caption = "The unique values of the race column in the general social survey data")
```

Table 2.7. The Unique Values of the Race Column in the General Social Survey Data

race	n
Other	1,947
Black	3,121
White	16,152

The race values are ok and no strange values are present.

2.5.1.5. The Reported Income Column

```
gss_cat2 %>% count(rincome) %>% flextable() %>% theme_box() %>%
set_caption(caption = "The unique values of the reported income
column in the general social survey data")
```

Table 2.8. The Unique Values of the Reported Income Column in the General Social Survey Data

rincome	n
No answer	183
Don't know	265
Refused	969
$25000 or more	7,200
$20000–24999	1,278
$15000–19999	1,044
$10000–14999	1,166
$8000–9999	340
$7000–7999	188
$6000–6999	215
$5000–5999	227
$4000–4999	225
$3000–3999	275
$1000–2999	394
Lt $1000	286
Not applicable	6,965

The "No answer," "Don't know," "Refused," and "Not applicable" are not real income categories and should be converted to NA or missing.

2.5.1.6. The Party id Column

```
gss_cat2 %>% count(partyid) %>% flextable() %>% theme_box() %>%
set_caption(caption = "The unique values of the party id column
in the general social survey data")
```

Table 2.9. The Unique Values of the Party id Column in the General Social Survey Data

partyid	**n**
No answer	154
Don't know	1
Other party	393
Strong republican	2,277
Not str republican	2,978
Ind,near rep	1,781
Independent	4,071
Ind,near dem	2,472
Not str democrat	3,639
Strong democrat	3,454

The "No answer" and "Don't know" values are not real party id values and should be converted to missing.

2.5.1.7. The Religion Column

```
gss_cat2 %>% count(relig) %>% flextable() %>% theme_box() %>%
set_caption(caption = "The unique values of the religion column
in the general social survey data")
```

Table 2.10. The Unique Values of the Religion Column in the General Social Survey Data

relig	**n**
No answer	93
Don't know	15
Inter-nondenominational	109
Native American	23
Christian	685
Orthodox-Christian	95
Moslem/Islam	104

Other eastern	32
Hinduism	71
Buddhism	147
Other	223
None	3,471
Jewish	387
Catholic	4,990
Protestant	10,775

The "No answer" and "Don't know" values are not real religion values and should be converted to missing.

2.5.1.8. The Denomination Column

```
gss_cat2 %>% count(denom) %>% flextable() %>% theme_box() %>%
set_caption(caption = "The unique values of the denomination
column in the general social survey data")
```

Table 2.11. The Unique Values of the Denomination Column in the General Social Survey Data

denom	**n**
No answer	117
Don't know	52
No denomination	1,676
Other	2,505
Episcopal	394
Presbyterian-dk wh	243
Presbyterian, merged	67
Other presbyterian	47
United Pres Ch in us	110
Presbyterian c in us	104
Lutheran-dk which	265
Evangelical luth	122
Other Lutheran	30
Wi Evan Luth synod	71
Lutheran-Mo synod	211
Luth Ch in America	71
Am Lutheran	146

Methodist-dk which	238
Other methodist	33
United methodist	1,054
Afr Meth ep Zion	32
Afr meth episcopal	77
Baptist-dk which	1,452
Other Baptists	213
Southern Baptist	1,525
Nat Bapt Conv USA	40
Nat Bapt Conv of am	76
Am Bapt Ch in USA	130
Am Baptist Asso	237
Not applicable	9,882

The "No answer," "Don't know," and "Not applicable" values are not real denomination values and should be converted to missing.

2.5.1.9. The TV Hours Column

```
gss_cat2 %>% count(tvhours) %>% flextable() %>% theme_box() %>%
set_caption(caption = "The unique values of the TV hours column
in the general social survey data")
```

Table 2.12. The Unique Values of the TV Hours Column in the General Social Survey Data

tvhours	n
0	675
1	2,333
2	3,021
3	1,947
4	1,403
5	695
6	477
7	119
8	261
9	19
10	122
11	9
12	96

13	9
14	24
15	17
16	10
17	2
18	7
20	14
21	2
22	2
23	1
24	22
	9,933

All values are ok and range from 0 to 24. Although values of 20,21,22,23, and 24 may seem unrealistic with only 4,3,2,1, and 0, respectively, remaining hours for other life activities, we keep them as they are reported by some respondents.

2.5.1.10. Convert Strange Values to missing in General Social Survey Data

We will apply the replace_with_na function on the gss_cat2 data with the argument replace = list. The list function will contain the following arguments:

- marital = "No answer" to replace the "No answer" value of marital to NA or missing.
- rincome = c("No answer", "Don't know", "Refused", "Not applicable") to replace these values of reported income to NA or missing.
- partyid = c("No answer", "Don't know") to replace these values of party id with missing.
- relig = c("No answer", "Don't know") to replace these values of religion with missing.
- denom = c("No answer", "Don't know", "Not applicable") to replace these values of the denomination with missing.

The resulting data is called "gss_cat3" and we use the glimpse function to get the data structure.

```
gss_cat3<-gss_cat2 %>%
replace_with_na(replace = list(marital="No answer",
rincome = c("No answer", "Don't know", "Refused", "Not
```

```
applicable”),
partyid = c(“No answer”, “Don’t know”),
relig = c(“No answer”, “Don’t know”),
denom = c(“No answer”, “Don’t know”,
“Not applicable”)))
glimpse(gss_cat3)
## Rows: 21,220
## Columns: 9
## $ year <int> 2000, 2000, 2000, 2000, 2000, 2000, 2000, 2000, 2000, 2000, 20…
## $ marital <fct> Never married, Divorced, Widowed, Never married, Divorced, Mar…
## $ age <int> 26, 48, 67, 39, 25, 25, 36, 44, 44, 47, 53, 52, 52, 51, 52, 40…
## $ race <fct> White, White, White, White, White, White, White, White, White,…
## $ rincome <fct> $8000 to 9999, $8000 to 9999, NA, NA, NA, $20000-24999, $250…
## $ partyid <fct> “Ind,near rep”, “Not str republican”, “Independent”, “Ind,near…
## $ relig <fct> Protestant, Protestant, Protestant, Orthodox-christian, None, …
## $ denom <fct> “Southern baptist”, “Baptist-dk which”, “No denomination”, NA,…
## $ tvhours <int> 12, NA, 2, 4, 1, NA, 3, NA, 0, 3, 2, NA, 1, NA, 1, 7, NA, 3, 3…
```

The resulting data has 21220 rows and the same 9 columns.

2.5.1.11. Checking the Cleaned Columns

2.5.1.11.1. The Marital Column

To see that our cleaning was correct, we use the count function on the cleaned columns. For the marital column.

```
gss_cat3 %>% count(marital) %>% flextable() %>% theme_box() %>%
set_caption(caption = “The unique values of the marital column after cleaning in the general social survey data”)
```

Table 2.13. The Unique Values of the Marital Column After Cleaning in the General Social Survey Data

marital	n
Never married	5,372
Separated	743
Divorced	3,367
Widowed	1,789
Married	9,932
	17

We see that the strange values are replaced with missing values with a total of 17.

2.5.1.11.2. The Reported Income Column

```
gss_cat3 %>% count(rincome) %>% flextable() %>% theme_box() %>%
set_caption(caption = "The unique values of the reported income
column after cleaning in the general social survey data")
```

Table 2.14. The Unique Values of the Reported Income Column After Cleaning in the General Social Survey Data

rincome	n
$25000 or more	7,200
$20000–24999	1,278
$15000–19999	1,044
$10000–14999	1,166
$8000–9999	340
$7000–7999	188
$6000–6999	215
$5000–5999	227
$4000–4999	225
$3000–3999	275
$1000–2999	394
Lt $1000	286
	8,382

We see that the strange values are replaced with missing values with a total of 8382.

2.5.1.11.3. The Party id Column

```
gss_cat3 %>% count(partyid) %>% flextable() %>% theme_box() %>%
set_caption(caption = "The unique values of the party id column
after cleaning in the general social survey data")
```

Table 2.15. The Unique Values of the Party id Column After Cleaning in the General Social Survey Data

partyid	n
Other party	393
Strong republican	2,277
Not str republican	2,978
Ind,near rep	1,781
Independent	4,071
Ind,near dem	2,472
Not str democrat	3,639
Strong democrat	3,454
	155

We see that the strange values are replaced with missing values with a total of 155.

2.5.1.11.4. The Religion Column

```
gss_cat3 %>% count(relig) %>% flextable() %>% theme_box() %>%
set_caption(caption = "The unique values of the religion column
after cleaning in the general social survey data")
```

Table 2.16. The Unique Values of the Religion Column After Cleaning in the General Social Survey Data

relig	n
Inter-nondenominational	109
Native american	23
Christian	685
Orthodox-christian	95
Moslem/islam	104
Other eastern	32
Hinduism	71

Buddhism	147
Other	223
None	3,471
Jewish	387
Catholic	4,990
Protestant	10,775
	108

We see that the strange values are replaced with missing values with a total of 108.

2.5.1.11.5. The Denomination Column

```
gss_cat3 %>% count(denom) %>% flextable() %>% theme_box() %>%
set_caption(caption = "The unique values of the denomination
column after cleaning in the general social survey data")
```

Table 2.17. The Unique Values of the Denomination Column After Cleaning in the General Social Survey Data

denom	**n**
No denomination	1,676
Other	2,505
Episcopal	394
Presbyterian-dk wh	243
Presbyterian, merged	67
Other presbyterian	47
United pres ch in us	110
Presbyterian c in us	104
Lutheran-dk which	265
Evangelical luth	122
Other lutheran	30
Wi evan luth synod	71
Lutheran-mo synod	211
Luth ch in america	71
Am lutheran	146
Methodist-dk which	238
Other methodist	33
United methodist	1,054

Afr meth ep zion	32
Afr meth episcopal	77
Baptist-dk which	1,452
Other baptists	213
Southern baptist	1,525
Nat bapt conv usa	40
Nat bapt conv of am	76
Am bapt ch in usa	130
Am baptist asso	237
	10,051

We see that the strange values are replaced with missing values with a total of 10051.

2.5.2. The BRFSS Data

2.5.2.1. The State Column

Similarly, we use the count function.

```
riskfactors %>% count(state) %>% flextable() %>% theme_box() %>%
set_caption(caption = "The unique values of the state column in
the BRFSS data")
```

Table 2.18. The Unique Values of the State Column in the BRFSS Data

state	n
1	5
2	1
5	2
6	12
8	7
9	7
10	3
11	4
12	10
13	2
15	9
16	1
17	1
18	4

19	3
20	5
21	5
22	5
23	3
24	3
25	11
26	6
27	4
28	6
29	3
30	5
31	9
32	3
33	1
34	12
35	5
36	2
37	5
38	2
39	6
40	3
41	4
42	5
44	3
45	6
46	3
47	3
48	9
49	7
50	4
51	2
53	9
54	2
55	1
56	6
66	1
72	5

All values are ok and range from 1 to 72. The interpretation of different numbers is explained above, and no strange values are present.

2.5.2.2. The Sex Column

```
riskfactors %>% count(sex) %>% flextable() %>% theme_box() %>%
set_caption(caption = "The unique values of the sex column in
the BRFSS data")
```

Table 2.19. The Unique Values of the Sex Column in the BRFSS Data

sex	n
Male	92
Female	153

All values are ok and no strange values are present.

2.5.2.3. The Age Column

```
riskfactors %>% count(age) %>% flextable() %>% theme_box() %>%
set_caption(caption = "The unique values of the age column in
the BRFSS data")
```

Table 2.20. The Unique Values of the Age Column in the BRFSS Data

age	n
7	1
9	3
20	1
21	1
22	1
23	2
25	1
26	1
27	2
28	1
29	2
31	4
32	2
33	2
34	3
37	5
38	3
39	1

40	2
41	4
42	3
43	3
44	2
45	5
46	3
47	3
48	3
49	3
50	8
51	4
52	7
53	1
54	8
55	3
56	6
57	7
58	6
59	10
60	3
61	5
62	12
63	2
64	9
65	4
66	7
67	4
68	4
69	6
70	6
71	2
72	3
73	2
74	1
75	5

76	1
77	4
78	3
79	4
80	7
81	2
82	2
83	3
84	2
85	4
86	2
87	2
88	3
89	1
90	1
92	1
97	1

The 7 and 9 years should be filtered out because this is an adult survey. The 7 and 9 values should be converted to missing values.

2.5.2.4. The weight_lbs Column

```
riskfactors %>% count(weight_lbs) %>% flextable() %>% theme_
box() %>%
set_caption(caption = "The unique values of the weight column in
the BRFSS data")
```

Table 2.21. The Unique Values of the Weight Column in the BRFSS Data

weight_lbs	n
96	1
98	1
100	1
104	1
105	1
107	1
110	5
113	2
117	3

118	5
120	1
123	1
125	7
127	1
128	2
130	4
132	1
133	1
135	5
138	2
140	10
141	1
143	1
144	2
145	5
146	1
148	3
150	10
151	2
152	1
153	1
155	3
156	1
157	1
158	1
160	13
163	1
164	1
165	7
166	1
169	1
170	13
175	12
178	1
179	1
180	11
183	1
184	2

185	3
186	1
189	1
190	6
192	1
193	1
194	1
195	9
196	1
198	1
200	10
201	1
205	2
208	3
210	2
212	2
215	1
218	1
220	2
222	1
223	2
225	3
230	3
235	1
238	1
240	1
241	1
242	1
245	1
250	3
255	2
260	3
265	1
270	2
285	1
300	4
410	1
	10

The weight values are ok and range from 96 to 410 pounds. There are 10 missing values.

2.5.2.5. The height_inch Column

```
riskfactors %>% count(height_inch) %>% flextable() %>% theme_box() %>%
set_caption(caption = "The unique values of the height column in the BRFSS data")
```

Table 2.22. The Unique Values of the Height Column in the BRFSS Data

height_inch	n
57	2
58	3
59	1
60	6
61	10
62	20
63	15
64	26
65	23
66	17
67	26
68	30
69	12
70	17
71	7
72	12
73	7
74	8
75	1
	2

The height values are ok and range from 57 to 75 inches. There are two missing values.

2.5.2.6. The bmi Column

```
riskfactors %>% count(bmi) %>% flextable() %>% theme_box() %>%
set_caption(caption = "The unique values of the BMI column in the BRFSS data")
```

Table 2.23. The Unique Values of the BMI Column in the BRFSS Data

bmi	n
14.21	1
16.34	1
17.34	1
17.98	1
18.33	1
18.36	2
18.84	1
18.92	1
19.05	1
19.24	1
19.53	1
19.57	1
20.06	1
20.13	1
20.16	1
20.22	1
20.30	1
20.40	1
20.64	1
20.66	1
20.70	1
20.77	1
20.95	1
20.99	1
21.33	1
21.34	1
21.35	1
21.46	1
21.53	1
21.75	1
21.87	1
22.09	1
22.19	2
22.20	1
22.34	1

22.36	1
22.41	1
22.42	1
22.44	1
22.51	2
22.54	1
22.64	1
22.76	1
22.86	2
22.91	2
23.04	1
23.08	1
23.14	2
23.16	1
23.22	1
23.23	1
23.31	1
23.35	2
23.45	1
23.54	4
23.62	1
23.70	1
23.72	2
23.74	2
23.80	1
23.83	1
23.94	1
24.01	1
24.05	1
24.08	2
24.26	1
24.38	1
24.44	3
24.46	4
24.71	1
24.74	1
24.80	1
24.85	1

24.94	1
25.01	1
25.07	1
25.11	1
25.12	1
25.16	2
25.18	2
25.44	1
25.46	1
25.56	2
25.75	1
25.88	3
25.90	5
26.09	1
26.49	1
26.51	1
26.66	5
26.68	1
26.69	1
26.70	1
26.83	1
26.91	1
27.08	1
27.18	1
27.25	1
27.32	2
27.52	3
27.56	1
27.95	1
28.04	3
28.19	1
28.30	1
28.38	1
28.40	2
28.65	1
28.76	1
28.79	1
28.86	1

28.95	2
29.00	1
29.04	1
29.18	1
29.33	2
29.36	1
29.56	1
29.59	1
29.60	1
29.71	1
29.73	1
29.91	1
30.02	3
30.10	1
30.17	1
30.18	1
30.24	1
30.61	2
30.91	1
31.07	1
31.16	1
31.24	1
31.35	1
31.39	3
31.52	1
31.65	1
31.68	1
31.69	1
31.95	1
32.00	2
32.06	1
32.07	2
32.10	1
32.35	1
32.52	1
32.68	2
32.81	1
32.99	2

33.05	1
33.35	1
33.68	1
34.08	1
34.10	1
34.28	1
34.37	2
34.41	1
34.53	1
34.66	1
35.00	1
35.74	1
35.78	1
36.10	2
36.47	1
36.54	1
36.66	1
36.87	1
38.09	1
38.60	1
38.82	1
38.86	1
39.94	1
40.44	1
40.86	1
42.29	1
43.14	1
43.36	1
43.67	1
43.99	1
49.02	1
50.03	1
51.60	1
51.61	1
55.72	1
	11

The BMI values are ok and range from 14.21 to 55.72. There are 11 missing values.

2.5.2.7. The Marital Column

```
riskfactors %>% count(marital) %>% flextable() %>% theme_box() %>%
set_caption(caption = "The unique values of the marital column in the BRFSS data")
```

Table 2.24. The Unique Values of the Marital Column in the BRFSS Data

marital	n
Married	131
Divorced	39
Widowed	41
Separated	3
NeverMarried	24
UnmarriedCouple	6
	1

The marital values are ok and there is 1 missing value.

2.5.2.8. The Pregnant Column

```
riskfactors %>% count(pregnant) %>% flextable() %>% theme_box() %>%
set_caption(caption = "The unique values of the pregnant column in the BRFSS data")
```

Table 2.25. The Unique Values of the Pregnant Column in the BRFSS Data

pregnant	n
Yes	2
No	28
	215

The pregnant values are ok and there are 215 missing values.

2.5.2.9. The Children Column

```
riskfactors %>% count(children) %>% flextable() %>% theme_box() %>%
set_caption(caption = "The unique values of the children column in the BRFSS data")
```

Table 2.26. The Unique Values of the Children Column in the BRFSS Data

children	n
0	190
1	20
2	23
3	10
4	2

The children's values are ok and range from 0 to 4. There are no missing values.

2.5.2.10. The Education Column

```
riskfactors %>% count(education) %>% flextable() %>% theme_box()
%>%
set_caption(caption = "The unique values of the education column
in the BRFSS data")
```

Table 2.27. The Unique Values of the Education Column in the BRFSS Data

education	n
1	1
2	10
3	14
4	85
5	59
6	75
	1

The education values are ok and range from 1 to 6 as explained before. There is 1 missing value.

2.5.2.11. The Employment Column

```
riskfactors %>% count(employment) %>% flextable() %>% theme_
box() %>%
set_caption(caption = "The unique values of the employment column
in the BRFSS data")
```

Table 2.28. The Unique Values of the Employment Column in the BRFSS Data

employment	n
1	92
2	21
3	6
4	11
5	17
7	80
8	18

The employment values are ok and range from 1 to 8 as explained before. There are no missing values.

2.5.2.12. The Income Column

```
riskfactors %>% count(income) %>% flextable() %>% theme_box() %>%
set_caption(caption = "The unique values of the income column in the BRFSS data")
```

Table 2.29. The Unique Values of the Income Column in the BRFSS Data

income	n
<10k	10
10–15k	18
15–20k	16
20–25k	19
25–35k	28
35–50k	38
50–75k	32
>75k	46
Dontknow	18
Refused	20

The “Dontknow” and “Refused” are not real income values and should be converted to missing values.

2.5.2.13. The Veteran Column

```
riskfactors %>% count(veteran) %>% flextable() %>% theme_box() %>%
```

```
set_caption(caption = "The unique values of the veteran column
in the BRFSS data")
```

Table 2.30. The Unique Values of the Veteran Column in the BRFSS Data

veteran	n
1	1
2	2
3	35
4	6
5	198
	3

The veteran values are ok and range from 1 to 5 as explained before. There are three missing values.

2.5.2.14. The Hispanic Column

```
riskfactors %>% count(hispanic) %>% flextable() %>% theme_box()
%>%
set_caption(caption = "The unique values of the hispanic column
in the BRFSS data")
```

Table 2.31. The Unique Values of the Hispanic Column in the BRFSS Data

Hispanic	n
Yes	22
No	221
	2

The Hispanic values are ok and there are two missing values.

2.5.2.15. The health_general Column

```
riskfactors %>% count(health_general) %>% flextable() %>%
theme_box() %>%
set_caption(caption = "The unique values of the health general
column in the BRFSS data")
```

Table 2.32. The Unique Values of the Health General Column in the BRFSS Data

health_general	n
Excellent	45
VeryGood	56

Good	82
Fair	40
Poor	20
Refused	2

The "Refused" value is not a real general health value and should be converted to a missing value.

2.5.2.16. The health_physical Column

```
riskfactors %>% count(health_physical) %>% flextable() %>%
theme_box() %>%
set_caption(caption = "The unique values of the health physical
column in the BRFSS data")
```

Table 2.33. The Unique Values of the Health Physical Column in the BRFSS Data

health_physical	n
–9	2
–7	6
0	139
1	11
2	17
3	12
4	4
5	8
6	2
7	8
8	2
10	2
12	1
14	2
15	3
20	3
25	1
28	1
30	21

The –7 and –9 values correspond to "Don't know/Not sure" and "Refused" respectively and are not real days numbers as explained before. So, they should be converted to missing values.

2.5.2.17. The health_mental Column

```
riskfactors %>% count(health_mental) %>% flextable() %>%
theme_box() %>%
set_caption(caption = "The unique values of the health mental column in the BRFSS data")
```

Table 2.34. The Unique Values of the Health Mental Column in the BRFSS Data

health_mental	n
–9	2
–7	5
0	170
1	9
2	12
3	1
4	2
5	10
7	4
10	1
15	7
16	1
20	6
30	15

Similarly, the –7 and –9 values are not real number of days and should be converted to missing values.

2.5.2.18. The health_poor Column

```
riskfactors %>% count(health_poor) %>% flextable() %>%
theme_box() %>%
set_caption(caption = "The unique values of the health poor column in the BRFSS data")
```

Table 2.35. The Unique Values of the Health Poor Column in the BRFSS Data

health_poor	n
–9	2
–7	4

0	73
1	8
2	5
3	4
4	2
5	3
7	2
10	2
12	1
14	2
15	3
20	2
25	3
30	16
	113

The –7 and –9 values are not real number of days and should be converted to missing values.

2.5.2.19. The health_cover Column

```
riskfactors %>% count(health_cover) %>% flextable() %>%
theme_box() %>%
set_caption(caption = "The unique values of the health cover column in the BRFSS data")
```

Table 2.36. The Unique Values of the Health Cover Column in the BRFSS Data

health_cover	**n**
Yes	217
No	28

The health cover values are ok and there are no missing values.

2.5.2.20. The provide_care Column

```
riskfactors %>% count(provide_care) %>% flextable() %>%
theme_box() %>%
set_caption(caption = "The unique values of the provide care column in the BRFSS data")
```

Table 2.37. The Unique Values of the Provide Care Column in the BRFSS Data

provide_care	n
Yes	61
No	181
	3

The provide care values are ok and there are three missing values.

2.5.2.21. The activity_limited Column

```
riskfactors %>% count(activity_limited) %>% flextable() %>%
theme_box() %>%
set_caption(caption = "The unique values of the activity limited
column in the BRFSS data")
```

Table 2.38. The Unique Values of the Activity Limited Column in the BRFSS Data

activity_limited	n
Yes	72
No	170
	3

The activity_limited values are ok and there are three missing values.

2.5.2.22. The drink_any Column

```
riskfactors %>% count(drink_any) %>% flextable() %>%
theme_box() %>%
set_caption(caption = "The unique values of the drink any column
in the BRFSS data")
```

Table 2.39. The Unique Values of the Drink Any Column in the BRFSS Data

drink_any	n
Yes	111
No	132
	2

The drink any values are ok and there are two missing values.

2.5.2.23. The drink_days Column

```
riskfactors %>% count(drink_days) %>% flextable() %>%
theme_box() %>%
```

```
set_caption(caption = "The unique values of the drink days column in the BRFSS data")
```

Table 2.40. The Unique Values of the Drink Days Column in the BRFSS Data

drink_days	n
–9	1
–7	4
1	22
2	11
3	6
4	12
5	3
7	1
8	2
9	6
10	4
12	1
13	5
15	7
17	5
20	3
21	4
25	1
30	13
	134

The –7 and –9 values are not real number of days and should be converted to missing values.

2.5.2.24. The drink_average Column

```
riskfactors %>% count(drink_average) %>% flextable() %>%
theme_box() %>%
set_caption(caption = "The unique values of the drink average column in the BRFSS data")
```

Table 2.41. The Unique Values of the Drink Average Column in the BRFSS Data

drink_average	n
–9	1
–7	5
1	57
2	26
3	11
4	4
5	1
6	2
7	1
8	1
9	1
	135

The –7 and –9 values are not real number of average drinks and should be converted to missing values.

2.5.2.25. The smoke_100 Column

```
riskfactors %>% count(smoke_100) %>% flextable() %>%
theme_box() %>%
set_caption(caption = "The unique values of the smoke 100 column in the BRFSS data")
```

Table 2.42. The Unique Values of the Smoke 100 Column in the BRFSS Data

smoke_100	n
Yes	117
No	126
	2

The smoke 100 values are ok and there are two missing values.

2.5.2.26. The smoke_days Column

```
riskfactors %>% count(smoke_days) %>% flextable() %>%
theme_box() %>%
set_caption(caption = "The unique values of the smoke days column in the BRFSS data")
```

Table 2.43. The Unique Values of the Smoke Days Column in the BRFSS Data

smoke_days	n
Everyday	26
Somedays	7
Not@All	84
	128

The strange "Not@All" value should be converted to "Notatall." There are 128 missing values.

2.5.2.27. The smoke_stop Column

```
riskfactors %>% count(smoke_stop) %>% flextable() %>%
theme_box() %>%
set_caption(caption = "The unique values of the smoke stop column
in the BRFSS data")
```

Table 2.44. The Unique Values of the Smoke Stop Column in the BRFSS Data

smoke_stop	n
Yes	19
No	14
	212

The smoke stop values are ok and there are 212 missing values.

2.5.2.28. The smoke_last Column

```
riskfactors %>% count(smoke_last) %>% flextable() %>%
theme_box() %>%
set_caption(caption = "The unique values of the smoke last column
in the BRFSS data")
```

Table 2.45. The Unique Values of the Smoke Last Column in the BRFSS Data

smoke_last	n
3	1
4	4
5	9
6	6
7	59

8	5
	161

The smoke last values are ok and range from 3 to 8 as explained before. There are 161 missing values.

2.5.2.29. The diet_fruit Column

```
riskfactors %>% count(diet_fruit) %>% flextable() %>%
theme_box() %>%
set_caption(caption = "The unique values of the diet fruit column
in the BRFSS data")
```

Table 2.46. The Unique Values of the Diet Fruit Column in the BRFSS Data

diet_fruit	n
–9	1
–7	4
0	2
6	1
12	10
24	8
36	2
48	2
52	29
60	1
104	18
120	1
156	25
209	18
261	7
313	1
365	63
730	28
1,095	13
1,460	2
2,555	1
	8

The –7 and –9 values are not real number of fruits and should be converted to missing values.

2.5.2.30. The diet_salad Column

```
riskfactors %>% count(diet_salad) %>% flextable() %>%
theme_box() %>%
set_caption(caption = "The unique values of the diet salad column in the BRFSS data")
```

Table 2.47. The Unique Values of the Diet Salad Column in the BRFSS Data

diet_salad	n
–9	1
–7	4
0	9
1	1
3	2
12	8
24	8
36	5
48	3
52	24
60	2
72	1
84	1
96	1
104	27
156	48
209	27
240	1
261	15
313	1
365	44
730	4
	8

The –7 and –9 values are not real number of green salads and should be converted to missing values.

2.5.2.31. The diet_potato Column

```
riskfactors %>% count(diet_potato) %>% flextable() %>%
theme_box() %>%
set_caption(caption = "The unique values of the diet potato column in the BRFSS data")
```

Table 2.48. The Unique Values of the Diet Potato Column in the BRFSS Data

diet_potato	n
–9	1
–7	5
0	13
2	2
5	2
12	17
24	26
25	1
36	5
48	2
52	43
104	45
120	1
144	1
156	31
180	2
209	15
261	12
365	8
521	1
730	3
1,095	1
	8

The –7 and –9 values are not real number of potato servings and should be converted to missing values.

2.5.2.32. The diet_carrot Column

```
riskfactors %>% count(diet_carrot) %>% flextable() %>%
```

```
theme_box() %>%
set_caption(caption = "The unique values of the diet carrot column in the BRFSS data")
```

Table 2.49. The Unique Values of the Diet Carrot Column in the BRFSS Data

diet_carrot	n
–9	1
–7	7
0	26
6	1
10	1
12	22
24	24
36	6
48	6
52	50
72	1
104	27
120	1
156	31
209	11
261	2
300	1
313	2
365	17
	8

The –7 and –9 values are not real number of carrots and should be converted to missing values.

2.5.2.33. The diet_vegetable Column

```
riskfactors %>% count(diet_vegetable) %>% flextable() %>%
theme_box() %>%
set_caption(caption = "The unique values of the diet vegetable column in the BRFSS data")
```

Table 2.50. The Unique Values of the Diet Vegetable Column in the BRFSS Data

diet_vegetable	n
–9	1
–7	8
0	3
10	1
24	5
52	9
60	1
96	1
104	10
156	22
180	1
209	8
261	12
313	4
365	90
521	1
626	1
730	43
1,095	11
1,460	4
1,825	1
	8

The –7 and –9 values are not real number of vegetables and should be converted to missing values.

2.5.2.34. The diet_juice Column

```
riskfactors %>% count(diet_juice) %>% flextable() %>%
theme_box() %>%
set_caption(caption = "The unique values of the diet juice column
in the BRFSS data")
```

Table 2.51. The Unique Values of the Diet Juice Column in the BRFSS Data

diet_juice	n
–9	2
–7	4
0	31

3	1
5	1
6	2
12	11
24	15
36	1
48	1
52	25
104	25
156	22
180	1
209	9
261	4
313	1
360	1
365	61
730	8
1,095	8
1,460	2
2,555	1
	8

The –7 and –9 values are not real number of fruit juices and should be converted to missing values.

2.5.2.35. Convert Strange Values to Suitable Values in BRFSS Data

We create another data frame "riskfactors2" by applying the following functions in sequence to the riskfactors data:

- **The replace_with_na Function:** This with the argument replace = list. The list function will contain the following arguments:
  - income = c("Dontknow", "Refused") to convert these values in the income column to missing.
  - health_general = "Refused" to convert this value in health_general column to missing.
  - health_physical = c(–7, –9) to convert these values in health_physical column to missing.

  - health_mental = c(–7, –9) to convert these values in health_mental column to missing.
  - health_poor = c(–7, –9) to convert these values in health_poor column to missing.
  - drink_days = c(–7, –9) to convert these values in drink_days column to missing.
  - drink_average = c(–7, –9) to convert these values in drink_average column to missing.
  - diet_fruit = c(–7, –9) to convert these values in diet_fruit column to missing.
  - diet_salad = c(–7, –9) to convert these values in diet_salad column to missing.
  - diet_potato = c(–7, –9) to convert these values in diet_potato column to missing.
  - diet_carrot = c(–7, –9) to convert these values in diet_carrot column to missing.
  - diet_vegetable = c(–7, –9) to convert these values in diet_vegetable column to missing.
  - diet_juice = c(–7, –9) to convert these values in diet_juice column to missing.
- **The Filter Function:** This with the argument age >=18 to keep only rows with age greater than or equal to 18 years.
- **The Mutate Function:** This to modify the smoke_days column using the if_else function with the arguments:
  - smoke_days==“Not@All” to test the condition if the value in the smoke_days is equal to “Not@All.”
  - “Notatall” so if the condition is true so the value of “Not@All” is replaced with “Notatall.”
  - smoke_days so if the condition is false, the value of smoke_days will be left as it is.

Finally, we use the glimpse function to get the data structure.

```
riskfactors2<-riskfactors %>%
replace_with_na(replace = list(income = c("Dontknow", "Refused"),
health_general = "Refused",
health_physical = c(-7, -9),
```

```
health_mental = c(-7, -9),
health_poor = c(-7, -9),
drink_days = c(-7, -9),
drink_average = c(-7, -9),
diet_fruit = c(-7, -9),
diet_salad = c(-7,-9),
diet_potato = c(-7, -9),
diet_carrot = c(-7, -9),
diet_vegetable = c(-7, -9),
diet_juice = c(-7, -9))) %>%
filter(age >=18) %>%
mutate(smoke_days = if_else(smoke_days=="Not@All",
"Notatall", smoke_days))
glimpse(riskfactors2)
## Rows: 241
## Columns: 34
## $ state <fct> 26, 40, 72, 42, 32, 19, 45, 56, 18, 8, 55, 48,
26, 12…
## $ sex <fct> Female, Female, Female, Male, Female, Male, Male,
Fem…
## $ age <int> 49, 48, 55, 42, 66, 66, 37, 62, 38, 42, 41, 64,
58, 8…
## $ weight_lbs <int> 190, 170, 163, 230, 135, 165, 150, 170,
146, 260, 192…
## $ height_inch <int> 64, 68, 64, 74, 62, 70, 68, 70, 70, 73,
72, 66, 62, N…
## $ bmi <dbl> 32.68, 25.90, 28.04, 29.59, 24.74, 23.72, 22.86,
24.4…
## $ marital <fct> Married, Divorced, Married, Married, Widowed,
Married…
## $ pregnant <fct> NA, NA, NA, NA, NA, NA, NA, NA, NA, No, NA,
NA, NA, N…
## $ children <int> 0, 0, 0, 1, 0, 0, 3, 0, 2, 3, 2, 0, 0, 0,
0, 0, 0, 0,…
## $ education <fct> 6, 5, 4, 6, 5, 5, 6, 6, 4, 5, 6, 4, 4, 3,
4, 4, 4, 6,…
## $ employment <fct> 2, 1, 5, 1, 1, 7, 2, 7, 1, 3, 1, 1, 1, 5,
```

```
1, 1, 2, 1,…
## $ income <fct> 35-50k, 35-50k, <10k, >75k, 50-75k, 35-50k,
>75k, <10…
## $ veteran <fct> 5, 5, 5, 5, 5, 3, 5, 5, 5, 5, 5, 3, 5, 5, 5,
5, 5, 5,…
## $ hispanic <fct> No, No, Yes, No, No, No, No, No, No, No, No,
No, No, …
## $ health_general <fct> Good, Fair, Fair, Excellent, Excellent,
Excellent, Ve…
## $ health_physical <int> 3, 4, 0, 0, 0, 0, 0, 30, 30, 0, 0, 0,
5, 0, 0, 3, 3, …
## $ health_mental <int> 15, 30, 0, 0, 0, 0, 0, 30, 30, 20, 0,
2, 0, 0, 30, 0,…
## $ health_poor <int> 2, 3, NA, NA, NA, NA, NA, 30, 14, 4, NA,
0, 3, NA, 0,…
## $ health_cover <fct> Yes, Yes, Yes, Yes, Yes, Yes, Yes, No,
Yes, Yes, Yes,…
## $ provide_care <fct> No, No, No, No, No, No, Yes, No, No, No,
No, No, No, …
## $ activity_limited <fct> Yes, No, No, No, No, No, No, No, Yes,
NA, No, No, No,…
## $ drink_any <fct> No, No, No, Yes, No, No, Yes, No, No, NA,
Yes, Yes, Y…
## $ drink_days <int> NA, NA, NA, 15, NA, NA, 2, NA, NA, NA, 4,
3, 1, NA, N…
## $ drink_average <int> NA, NA, NA, NA, NA, NA, 2, NA, NA, NA,
2, 5, 1, NA, N…
## $ smoke_100 <fct> No, No, No, No, Yes, No, No, Yes, Yes, Yes,
No, Yes, …
## $ smoke_days <chr> NA, NA, NA, NA, “Everyday”, NA, NA,
“Notatall”, “Ever…
## $ smoke_stop <fct> NA, NA, NA, NA, Yes, NA, NA, NA, Yes, NA,
NA, NA, NA,…
## $ smoke_last <fct> NA, NA, NA, NA, NA, NA, NA, 7, NA, 5, NA,
7, 7, NA, 6…
## $ diet_fruit <int> 1095, 52, 36, NA, NA, 24, 52, 156, 24, NA,
365, 104, …
## $ diet_salad <int> 261, 209, 156, NA, 261, 52, 156, 24, 84,
NA, 156, 52,…
```

```
## $ diet_potato <int> 104, 52, 52, NA, 209, 104, 24, 52, 144, NA, 52, 104, …
## $ diet_carrot <int> 156, 0, 24, NA, 261, 52, 24, 104, 24, NA, 156, 0, 104…
## $ diet_vegetable <int> 521, 52, 24, NA, 365, 365, 730, 365, 0, NA, 1095, 24,…
## $ diet_juice <int> 12, 0, 24, NA, 104, 365, 104, 0, 0, NA, 261, 12, 104,…
```

The resulting data has 241 rows and the same 34 columns. To see that our cleaning was correct, we use the count function on the cleaned columns.

2.5.2.36. Check the Cleaned Columns in the BRFSS Data

2.5.2.36.1. The Income Column

```
riskfactors2 %>% count(income) %>% flextable() %>% theme_box() %>%
set_caption(caption = "The unique values of the income column after cleaning in the BRFSS data")
```

Table 2.52. The Unique Values of the Income Column After Cleaning in the BRFSS Data

income	n
<10k	10
10–15k	18
15–20k	15
20–25k	19
25–35k	28
35–50k	38
50–75k	32
>75k	46
	35

We see that the strange values are replaced with missing values with a total of 35 missing.

2.5.2.36.2. The health_general Column

```
riskfactors2 %>% count(health_general) %>% flextable() %>%
theme_box() %>%
set_caption(caption = "The unique values of the health general column after cleaning in the BRFSS data")
```

Table 2.53. The Unique Values of the Health General Column After Cleaning in the BRFSS Data

health_general	n
Excellent	45
VeryGood	56
Good	80
Fair	38
Poor	20
	2

We see that the strange values of heath_general are replaced with missing values with a total of 2 missing.

2.5.2.36.3. The health_physical Column

```
riskfactors2 %>% count(health_physical) %>% flextable() %>%
theme_box() %>%
set_caption(caption = "The unique values of the health physical column after cleaning in the BRFSS data")
```

Table 2.54. The Unique Values of the Health Physical Column After Cleaning in the BRFSS Data

health_physical	n
0	137
1	11
2	17
3	12
4	4
5	8
6	2
7	8
8	2
10	2
12	1
14	2
15	3
20	3
25	1
28	1
30	20
	7

We see that the strange values of heath_physical are replaced with missing values with a total of 7 missing.

2.5.2.36.4. The health_mental Column

```
riskfactors2 %>% count(health_mental) %>% flextable() %>%
theme_box() %>%
set_caption(caption = "The unique values of the health mental column after cleaning in the BRFSS data")
```

Table 2.55. The Unique Values of the Health Mental Column After Cleaning in the BRFSS Data

health_mental	n
0	168
1	9
2	12
3	1
4	2
5	10
7	4
10	1
15	6
16	1
20	6
30	15
	6

We see that the strange values of heath_mental are replaced with missing values with a total of 6 missing.

2.5.2.36.5. The health_poor Column

```
riskfactors2 %>% count(health_poor) %>% flextable() %>%
theme_box() %>%
set_caption(caption = "The unique values of the health poor column after cleaning in the BRFSS data")
```

Table 2.56. The Unique Values of the Health Poor Column After Cleaning in the BRFSS Data

health_ poor	n
0	73
1	8
2	5
3	4
4	2
5	3
7	2
10	2
12	1
14	2
15	3
20	2
25	1
30	16
	117

We see that the strange values of heath_poor are replaced with missing values with a total of 117 missing.

2.5.2.36.6. The drink_days Column

```
riskfactors2 %>% count(drink_days) %>% flextable() %>%
theme_box() %>%
set_caption(caption = "The unique values of the drink days column after cleaning in the BRFSS data")
```

Table 2.57. The Unique Values of the Drink Days Column After Cleaning in the BRFSS Data

drink_days	n
1	22
2	10
3	6
4	12
5	3

7	1
8	2
9	6
10	4
12	1
13	5
15	7
17	5
20	3
21	4
25	1
30	13
	136

We see that the strange values of drink days are replaced with missing values.

2.5.2.36.7. The drink_average Column

```
riskfactors2 %>% count(drink_average) %>% flextable() %>%
theme_box() %>%
set_caption(caption = "The unique values of the drink average column after cleaning in the BRFSS data")
```

Table 2.58. The Unique Values of the Drink Average Column After Cleaning in the BRFSS Data

drink_average	**n**
1	56
2	26
3	11
4	4
5	1
6	2
7	1
8	1
9	1
	138

We see that the strange values of the drink average are replaced with missing values.

2.5.2.36.8. The diet_fruit Column

```
riskfactors2 %>% count(diet_fruit) %>% flextable() %>%
theme_box() %>%
set_caption(caption = "The unique values of the diet fruit column
after cleaning in the BRFSS data")
```

Table 2.59. The Unique Values of the Diet Fruit Column After Cleaning in the BRFSS Data

diet_fruit	n
0	2
6	1
12	10
24	8
36	2
48	2
52	27
60	1
104	18
120	1
156	25
209	17
261	7
313	1
365	63
730	27
1,095	13
1,460	2
2,555	1
	13

We see that the strange values of diet fruit are replaced with missing values.

2.5.2.36.9. The diet_salad Column

```
riskfactors2 %>% count(diet_salad) %>% flextable() %>%
theme_box() %>%
set_caption(caption = "The unique values of the diet salad column
after cleaning in the BRFSS data")
```

Table 2.60. The Unique Values of the Diet Salad Column After Cleaning in the BRFSS Data

diet_salad	n
0	9
1	1
3	2
12	8
24	8
36	5
48	3
52	23
60	2
72	1
84	1
96	1
104	26
156	48
209	27
240	1
261	14
313	1
365	44
730	4
	12

We see that the strange values of diet salad are replaced with missing values.

2.5.2.36.10. The diet_potato Column

```
riskfactors2 %>% count(diet_potato) %>% flextable() %>%
theme_box() %>%
set_caption(caption = "The unique values of the diet potato
column after cleaning in the BRFSS data")
```

Table 2.61. The Unique Values of the Diet Potato Column After Cleaning in the BRFSS Data

diet_potato	n
0	13
2	2
5	2
12	17

24	26
25	1
36	5
48	2
52	42
104	44
120	1
144	1
156	31
180	2
209	14
261	11
365	8
521	1
730	3
1,095	1
	14

We see that the strange values of diet potato are replaced with missing values.

2.5.2.36.11. The diet_carrot Column

```
riskfactors2 %>% count(diet_carrot) %>% flextable() %>%
theme_box() %>%
set_caption(caption = "The unique values of the diet carrot column after cleaning in the BRFSS data")
```

Table 2.62. The Unique Values of the Diet Carrot Column After Cleaning in the BRFSS Data

diet_carrot	n
0	25
6	1
10	1
12	22
24	24
36	6
48	6
52	48

72	1
104	27
120	1
156	30
209	11
261	2
300	1
313	2
365	17
	16

We see that the strange values of diet carrot are replaced with missing values.

2.5.2.36.12. The diet_vegetable Column

```
riskfactors2 %>% count(diet_vegetable) %>% flextable() %>%
theme_box() %>%
set_caption(caption = "The unique values of the diet vegetable
column after cleaning in the BRFSS data")
```

Table 2.63. The Unique Values of the Diet Vegetable Column After Cleaning in the BRFSS Data

diet_vegetable	**n**
0	3
10	1
24	5
52	9
60	1
96	1
104	9
156	21
180	1
209	8
261	11
313	3
365	90
521	1

626	1
730	43
1,095	11
1,460	4
1,825	1
	17

We see that the strange values of diet vegetable are replaced with missing values.

2.5.2.36.13. The diet_juice Column

```
riskfactors2 %>% count(diet_juice) %>% flextable() %>%
theme_box() %>%
set_caption(caption = "The unique values of the diet juice column
after cleaning in the BRFSS data")
```

Table 2.64. The Unique Values of the Diet Juice Column After Cleaning in the BRFSS Data

diet_juice	n
0	31
3	1
5	1
6	2
12	11
24	15
36	1
48	1
52	25
104	23
156	21
180	1
209	9
261	4
313	1
360	1
365	60
730	8

1,095	8
1,460	2
2,555	1
	14

We see that the strange values of diet juice are replaced with missing values.

2.5.2.36.14. The Age Column

```
riskfactors2 %>% count(age) %>% flextable() %>%
theme_box() %>%
set_caption(caption = "The unique values of the age column after cleaning in the BRFSS data")
```

Table 2.65. The Unique Values of the Age Column After Cleaning in the BRFSS Data

age	n
20	1
21	1
22	1
23	2
25	1
26	1
27	2
28	1
29	2
31	4
32	2
33	2
34	3
37	5
38	3
39	1
40	2
41	4
42	3
43	3
44	2

45	5
46	3
47	3
48	3
49	3
50	8
51	4
52	7
53	1
54	8
55	3
56	6
57	7
58	6
59	10
60	3
61	5
62	12
63	2
64	9
65	4
66	7
67	4
68	4
69	6
70	6
71	2
72	3
73	2
74	1
75	5
76	1
77	4
78	3
79	4
80	7

81	2
82	2
83	3
84	2
85	4
86	2
87	2
88	3
89	1
90	1
92	1
97	1

We see that the age column now contains years of at least 18 as expected.

2.5.2.36.15. The smoke_days Column

```
riskfactors2 %>% count(smoke_days) %>% flextable() %>%
theme_box() %>%
set_caption(caption = "The unique values of the smoke days after
cleaning in the BRFSS data")
```

Table 2.66. The Unique Values of the Smoke Days After Cleaning in the BRFSS Data

smoke_days	**n**
Everyday	26
Notatall	83
Somedays	7
	125

We see that the "Not@All" value is now replaced with "Notatall" in the smoke days column.

2.6. WRITING THE DATA AS CSV FILES

The cleaned general social survey data "gss_cat3" can be saved as a csv (comma separated value) file (called gss_dat) inside the "Documents" folder which is inside the "Dr Mohsen" folder which is inside the "Users" folder inside the C compartment of the used computer.

We use the write_csv function with the arguments:

- gss_cat3 which is the cleaned data.
- file = "C:/Users/Dr Mohsen/Documents/gss_dat.csv" which is the path we want to save the gss_dat csv data in. We add the extension ".csv" because we want to write this data as csv data.

```
write_csv(gss_cat3, file = "C:/Users/Dr Mohsen/Documents/gss_
dat.csv")
```

Similarly, we do the same for the cleaned BRFSS data "riskfactors2" and called it brfss_dat. Similarly, we add the extension ".csv" because we want to write this data as csv data.

```
write_csv(riskfactors2, file = "C:/Users/Dr Mohsen/Documents/
brfss_dat.csv")
```

Chapter **3**

Splitting Data

Contents

3.1. READING THE CLEANED DATA

In Chapter 2, we saved the cleaned data in our Documents folder. Because these data are csv (comma-separated value) files so we use the read_csv function from the readr package (part of tidyverse package). We begin loading the tidyverse and flextable (for creating tables) packages using the library function.

```
library(tidyverse)
library(flextable)
```

3.1.1. The General Social Survey Data

We read the cleaned general social survey data (gss_dat.csv) using the same path, that this data was saved at, as an argument to the read_csv function.

The created data is called "dat_gss" and we use the glimpse function to see the data structure.

```
dat_gss<-read_csv("C:/Users/Dr Mohsen/Documents/gss_dat.csv")
glimpse(dat_gss)
## Rows: 21,220
## Columns: 9
## $ year <dbl> 2000, 2000, 2000, 2000, 2000, 2000, 2000, 2000, 2000, 2000, 20…
## $ marital <chr> "Never married", "Divorced", "Widowed", "Never married", "Divo…
## $ age <dbl> 26, 48, 67, 39, 25, 25, 36, 44, 44, 47, 53, 52, 52, 51, 52, 40…
## $ race <chr> "White", "White", "White", "White", "White", "White", "White",…
## $ rincome <chr> "$8000 to 9999", "$8000 to 9999", NA, NA, NA, "$20000-24999"…
## $ partyid <chr> "Ind,near rep", "Not str republican", "Independent", "Ind,near…
## $ relig <chr> "Protestant", "Protestant", "Protestant", "Orthodox-christian"…
## $ denom <chr> "Southern baptist", "Baptist-dk which", "No denomination", NA,…
## $ tvhours <dbl> 12, NA, 2, 4, 1, NA, 3, NA, 0, 3, 2, NA, 1, NA, 1, 7, NA, 3, 3…
```

The data contains 21220 rows (respondents) and 9 columns. The meaning of different columns can be found in Chapter 2.

3.1.2. The Behavioral Risk Factor Surveillance System (BRFSS) Survey Data

Similarly, we read the cleaned BRFSS data (brfss_dat.csv) using the same path, that this data was saved at, as an argument to the read_csv function.

The created data is called "dat_brfss" and we use the glimpse function to see the data structure.

```
dat_brfss<-read_csv("C:/Users/Dr    Mohsen/Documents/brfss_dat.
csv")
glimpse(dat_brfss)
## Rows: 241
## Columns: 34
## $ state <dbl> 26, 40, 72, 42, 32, 19, 45, 56, 18, 8, 55, 48,
26, 12…
## $ sex <chr> "Female", "Female", "Female", "Male", "Female",
"Male…
## $ age <dbl> 49, 48, 55, 42, 66, 66, 37, 62, 38, 42, 41, 64,
58, 8…
## $ weight_lbs <dbl> 190, 170, 163, 230, 135, 165, 150, 170,
146, 260, 192…
## $ height_inch <dbl> 64, 68, 64, 74, 62, 70, 68, 70, 70, 73,
72, 66, 62, N…
## $ bmi <dbl> 32.68, 25.90, 28.04, 29.59, 24.74, 23.72, 22.86,
24.4…
## $ marital <chr> "Married", "Divorced", "Married", "Married",
"Widowed…
## $ pregnant <chr> NA, NA, NA, NA, NA, NA, NA, NA, NA, "No",
NA, NA, NA,…
## $ children <dbl> 0, 0, 0, 1, 0, 0, 3, 0, 2, 3, 2, 0, 0, 0,
0, 0, 0, 0,…
## $ education <dbl> 6, 5, 4, 6, 5, 5, 6, 6, 4, 5, 6, 4, 4, 3,
4, 4, 4, 6,…
## $ employment <dbl> 2, 1, 5, 1, 1, 7, 2, 7, 1, 3, 1, 1, 1, 5,
1, 1, 2, 1,…
## $ income <chr> "35-50k", "35-50k", "<10k", ">75k", "50-75k",
```

```
"35-50k…
## $ veteran <dbl> 5, 5, 5, 5, 5, 3, 5, 5, 5, 5, 5, 3, 5, 5, 5, 5, 5, 5,…
## $ hispanic <chr> "No", "No", "Yes", "No", "No", "No", "No", "No", "No"…
## $ health_general <chr> "Good", "Fair", "Fair", "Excellent", "Excellent", "Ex…
## $ health_physical <dbl> 3, 4, 0, 0, 0, 0, 0, 30, 30, 0, 0, 0, 5, 0, 0, 3, 3, …
## $ health_mental <dbl> 15, 30, 0, 0, 0, 0, 0, 30, 30, 20, 0, 2, 0, 0, 30, 0,…
## $ health_poor <dbl> 2, 3, NA, NA, NA, NA, NA, 30, 14, 4, NA, 0, 3, NA, 0,…
## $ health_cover <chr> "Yes", "Yes", "Yes", "Yes", "Yes", "Yes", "Yes", "No"…
## $ provide_care <chr> "No", "No", "No", "No", "No", "No", "Yes", "No", "No"…
## $ activity_limited <chr> "Yes", "No", "No", "No", "No", "No", "No", "No", "Yes…
## $ drink_any <chr> "No", "No", "No", "Yes", "No", "No", "Yes", "No", "No…
## $ drink_days <dbl> NA, NA, NA, 15, NA, NA, 2, NA, NA, NA, 4, 3, 1, NA, N…
## $ drink_average <dbl> NA, NA, NA, NA, NA, NA, 2, NA, NA, NA, 2, 5, 1, NA, N…
## $ smoke_100 <chr> "No", "No", "No", "No", "Yes", "No", "No", "Yes", "Ye…
## $ smoke_days <chr> NA, NA, NA, NA, "Everyday", NA, NA, "Notatall", "Ever…
## $ smoke_stop <chr> NA, NA, NA, NA, "Yes", NA, NA, NA, "Yes", NA, NA, NA,…
## $ smoke_last <dbl> NA, NA, NA, NA, NA, NA, NA, 7, NA, 5, NA, 7, 7, NA, 6…
## $ diet_fruit <dbl> 1095, 52, 36, NA, NA, 24, 52, 156, 24, NA, 365, 104, …
## $ diet_salad <dbl> 261, 209, 156, NA, 261, 52, 156, 24, 84, NA, 156, 52,…
## $ diet_potato <dbl> 104, 52, 52, NA, 209, 104, 24, 52, 144, NA, 52, 104, …
```

```
## $ diet_carrot <dbl> 156, 0, 24, NA, 261, 52, 24, 104, 24, NA,
156, 0, 104…
## $ diet_vegetable <dbl> 521, 52, 24, NA, 365, 365, 730, 365,
0, NA, 1095, 24,…
## $ diet_juice <dbl> 12, 0, 24, NA, 104, 365, 104, 0, 0, NA,
261, 12, 104,…
```

The data contains 241 rows and 34 columns. The meaning of different columns can be found in Chapter 2.

3.2. RESAMPLING APPROACHES

Generally, in machine learning:

1. We split our data randomly into a training set (70–80% of the whole data for building the predictive model) and a testing set (20–30% of the whole data for evaluating the model performance). This step is called the *initial split*.
2. Generate different resamples (different versions) of the training data and fit the different machine learning models to these resamples. The resamples of the training data can be created using different methods:
   - V-fold cross-validation;
   - Monte-Carlo cross-validation;
   - Bootstrap resampling.
3. Estimate the different models' performance on the different resamples of the training data.
4. Fit the best model on the testing data created in step 1.

In addition, the resamples of original data can also be used to estimate the sampling distribution of a test statistic.

The rsample R package (part of the tidymodels package) contains functions to create different types of resamples that will be discussed in the next sections of this chapter.

3.3. INITIAL SPLITS

3.3.1. Initial Split of General Social Survey (gss) Data

To split the general social survey data into the training and testing data, we use the initial_split function from the rsample package (part of the tidymodels package).

Because we are using functions from the rsample or tidymodels package, so we load the tidymodels package using the library function.

Also, we use the set.seed function, before using the initial_split function, with any number to make the splitting reproducible.

We create an object "split_gss" that contains the result of applying the initial_split function on dat_gss data.

```
library(tidymodels)
set.seed(123)
split_gss<-initial_split(dat_gss)
split_gss
## <Training/Testing/Total>
## <15915/5305/21220>
```

- We see that training data has 15915 rows and the testing data has 5305 rows with a total of 21220 which is the total rows of original data.
- The split_gss object is a rsplit object with each observation or row assigned to one of the training or testing data.
- The default proportion of training data is 75% and testing data is 25%. We can see that by dividing the number of training data rows by the total rows of original data. 15915/21220 = 0.75 or 75%.
- We can control the proportion of training data by using the prop argument. For example, by using prop = 0.7 argument.

```
set.seed(123)
split_gss<-initial_split(dat_gss, prop = 0.7)
split_gss
## <Training/Testing/Total>
## <14853/6367/21220>
```

- We see that training data has 14853 rows and the testing data has 6367 rows with a total of 21220 which is the total rows of original data.
- The proportion of training data is 70% and so the testing data proportion is 30%. We can see that by dividing the number of training data rows by the total rows of original data. 14853/21220 = 0.70 or 70%.

3.3.2. Exploring the Splitting Pattern of gss Data

- To see which rows are included in the training data and which are included in the testing data, we use the mutate function on the dat_gss data with 2 arguments:

  ++ id = row_number() to add an id column to the data that will contain the row numbers from 1 to 21220 using the row_number function.

  ++ .before = 1 to add the id column before the 1st column of the original data.

We called the resulting data "dat_gss2." Then, we use the dim function to see the data dimensions.

```
dat_gss2<-dat_gss %>% mutate(id = row_number(), .before = 1)
dim(dat_gss2)
## [1] 21220 10
```

The data has 21220 rows (1st number) and 10 columns (2nd number). The data has 10 columns instead of 9 because of the extra id column.

To explore the data, we use the head function with the dat_gss2 data and 10 as the 2nd argument to see the first 10 rows of this data.

```
head(dat_gss2,10) %>% flextable() %>% theme_box() %>%
set_caption(caption = "The first 10 rows of the general social
survey data after adding an id column")
```

Table 3.1. The First 10 Rows of the General Social Survey Data After Adding an id Column

id	year	marital	age	race	rincome	partyid	relig	denom	tvhours
1	2,000	Never married	26	White	$8000 to 9999	Ind,near rep	Protestant	Southern baptist	12
2	2,000	Divorced	48	White	$8000 to 9999	Not str republican	Protestant	Baptist-dk which	
3	2,000	Widowed	67	White	–	Independent	Protestant	No denomination	2

4	2,000	Never married	39	White	–	Ind,near rep	Orthodox-christian	–	4
5	2,000	Divorced	25	White	–	Not str democrat	None	–	1
6	2,000	Married	25	White	$20000–24999	Strong democrat	Protestant	Southern baptist	
7	2,000	Never married	36	White	$25000 or more	Not str republican	Christian	–	3
8	2,000	Divorced	44	White	$7000 to 7999	Ind,near dem	Protestant	Lutheran-mo synod	
9	2,000	Married	44	White	$25000 or more	Not str democrat	Protestant	Other	0
10	2,000	Married	47	White	$25000 or more	Strong republican	Protestant	Southern baptist	3

We see that the id column has values from 1 to 10 with a step of 1 as expected because these are the 1st 10 rows.

- Then, we apply the initial_split function on the dat_gss2 data.

```
set.seed(123)
split_gss<-initial_split(dat_gss2, prop = 0.7)
split_gss
## <Training/Testing/Total>
## <14853/6367/21220>
```

- We see again that training data has 14853 rows and the testing data has 6367 rows with a total of 21220 which is the total rows of original data.
- To get the actual training data (called train_gss), we use:

  ++ The training function on the split_gss object, then:

  ++ The arrange function to arrange the data by the id column in ascending order.
- Then, we use the head function with 10 argument to see the first 10 rows of this training data.

```
train_gss<-training(split_gss) %>% arrange(id)
head(train_gss,10) %>% flextable() %>% theme_box() %>%
set_caption(caption = "The first 10 rows of the training data
from the general social survey data")
```

Table 3.2. The First 10 Rows of the Training Data from the General Social Survey Data

id	year	marital	age	race	rincome	partyid	relig	denom	tvhours
1	2,000	Never married	26	White	$8000 to 9999	Ind,near rep	Protestant	Southern baptist	12
2	2,000	Divorced	48	White	$8000 to 9999	Not str republican	Protestant	Baptist-dk which	
4	2,000	Never married	39	White	–	Ind,near rep	Orthodox-christian	–	4
5	2,000	Divorced	25	White	–	Not str democrat	None	–	1
6	2,000	Married	25	White	$20000–24999	Strong democrat	Protestant	Southern baptist	–
7	2,000	Never married	36	White	$25000 or more	Not str republican	Christian	–	3
9	2,000	Married	44	White	$25000 or more	Not str democrat	Protestant	Other	0
10	2,000	Married	47	White	$25000 or more	Strong republican	Protestant	Southern baptist	3
11	2,000	Married	53	White	$25000 or more	Not str democrat	Protestant	Other	2
13	2,000	Married	52	White	$25000 or more	Strong democrat	Protestant	Southern baptist	1

- The rows included in the training data are 1,2,4,5,6,7,9,10,11,13, etc.

- Using the testing function, we can get the actual testing data (called test_gss) and also arrange it by the id column in ascending order.

```
test_gss<-testing(split_gss) %>% arrange(id)
head(test_gss,10) %>% flextable() %>% theme_box() %>%
set_caption(caption = "The first 10 rows of the testing data from
the general social survey data")
```

Table 3.3. The First 10 Rows of the Testing Data from the General Social Survey Data

id	year	marital	age	race	rincome	partyid	relig	denom	tvhours
3	2,000	Widowed	67	White		Indepen-dent	Protes-tant	No de-nomi-nation	2
8	2,000	Divorced	44	White	$7000 to 7999	Ind,near dem	Protes-tant	Luther-an-mo synod	
12	2,000	Married	52	White	$25000 or more	Ind,near rep	None	–	
23	2,000	Never married	19	White	–	Indepen-dent	None	–	2
24	2,000	Widowed	54	White	$25000 or more	Ind,near rep	Chris-tian	–	1
29	2,000	Divorced	72	White	–	Strong demo-crat	Protes-tant	South-ern baptist	7
34	2,000	Never married	37	White	$25000 or more	Indepen-dent	None	–	–
35	2,000	Married	22	White	$10000–14999	Ind,near dem	Protes-tant	Other	–
39	2,000	Never married	29	White	$25000 or more	Ind,near rep	Catho-lic	–	2
40	2,000	Never married	57	White	–	Strong republi-can	Protes-tant	South-ern baptist	1

- The rows included in the testing data are 3,8,12,23, etc. These rows were not included in the training data.

Alternatively, we can use the tidy function on the split_gss object to detect which row is for training data and which row is for the testing data.

```
tidy(split_gss)
```

```
## # A tibble: 21,220 × 2
## Row Data
## <int> <chr>
## 1 1 Analysis
## 2 2 Analysis
## 3 4 Analysis
## 4 5 Analysis
## 5 6 Analysis
## 6 7 Analysis
## 7 9 Analysis
## 8 10 Analysis
## 9 11 Analysis
## 10 13 Analysis
## # i 21,210 more rows
```

The resulting data is 21220 rows and 2 columns:

- Row which is the row number from 1 to 21220.
- Data which is a character column for the analysis data (training data) or assessment (testing) data.
- By using the count function with Data argument after the tidy function, we can see how many rows were for the training data and how many for the testing data.

```
tidy(split_gss) %>% count(Data) %>% flextable() %>% theme_box()
%>%
set_caption(caption = "The number of rows in the training and testing data of the general social survey data")
```

Table 3.4. The Number of Rows in the Training and Testing Data of the General Social Survey Data

Data	n
Analysis	14,853
Assessment	6,367

As expected, the number of rows in training (analysis) data is 14853 rows and in testing (assessment) data is 6367 rows.

3.3.3. Plotting the Splitting Pattern of gss Data

We can also plot which row was for the training data and which was for the testing data as a heat map by using the functions after the tidy function:

- The ggplot function with the arguments aes(x = Data to plot Data type on the x-axis, y = Row to plot the row number on the y-axis, fill = Data to get a separate filling color for each Data type.
- The geom_tile function to plot a heat map.
- The scale_fill_viridis_d function uses the viridis colors, perceived by viewers with common forms of color blindness, for color filling.
- The theme_classic function removes the default grey background and white grid lines.
- The labs function with a title argument to add a plot title.

```
tidy(split_gss) %>% ggplot(aes(x = Data, y = Row, fill = Data))+
geom_tile()+ scale_fill_viridis_d()+ theme_classic()+
labs(title = "The assignment of different rows in the general
social survey data to training or testing data")
```

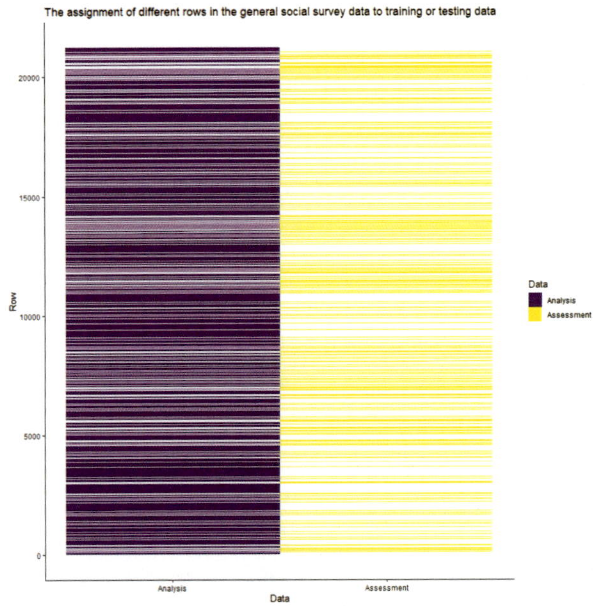

The heat map is overcrowded because we have 21220 rows in our data. To get a less crowded plot, we can filter the data for the 1st 20 rows using the filter function with the argument Row <= 20 to get the row number equal to or less than 20.

We also use the geom_text function with the arguments:

- aes(label = Row) to add a text label of row number to each tile.
- color = "white" to color the text by white.

```
tidy(split_gss) %>% filter(Row <= 20) %>%
ggplot(aes(x = Data, y = Row, fill = Data))+
geom_tile()+ scale_fill_viridis_d()+ theme_classic()+
geom_text(aes(label = Row), color = "white")+
labs(title = "The assignment of first 20 rows in the general
social survey data to training or testing data")
```

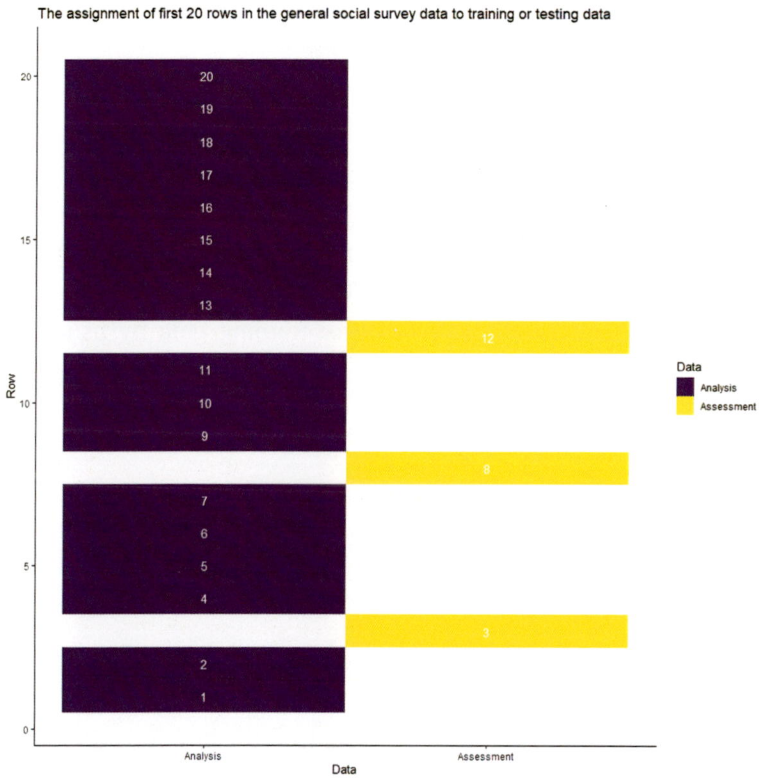

- For the row numbers from 1 to 20, only row numbers 3,8,12 were included in testing (assessment) data, and all other rows were included in training (analysis) data.
- There is no overlapping between the row numbers in the training and testing data meaning that each row is either included in the training or testing data.

3.3.4. Initial Split of BRFSS Data

- To make the splitting reproducible, we use the set.seed function with any number before using the initial_split function.
- We create an object "split_brfss" that contains the result of applying the initial_split function on dat_brfss data.

```
set.seed(123)
split_brfss<-initial_split(dat_brfss)
split_brfss
## <Training/Testing/Total>
## <180/61/241>
```

- We see that training data has 180 rows and the testing data has 61 rows with a total of 241 which is the total rows of original data.
- The split_brfss object is a rsplit object with each observation or row assigned to one of the training or testing data.
- The default proportion of training data is 75% and testing data is 25%. We can see that by dividing the number of training data rows by the total rows of original data. 180/241 = 0.75 or 75%.
- We can change the proportion of training data by using the prop argument as done previously.

```
set.seed(123)
split_brfss<-initial_split(dat_brfss, prop = 0.7)
split_brfss
## <Training/Testing/Total>
## <168/73/241>
```

- We see that training data has 168 rows and the testing data has 73 rows with a total of 241 which is the total rows of original data.
- The proportion of training data is 70% and so the testing data proportion is 30%. We can see that by dividing the number of training data rows by the total rows of original data. 168/241 = 0.70 or 70%.

3.3.5. Exploring the Splitting Pattern of BRFSS Data

- To see which rows are included in the training data and which are included in the testing data, we use the mutate function on dat_brfss data with 2 arguments:

++ id = row_number() to add an id column to the data that will contain the row numbers from 1 to 241 using the row_number function.

++ .before = 1 to add the id column before the 1st column of the original data.

We called the resulting data "dat_brfss2." Then, we use the dim function to see the data dimensions.

```
dat_brfss2<-dat_brfss %>% mutate(id = row_number(), .before = 1)
dim(dat_brfss2)
## [1] 241 35
```

The data has 241 rows (1st number) and 35 columns (2nd number). The dat_brfss2 data has 35 columns instead of 34 because of the extra id column.

Then, We use the head function with 10 as the 2nd argument to see the first 10 rows of this data. Because the dat_brfss2 data contains 35 columns so we use the select function, after the head function, with the argument 1:10 to select the first 10 columns of this wide data.

```
head(dat_brfss2,10) %>% select(1:10) %>% flextable() %>%
theme_box() %>%
set_caption(caption = "The first 10 rows and 10 columns of the
BRFSS data after adding an id column")
```

Table 3.5. The First 10 Rows and 10 Columns of the BRFSS Data After Adding an id Column

id	state	sex	age	weight_lbs	height_inch	bmi	marital	preg-nant	chil-dren
1	26	Female	49	190	64	32.68	Married	–	0
2	40	Female	48	170	68	25.90	Di-vorced	–	0
3	72	Female	55	163	64	28.04	Married	–	0
4	42	Male	42	230	74	29.59	Married	–	1
5	32	Female	66	135	62	24.74	Wid-owed	–	0
6	19	Male	66	165	70	23.72	Married	–	0
7	45	Male	37	150	68	22.86	Married	–	3
8	56	Female	62	170	70	24.44	Never-Married	–	0

9	18	Male	38	146	70	20.99	Married	–	2
10	8	Female	42	260	73	34.37	Sepa-rated	No	3

We see that the id column has values from 1 to 10 with a step of 1 as expected because these are the 1st 10 rows.

- Then, we apply the initial_split function to this data.

```
set.seed(123)
split_brfss<-initial_split(dat_brfss2, prop = 0.7)
split_brfss
## <Training/Testing/Total>
## <168/73/241>
```

- We see again that training data has 168 rows and the testing data has 73 rows with a total of 241 which is the total rows of original data.
- To get the actual training data (called train_brfss), we use:

  ++ The training function on the split_brfss object, then:

  ++ The arrange function to arrange the data by the id column in ascending order.
- Then, we use the head function with 10 argument, followed by the select function, to see the first 10 rows and columns of this training data.

```
train_brfss<-training(split_brfss) %>% arrange(id)
head(train_brfss,10) %>% select(1:10) %>% flextable() %>%
theme_box() %>%
set_caption(caption = "The first 10 rows and 10 columns of the training data from the BRFSS data")
```

Table 3.6. The First 10 Rows and 10 Columns of the Training Data from the BRFSS Data

Id	state	sex	age	weight_lbs	height_inch	bmi	marital	preg-nant	chil-dren
1	26	Female	49	190	64	32.68	Married	–	0
4	42	Male	42	230	74	29.59	Married	–	1
5	32	Female	66	135	62	24.74	Widowed	–	0
6	19	Male	66	165	70	23.72	Married	–	0
7	45	Male	37	150	68	22.86	Married	–	3

8	56	Female	62	170	70	24.44	Never-Married	–	0
9	18	Male	38	146	70	20.99	Married	–	2
11	55	Male	41	192	72	26.09	Married	–	2
13	26	Female	58	200	62	36.66	Married	–	0
14	12	Female	85	166	–	–	Widowed	–	0

- The rows included in training data are 1,4,5,6,7,8,9, etc.
- Using the testing function, we can get the actual testing data (called test_brfss) and also arrange it by the id column in ascending order.

```
test_brfss<-testing(split_brfss) %>% arrange(id)
head(test_brfss,10) %>% select(1:10) %>% flextable() %>%
theme_box() %>%
set_caption(caption = "The first 10 rows and 10 columns of the testing data from the BRFSS data")
```

Table 3.7. The First 10 Rows and 10 Columns of the Testing Data from the BRFSS Data

id	state	sex	age	weight_lbs	height_inch	bmi	marital	pregnant	children
2	40	Female	48	170	68	25.90	Divorced	–	0
3	72	Female	55	163	64	28.04	Married	–	0
10	8	Female	42	260	73	34.37	Separated	No	3
12	48	Male	64	155	66	25.07	Divorced	–	0
15	48	Female	63		67	–	Divorced	–	0
18	47	Male	70	175	73	23.14	Married	–	0
19	9	Female	80	160	63	28.40	Divorced	–	0
28	53	Female	64	160	64	27.52	Married	–	0
29	40	Female	31	156	64	26.83	Separated	No	4
31	15	Female	62	135	65	22.51	Married	–	0

- The rows included in the testing data are 2,3,10, etc. These rows were not included in the training data.

Alternatively, we can use the tidy function on the split_brfss object to detect which row is for training data and which row is for the testing data.

```
tidy(split_brfss)
## # A tibble: 241 × 2
## Row Data
```

```
## <int> <chr>
## 1 1 Analysis
## 2 4 Analysis
## 3 5 Analysis
## 4 6 Analysis
## 5 7 Analysis
## 6 8 Analysis
## 7 9 Analysis
## 8 11 Analysis
## 9 13 Analysis
## 10 14 Analysis
## # i 231 more rows
```

The resulting data is 241 rows and 2 columns:

- Row column which is the row number from 1 to 241.
- Data column which is a character column for the analysis data (training data) or assessment (testing) data.
- By using the count function with Data argument after the tidy function, we can see how many rows were for the training data and how many for the testing data.

```
tidy(split_brfss) %>% count(Data) %>% flextable() %>% theme_
box() %>%
set_caption(caption = "The number of rows in the training and
testing data of the BRFSS data")
```

Table 3.8. The Number of Rows in the Training and Testing Data of the BRFSS Data

Data	n
Analysis	168
Assessment	73

As expected, the number of rows in training (analysis) data is 168 rows and in testing (assessment) data is 73 rows.

3.3.6. Plotting the Splitting Pattern of BRFSS Data

We can also plot which row was for the training data and which was for the testing data as a heat map as described previously.

```
tidy(split_brfss) %>% ggplot(aes(x = Data, y = Row, fill =
Data))+
geom_tile()+ scale_fill_viridis_d()+ theme_classic()+
labs(title = "The assignment of different rows in the BRFSS data
to training or testing data")
```

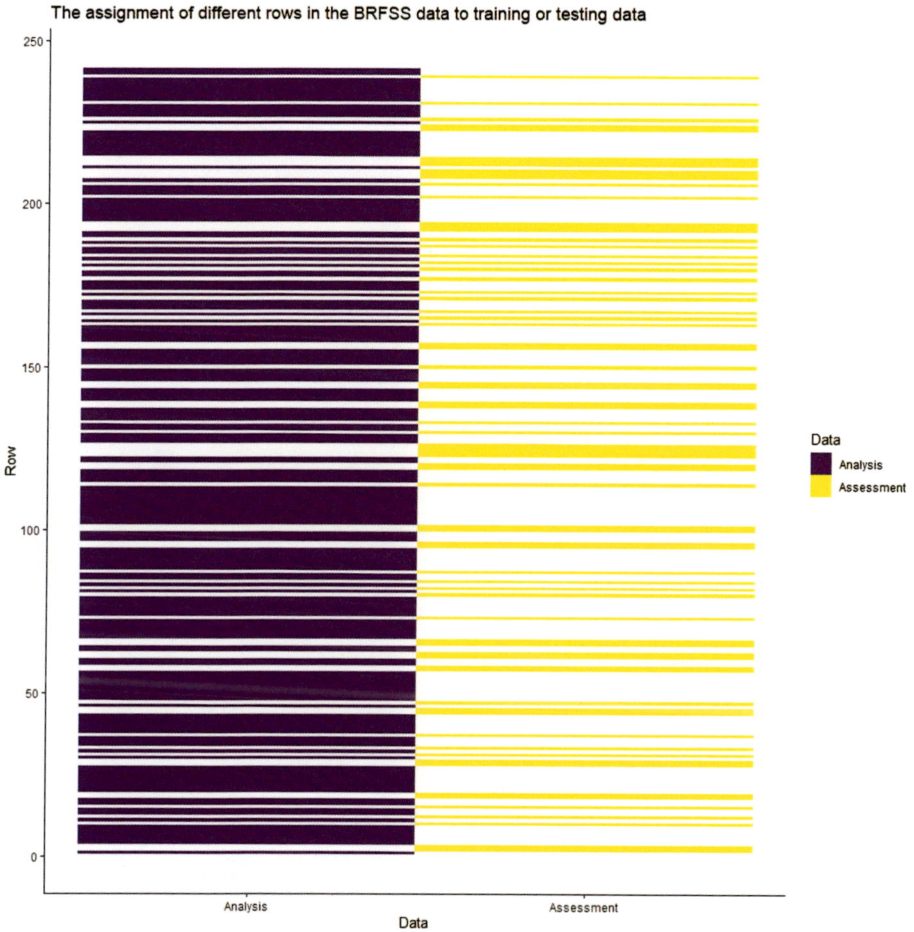

- To get a less crowded plot, we can filter the data for the 1st 30 rows using the filter function with the argument Row <= 30 to get the row number equal to or less than 30.
- We also use the geom_text function to add a text label of row number to each tile as described before. In addition, we add the argument color = "black" inside the geom_tile function to add a black border around each tile.

```
tidy(split_brfss) %>% filter(Row <= 30) %>%
ggplot(aes(x = Data, y = Row, fill = Data))+
geom_tile(color = "black")+ scale_fill_viridis_d()+ theme_classic()+
geom_text(aes(label = Row), color = "white")+
labs(title = "The assignment of first 30 rows in the BRFSS data to training or testing data")
```

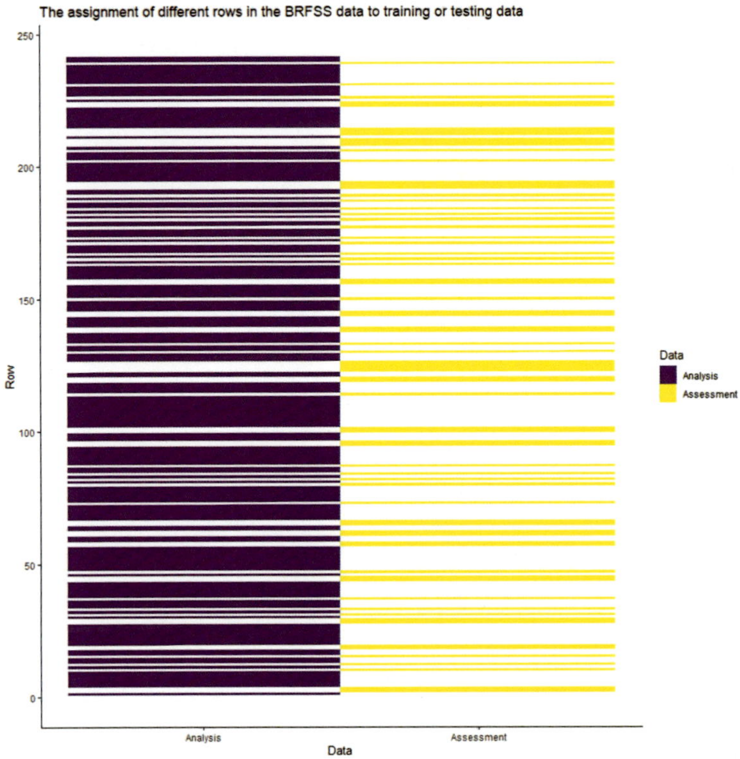

- For the row numbers from 1 to 30, only row numbers 2,3,10,12,15,18,19,28, and 29 were included in testing (assessment) data, and all other rows were included in training (analysis) data.
- There is no overlapping between the row numbers in the training and testing data meaning that each row is either included in the training or testing data.
- In conclusion, we will use the train_gss and train_brfss data to generate different resamples (different versions) of these training data.

3.4. V-FOLD CROSS-VALIDATION

- To estimate the model performance on training data, we split our training data into one part for model fitting (analysis data) and one part for measuring performance (assessment data). Typically, we split the training data into analysis and assessment data multiple times to get stable estimates of model performance.
- The most common method for estimating model performance is V-fold cross-validation or k-fold cross-validation where:
  - We split the training data into V groups or folds of roughly equal size.
  - The analysis data is made up of grouping the V–1 folds, and the remaining fold is used as the assessment data. In that case, we have created V resamples of training data.
  - For each V resample, we fit the model on the analysis data, test the model on the assessment data, and record the model performance.
  - Repeat step 3 until each of the V folds has served as the assessment data. So, we will have V different performance metrics.
  - Compute the average of the V performance metrics.

In this way, each row in our data is used in exactly one assessment data.

3.4.1. V-Fold Cross-Validation of General Social Survey Training Data

3.4.1.1. The 5-Fold Cross-Validation of General Social Survey Training Data

- We can split the training data into 5 folds using the vfold_cv function with the arguments:

  ++ train_gss which is our training data.

  ++ v = 5 to split the training data into 5 folds of nearly equal size.

  We also use the set.seed function to make the splitting reproducible before using the vfold_cv function.

```
set.seed(123)
folds<-vfold_cv(train_gss, v = 5)
```

```
folds
## # 5-fold cross-validation
## # A tibble: 5 × 2
## splits id
## <list> <chr>
## 1 <split [11882/2971]> Fold1
## 2 <split [11882/2971]> Fold2
## 3 <split [11882/2971]> Fold3
## 4 <split [11883/2970]> Fold4
## 5 <split [11883/2970]> Fold5
```

We see:

- We have 5 different rows. Each row corresponds to 1 resample of training data.
- Each row has a total rows of 14853 which is the number of rows in training data. 11882 + 2971 = 11883 + 2970 = 14853.
- Within each row, 4 of the 5 folds were grouped in the analysis data with 11882 or 11883 rows and the remaining fold was reserved as the assessment data with 2971 or 2970 rows.
- In each row, a separate fold of the 5 folds was reserved as the assessment data.
- The assessment data is about 1/5 of the total rows of training data because we have used the argument v = 5.

3.4.1.2. Exploring 5-Fold Cross-Validation of gss Training Data

- We can use the tidy function on the folds object to detect which row is for training data and which row is for the testing data within each resample.

```
tidy(folds)
## # A tibble: 74,265 × 3
## Row Data Fold
## <int> <chr> <chr>
## 1 1 Analysis Fold1
## 2 1 Analysis Fold2
## 3 1 Analysis Fold4
```

```
## 4 1 Analysis Fold5
## 5 2 Analysis Fold2
## 6 2 Analysis Fold3
## 7 2 Analysis Fold4
## 8 2 Analysis Fold5
## 9 3 Analysis Fold1
## 10 3 Analysis Fold2
## # i 74,255 more rows
```

- The resulting data is 74265 rows because we have 5 resamples of training data with 14853 rows. 14853 × 5 = 74265.
- We have 3 columns:

  ++ The Row column which is the row number from 1 to 14853.

  ++ The Data column which is a character column for the analysis data (training data) or assessment (testing) data.

  ++ The Fold column which is for the resample (fold) number.
- For example, we see that row 1 is included in resample 1,2,4,5 in the analysis (training) data and so is included in resample 3 in the assessment (testing) data.
- Row 2 is included in resample 2,3,4,5 in the analysis (training) data and so is included in resample 1 in the assessment (testing) data.
- By using the count function with Data and fold argument after the tidy function, we can see how many rows were for the training data and how many rows were for the testing data in each resample.
- We arrange the result by fold or resample number using the arrange function.

```
tidy(folds) %>% count(Data,Fold) %>% arrange(Fold) %>%
flextable() %>% theme_box() %>%
set_caption(caption = "The number of rows in the training and testing data of 5 resamples of the general social training data created by 5-fold cross-validation")
```

Table 3.9. The Number of Rows in the Training and Testing Data of 5 Resamples of the General Social Training Data Created by 5-Fold Cross-Validation

Data	Fold	n
Analysis	Fold1	11,882

Assessment	Fold1	2,971
Analysis	Fold2	11,882
Assessment	Fold2	2,971
Analysis	Fold3	11,882
Assessment	Fold3	2,971
Analysis	Fold4	11,883
Assessment	Fold4	2,970
Analysis	Fold5	11,883
Assessment	Fold5	2,970

- For some resamples, the number of rows in training (analysis) data is 11882 rows (4/5 X 14853) and in testing (assessment) data is 2971 rows (1/5 X 14853) as in resample 1,2,3.
- In other resamples, the number of rows in training (analysis) data is 11883 rows (4/5 X 14853) and in testing (assessment) data is 2970 rows (1/5 X 14853) as in resamples 4 and 5.

3.4.1.3. Plotting 5-Fold Cross-Validation of gss Training Data

We can also plot which row was for the training data and which was for the testing data as a heatmap within each resample by using the functions:

- The ggplot function with the arguments aes(x = Data to plot Data type on the x-axis, y = Row to plot the row number on the y-axis, fill = Data to get a separate filling color for each Data type.
- The geom_tile function to plot a heatmap.
- The scale_fill_viridis_d function uses the viridis colors, perceived by viewers with common forms of color blindness, for color filling.
- The theme_classic function removes the default grey background and white grid lines.
- The facet_wrap function with the arguments:

  ++ vars(Fold) to plot a separate graph for each fold or resample.

  ++ nrow = 1 to make all 5 graphs in 1 row.
- The labs function with a title argument to add a plot title. In addition, we add the "\n" within the title to make it in 2 lines.

```
tidy(folds) %>% ggplot(aes(x = Data, y = Row, fill = Data))+
geom_tile()+ scale_fill_viridis_d()+ theme_classic()+
facet_wrap(vars(Fold), nrow = 1)+
```

```
labs(title = "The assignment of different rows in 5 resamples of the general social survey training data\n to analysis or assessment data created by 5-fold cross-validation")
```

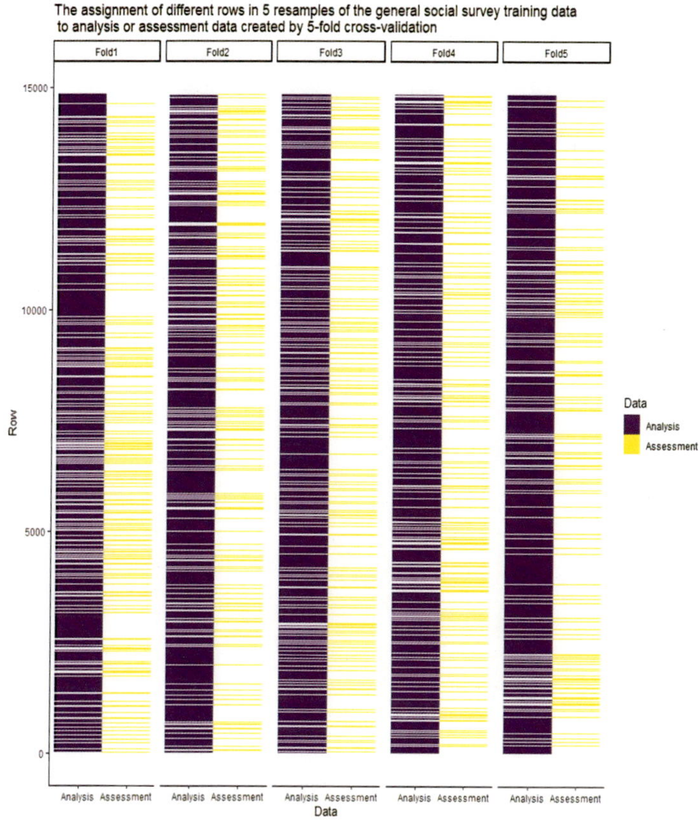

The heat map is overcrowded because we have 14853 rows in our training data. To get a less crowded plot, we can filter the data for the 1st 20 rows using the filter function with the argument Row <= 20 to get the row number equal to or less than 20 after the tidy function.

In addition, we add the argument color = "black" inside the geom_tile function to make the tiles with black borders and use the geom_text function to add text labels to each tile as described previously.

```
tidy(folds) %>% filter(Row <= 20) %>%
ggplot(aes(x = Data, y = Row, fill = Data))+
geom_tile(color = "black")+ scale_fill_viridis_d()+ theme_classic()+
```

```
geom_text(aes(label = Row), color = "white")+
facet_wrap(vars(Fold), nrow = 1)+
labs(title = "The assignment of first 20 rows in 5 resamples of the general social survey training data\n to analysis or assessment data created by 5-fold cross-validation")
```

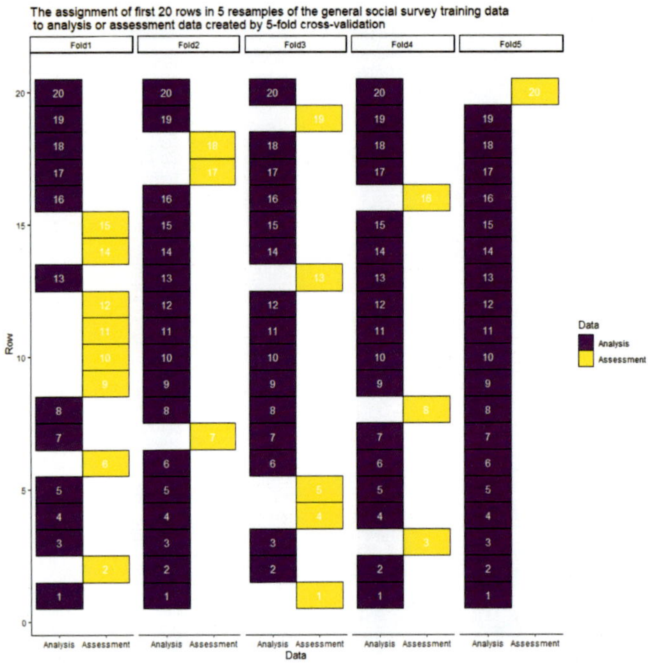

- There is no overlapping between the row numbers in the analysis and assessment data within each resample meaning that each row is either included in the analysis or assessment data within each resample.
- Any row is included only once in 1 assessment data across the 5 resamples. For example, row 20 is only included in assessment data in resample 5 and in analysis data in the other 4 resamples.
- For row number 1, it is only included in assessment data in resample 3 and in analysis data in the other 4 resamples, and so on.

3.4.1.4. 10-Fold Cross-Validation of gss Training Data

- Another and more common example is to split the data into 10 folds using the v = 10 argument.
- We also use the set.seed function to make the splitting reproducible.

```
set.seed(123)
folds<-vfold_cv(train_gss, v = 10)
folds
## # 10-fold cross-validation
## # A tibble: 10 × 2
## splits id
## <list> <chr>
## 1 <split [13367/1486]> Fold01
## 2 <split [13367/1486]> Fold02
## 3 <split [13367/1486]> Fold03
## 4 <split [13368/1485]> Fold04
## 5 <split [13368/1485]> Fold05
## 6 <split [13368/1485]> Fold06
## 7 <split [13368/1485]> Fold07
## 8 <split [13368/1485]> Fold08
## 9 <split [13368/1485]> Fold09
## 10 <split [13368/1485]> Fold10
```

We see:

- We have 10 different rows. Each row corresponds to 1 resample of training data.
- Each row has a total rows of 14853 which is the number of rows in training data. 13367 + 1486 = 13368 + 1485 = 14853.
- Within each row, 9 of the 10 folds were grouped in the analysis data with 13367 or 13368 rows and the remaining fold was reserved as the assessment data with 1486 or 1485 rows.
- In each row, a separate fold of the 10 folds was reserved as the assessment data.
- The assessment data is about 0.1 of the total rows of training data because we have used the argument v = 10.

3.4.1.5. Exploring 10-Fold Cross-Validation of gss Training Data

- We can use the tidy function on the folds object to detect which row is for training data and which row is for the testing data within each resample.

```
tidy(folds)
## # A tibble: 148,530 × 3
## Row Data Fold
## <int> <chr> <chr>
## 1 1 Analysis Fold01
## 2 1 Analysis Fold02
## 3 1 Analysis Fold04
## 4 1 Analysis Fold05
## 5 1 Analysis Fold06
## 6 1 Analysis Fold07
## 7 1 Analysis Fold08
## 8 1 Analysis Fold09
## 9 1 Analysis Fold10
## 10 2 Analysis Fold02
## # i 148,520 more rows
```

- The resulting data is 148,530 rows because we have 10 resamples of training data with 14853 rows. 14853 × 10 = 148530.
- We have 3 columns:

  ++ The Row column which is the row number from 1 to 14853.

  ++ The Data column which is a character column for the analysis data (training data) or assessment (testing) data.

  ++ The Fold column which is for the resample (fold) number.
- For example, we see that row 1 is included in all resamples in the analysis (training) data except in resample 3 and so is included in resample 3 in the assessment (testing) data.
- By using the count function with Data and fold argument after the tidy function, we can see how many rows were for the training data and how many rows were for the testing data in each resample.
- We arrange the result by fold or resample number.

```
tidy(folds) %>% count(Data,Fold) %>% arrange(Fold) %>%
flextable() %>% theme_box() %>%
set_caption(caption = "The number of rows in the training and testing data of 10 resamples of the general social survey data created by 10-fold cross-validation")
```

Table 3.10. The Number of Rows in the Training and Testing Data of 10 Resamples of the General Social Survey Data Created by 10-Fold Cross-Validation

Data	Fold	n
Analysis	Fold01	13,367
Assessment	Fold01	1,486
Analysis	Fold02	13,367
Assessment	Fold02	1,486
Analysis	Fold03	13,367
Assessment	Fold03	1,486
Analysis	Fold04	13,368
Assessment	Fold04	1,485
Analysis	Fold05	13,368
Assessment	Fold05	1,485
Analysis	Fold06	13,368
Assessment	Fold06	1,485
Analysis	Fold07	13,368
Assessment	Fold07	1,485
Analysis	Fold08	13,368
Assessment	Fold08	1,485
Analysis	Fold09	13,368
Assessment	Fold09	1,485
Analysis	Fold10	13,368
Assessment	Fold10	1,485

- For some resamples, the number of rows in training (analysis) data is 13367 rows (9/10 X 14853) and in testing (assessment) data is 1486 rows (1/10 X 14853) as in resample 1,2,3.
- In other resamples, the number of rows in training (analysis) data is 13,368 rows (9/10 X 14853) and in testing (assessment) data is 1485 rows (1/10 X 14853) as in resample 4,5,6,7,8,9, and 10.

3.4.1.6. Plotting 10-Fold Cross-Validation of gss Training Data

We can also plot which row was for the training data and which was for the testing data as a heat map within each resample by using the previously described functions.

However, we will use nrow = 2 within the facet_wrap function to make all 10 graphs in 2 rows.

```
tidy(folds) %>% ggplot(aes(x = Data, y = Row, fill = Data))+
geom_tile()+ scale_fill_viridis_d()+ theme_classic()+
facet_wrap(vars(Fold), nrow = 2)+
labs(title = "The assignment of different rows in 10 resamples of the general social survey training data\n to analysis or assessment data created by 10-fold cross-validation")
```

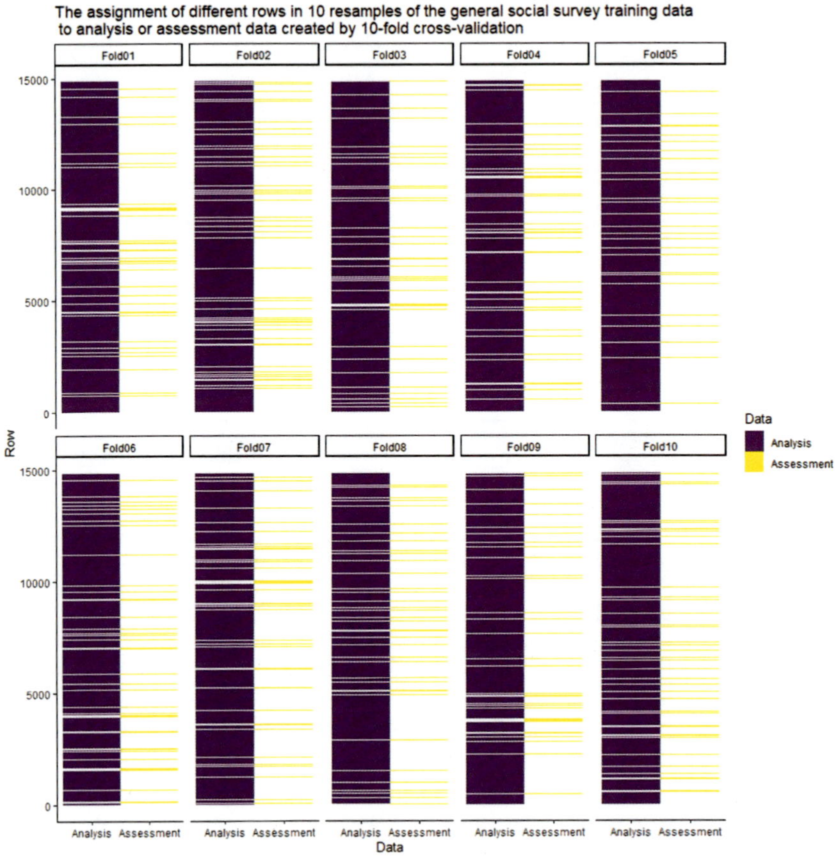

The heat map is overcrowded because we have 14853 rows in our training data. To get a less crowded plot, we can filter the data for the 1st 20 rows using the filter function with the argument Row <= 20 to get the row number equal to or less than 20 after the tidy function.

In addition, we add the argument color = "black" inside the geom_tile function to make the tiles with black borders and use the geom_text function to add text labels to each tile as described previously.

```
tidy(folds) %>% filter(Row <= 20) %>%
ggplot(aes(x = Data, y = Row, fill = Data))+
geom_tile(color = “black”)+ scale_fill_viridis_d()+ theme_classic()+
geom_text(aes(label = Row), color = “white”)+
facet_wrap(vars(Fold), nrow = 2)+
labs(title = “The assignment of first 20 rows in 10 resamples of the general social survey training data\n to analysis or assessment data created by 10-fold cross-validation”)
```

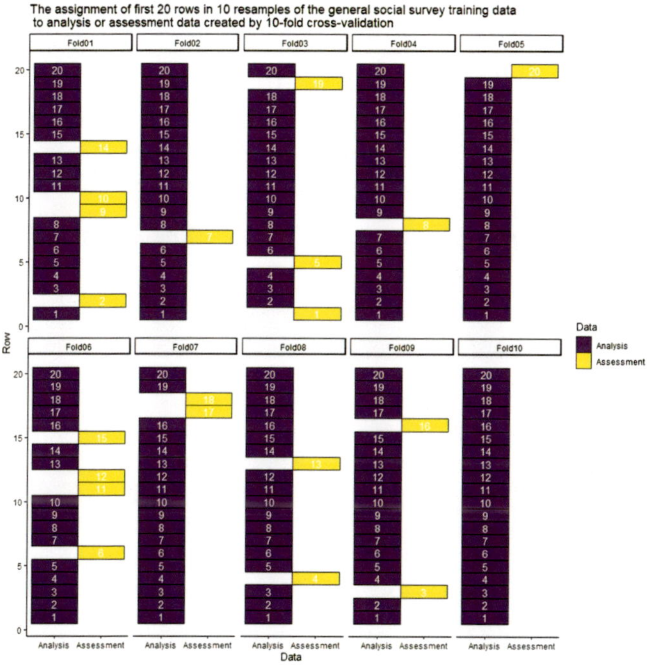

- There is no overlapping between the row numbers in the analysis and assessment data within each resample meaning that each row is either included in the analysis or assessment data within each resample.
- Any row is included only once in 1 assessment data across the 10 resamples. For example, row 20 is only included in assessment data in resample 5 and in analysis data in the other 9 resamples.
- Row number 1 is only included in assessment data in resample 3 and in analysis data in the other 9 resamples, and so on.

3.4.1.7. Fit a Linear Model to 10 Resamples of gss Training Data

- To fit a linear model on the analysis data and test the model performance on the assessment data of the 10 resamples of folds data, we use the fit_resamples function with the arguments:
  - ++ linear_reg with the arguments mode = "regression" and engine = "lm" which defines a linear regression model for predicting numeric outcomes using the lm function discussed in Chapter 1.
  - ++ tvhours ~ age + marital+ rincome which is the model formula meaning that we want to predict tv hours (numeric outcome) using the respondent's age, marital status, and reported income.
  - ++ folds which are the 10 resamples created above, each containing analysis data for fitting the model and assessment data for testing the model performance.

```
lm_res<- fit_resamples(linear_reg(mode = "regression",
engine = "lm"),
tvhours ~ age + marital+ rincome,
folds)
lm_res
## # Resampling results
## # 10-fold cross-validation
## # A tibble: 10 × 4
## splits id .metrics .notes
## <list> <chr> <list> <list>
## 1 <split [13367/1486]> Fold01 <tibble [2 × 4]> <tibble [0 × 3]>
## 2 <split [13367/1486]> Fold02 <tibble [2 × 4]> <tibble [0 × 3]>
## 3 <split [13367/1486]> Fold03 <tibble [2 × 4]> <tibble [0 × 3]>
## 4 <split [13368/1485]> Fold04 <tibble [2 × 4]> <tibble [0 × 3]>
## 5 <split [13368/1485]> Fold05 <tibble [2 × 4]> <tibble [0 × 3]>
## 6 <split [13368/1485]> Fold06 <tibble [2 × 4]> <tibble [0 × 3]>
## 7 <split [13368/1485]> Fold07 <tibble [2 × 4]> <tibble [0 ×
```

```
3]>
## 8 <split [13368/1485]> Fold08 <tibble [2 × 4]> <tibble [0 ×
3]>
## 9 <split [13368/1485]> Fold09 <tibble [2 × 4]> <tibble [0 ×
3]>
## 10 <split [13368/1485]> Fold10 <tibble [2 × 4]> <tibble [0 ×
3]>
```

The resulting object "lm_res" contains the results of applying this linear model on these 10 rows or resamples of training data. It contains 4 columns:

- The splits column is a list of each combination of analysis and assessment data.
- The id column is an id column or resample number.
- The 1st 2 columns are the same as that of the folds data.
- The .metrics column is a list of performance metrics of applying the linear model to the corresponding assessment data (1486 or 1485 rows). Each performance metric is saved in 2 rows and 4 columns [2 X 4] tibble or data frame. These will be extracted in the next step.
- The .notes column is a list of notes or warnings when applying the linear model to each analysis data (13367 or 13368 rows). Each note is saved in 0 rows and 3 columns [0 X 3] tibble or data frame meaning that there are no notes when applying this model to each analysis data.

To extract the 10 performance metrics for each combination of analysis and assessment data, we use the collect_metrics function on the lm_res object.

```
lm_res %>% collect_metrics() %>% flextable() %>% theme_box() %>%
set_caption(caption = "The mean RMSE and R squared of linear
model on 10 resamples of the general social survey training data
created by 10-fold cross-validation")
```

Table 3.11. The Mean RMSE and R Squared of Linear Model on 10 Resamples of the General Social Survey Training Data Created by 10-Fold Cross-Validation

.metric	.estimator	mean	n	std_err	.config
rmse	standard	2.07034906	10	0.07827117	Preprocessor1_ Model1
rsq	standard	0.04680704	10	0.00645303	Preprocessor1_ Model1

- The default behavior of the collect_metrics function is to summarize all performance metrics (n = 10) into their mean.
- The default calculated performance metrics for regression models are:
  - ++ RMSE or root mean squared error with a mean value of 2.07.
  - ++ Rsq or R squared with a mean value of 0.047 or 4.7%.
- To get the 10 performance metrics, we use the argument summarize = FALSE inside the collect_metrics function.

```
lm_res %>% collect_metrics(summarize = FALSE) %>% flextable() %>%
theme_box() %>%
set_caption(caption = "The RMSE and R squared of linear model on 10 resamples of the general social survey training data created by 10-fold cross-validation")
```

Table 3.12. The RMSE and R Squared of Linear Model on 10 Resamples of the General Social Survey Training Data Created by 10-Fold Cross-Validation

id	**.metric**	**.estimator**	**.estimate**	**.config**
Fold01	rmse	standard	2.12147640	Preprocessor1_Model1
Fold01	rsq	standard	0.08229515	Preprocessor1_Model1
Fold02	rmse	standard	2.08111902	Preprocessor1_Model1
Fold02	rsq	standard	0.03078954	Preprocessor1_Model1
Fold03	rmse	standard	2.64122970	Preprocessor1_Model1
Fold03	rsq	standard	0.01442343	Preprocessor1_Model1
Fold04	rmse	standard	2.18893393	Preprocessor1_Model1
Fold04	rsq	standard	0.06007981	Preprocessor1_Model1
Fold05	rmse	standard	1.92721411	Preprocessor1_Model1
Fold05	rsq	standard	0.05786171	Preprocessor1_Model1
Fold06	rmse	standard	1.79859209	Preprocessor1_Model1
Fold06	rsq	standard	0.03540502	Preprocessor1_Model1
Fold07	rmse	standard	1.77102798	Preprocessor1_Model1

Fold07	rsq	standard	0.04776312	Preprocessor1_Model1
Fold08	rmse	standard	2.15657309	Preprocessor1_Model1
Fold08	rsq	standard	0.04071703	Preprocessor1_Model1
Fold09	rmse	standard	1.93902372	Preprocessor1_Model1
Fold09	rsq	standard	0.06812393	Preprocessor1_Model1
Fold10	rmse	standard	2.07830057	Preprocessor1_Model1
Fold10	rsq	standard	0.03061169	Preprocessor1_Model1

- The resulting table has 20 rows because each resample has 2 rows one for RMSE and one for R-squared.
- To get the common summary statistics of RMSE and R squared across the 10 resamples of training data, we use the following functions after the collect_metrics function with summarize = FALSE argument:
  - ++ The group_by function with the .metric argument to split the 20 rows of data into 2 data with 10 rows each, one for RMSE and one for R squared.
  - ++ The get_summary_stats function (from the rstatix package) with the arguments:

+++ .estimate to get the summary statistics of the .estimate column.

+++ type = "common" to get the common summary statistics of the .estimate column.

Then, we convert the result to a table as discussed in previous chapters.

We will load the rstatix package first using the library function to use the get_summary_stats function from this package.

```
library(rstatix)
lm_res %>% collect_metrics(summarize = FALSE) %>% group_by(.
metric) %>%
get_summary_stats(.estimate, type = "common") %>%
flextable() %>% theme_box() %>%
set_caption(caption = "The common summary statistics of RMSE and
R squared across the 10 resamples of the general social survey
training data created by 10-fold cross-validation")
```

Table 3.13. The Common Summary Statistics of RMSE and R Squared Across the 10 Resamples of the General Social Survey Training Data Created by 10-Fold Cross-Validation

.metric	variable	n	min	max	median	iqr	mean	sd	se	ci
rmse	.estimate	10	1.771	2.641	2.080	0.218	2.070	0.248	0.078	0.177
rsq	.estimate	10	0.014	0.082	0.044	0.028	0.047	0.020	0.006	0.015

We see that:

- n = 10 because we have 10 resamples of training data.
- The minimum RMSE = 1.771 and maximum RMSE = 2.641.
- The minimum R squared = 0.014 or 1.4% and the maximum R squared = 0.082 or 8.2%.
- The mean RMSE and R squared value are the same as calculated by the collect_metrics function without using the summarize = FALSE argument.

3.4.1.8. Plot the Performance Metrics of the Linear Model on 10 Resamples of gss Training Data

We can also plot the different RMSE and R squared values for the 10 resamples using the following functions after the collect_metrics function:

- The ggplot function with the argument aes(x = id, y = .estimate, color = .metric) to plot id on the x-axis, .estimate value on the y-axis, and coloring by the .metric type (RMSE or Rsquared).
- The geom_point function to plot a scatter plot of points.
- The geom_line with the argument aes(group = .metric) plots a separate line for each performance metric (RMSE or R squared).
- The facet_wrap function with the arguments:
  - ++ vars(.metric) to plot a separate plot for each metric.
  - ++ scales = "free" so each plot has its own x and y-axis values.
  - ++ nrow = 2 to make the 2 plots in 2 rows.
- The labs function with the title argument to add a plot title, the x argument to add an x-axis title, the y argument to add a y-axis title, and the color argument to add a legend title.
- The theme_classic function removes the grey background and the white grid lines of the default ggplot.

```
lm_res %>% collect_metrics(summarize = FALSE) %>%
ggplot(aes(x = id, y = .estimate, color = .metric))+
geom_point()+ geom_line(aes(group = .metric))+
facet_wrap(vars(.metric), scales = "free", nrow = 2)+
labs(title = "The RMSE and R squared of linear model on 10 resamples of the general social survey training data\n created by 10-fold cross-validation",
x = "Resample", y = "Performance metric",
color = "Performance metric")+
theme_classic()
```

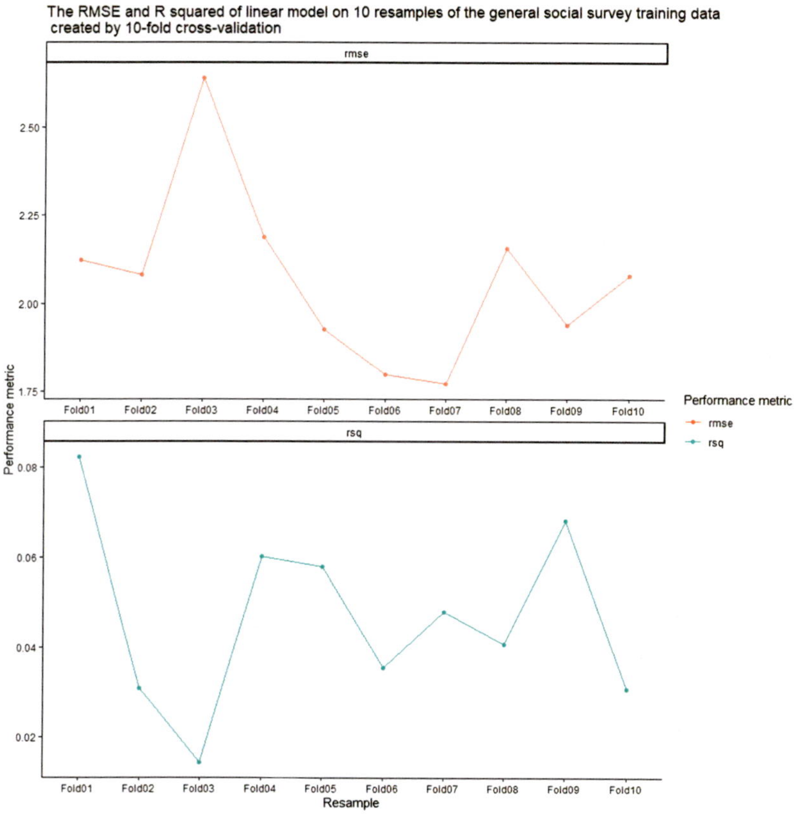

We see that:

- The lowest (best) RMSE value was for fold07 or resample 7.
- The highest (best) R squared was for fold01 or resample 1.
- The highest (worst) RMSE value was for fold03 or resample 3 which also has the lowest (worst) R squared.

One disadvantage of V-fold cross-validation is producing noisy or high-variance estimates of performance metrics when compared to other resampling methods. To reduce that variance, it's often recommended to do repeated cross-validation or run the V-fold resampling procedure multiple times for your data which will be discussed in the next section.

3.4.1.9. Repeated 10-Fold Cross-Validation of gss Training Data

- To perform repeated 10-fold cross-validation, we can use the repeats argument inside the vfold_cv function.
- So we split the gss training data into 10 folds using the v = 10 argument and repeat this process 3 times using the repeats = 3 argument so the result is 30 different resamples of gss training data.
- We also use the set.seed function to make the splitting reproducible.

```
set.seed(123)
folds<-vfold_cv(train_gss, v = 10, repeats = 3)
folds
## # 10-fold cross-validation repeated 3 times
## # A tibble: 30 × 3
## splits id id2
## <list> <chr> <chr>
## 1 <split [13367/1486]> Repeat1 Fold01
## 2 <split [13367/1486]> Repeat1 Fold02
## 3 <split [13367/1486]> Repeat1 Fold03
## 4 <split [13368/1485]> Repeat1 Fold04
## 5 <split [13368/1485]> Repeat1 Fold05
## 6 <split [13368/1485]> Repeat1 Fold06
## 7 <split [13368/1485]> Repeat1 Fold07
## 8 <split [13368/1485]> Repeat1 Fold08
## 9 <split [13368/1485]> Repeat1 Fold09
## 10 <split [13368/1485]> Repeat1 Fold10
## # i 20 more rows
```

We see that:

- We have 30 different rows. Each row corresponds to 1 resample of training data.

- Each row has 2 id values. id for the repeat number from 1 to 3 and id2 for the resample number from 1 to 10 within that repeat.
- Each row has a total rows of 14853 which is the number of rows in training data. 13367 + 1486 = 13368 + 1485 = 14853.
- Within each row, 9 of the 10 folds were grouped in the analysis data with 13367 or 13368 rows and the remaining fold was reserved as the assessment data with 1486 or 1485 rows.
- In each row, a separate fold of the 10 folds was reserved as the assessment data.
- The assessment data is about 0.1 of the total rows of training data because we have used the argument v = 10.

3.4.1.10. Exploring the Repeated 10-Fold Cross-Validation of gss Training Data

- We can use the tidy function on the folds object to detect which row is for training data and which row is for the testing data within each resample and repeat.

```
tidy(folds)
## # A tibble: 445,590 × 4
## Row Data Repeat Fold
## <int> <chr> <chr> <chr>
## 1 1 Analysis Repeat1 Fold01
## 2 1 Analysis Repeat1 Fold02
## 3 1 Analysis Repeat1 Fold04
## 4 1 Analysis Repeat1 Fold05
## 5 1 Analysis Repeat1 Fold06
## 6 1 Analysis Repeat1 Fold07
## 7 1 Analysis Repeat1 Fold08
## 8 1 Analysis Repeat1 Fold09
## 9 1 Analysis Repeat1 Fold10
## 10 1 Analysis Repeat2 Fold01
## # i 445,580 more rows
```

- The resulting data is 445,590 rows because we have 30 resamples of training data with 14853 rows. 14853 × 30 = 445,590.
- We have 4 columns:

- `++ The Row column which is the row number from 1 to 14853.`
- `++ The Data column which is a character column for the analysis data (training data) or assessment (testing) data.`
- `++ The Repeat column for the repeat number of 1,2, or 3.`
- `++ The Fold column which is for the resample (fold) number from 1 to 10.`

- By using the count function with Data, Repeat, and fold argument after the tidy function, we can see how many rows were for the training data and how many rows were for the testing data in each resample.
- We arrange the result by fold and repeat number.

```
tidy(folds) %>% count(Data,Repeat,Fold) %>% arrange(Fold,Repeat)
%>%
flextable() %>% theme_box() %>%
set_caption(caption = "The number of rows in the training and
testing data of 30 resamples of the gss training data created by
repeated 10-fold cross-validation")
```

Table 3.14. The Number of Rows in the Training and Testing Data of 30 Resamples of the gss Training Data Created by Repeated 10-Fold Cross-Validation

Data	Repeat	Fold	n
Analysis	Repeat1	Fold01	13,367
Assessment	Repeat1	Fold01	1,486
Analysis	Repeat2	Fold01	13,367
Assessment	Repeat2	Fold01	1,486
Analysis	Repeat3	Fold01	13,367
Assessment	Repeat3	Fold01	1,486
Analysis	Repeat1	Fold02	13,367
Assessment	Repeat1	Fold02	1,486
Analysis	Repeat2	Fold02	13,367
Assessment	Repeat2	Fold02	1,486
Analysis	Repeat3	Fold02	13,367
Assessment	Repeat3	Fold02	1,486

Analysis	Repeat1	Fold03	13,367
Assessment	Repeat1	Fold03	1,486
Analysis	Repeat2	Fold03	13,367
Assessment	Repeat2	Fold03	1,486
Analysis	Repeat3	Fold03	13,367
Assessment	Repeat3	Fold03	1,486
Analysis	Repeat1	Fold04	13,368
Assessment	Repeat1	Fold04	1,485
Analysis	Repeat2	Fold04	13,368
Assessment	Repeat2	Fold04	1,485
Analysis	Repeat3	Fold04	13,368
Assessment	Repeat3	Fold04	1,485
Analysis	Repeat1	Fold05	13,368
Assessment	Repeat1	Fold05	1,485
Analysis	Repeat2	Fold05	13,368
Assessment	Repeat2	Fold05	1,485
Analysis	Repeat3	Fold05	13,368
Assessment	Repeat3	Fold05	1,485
Analysis	Repeat1	Fold06	13,368
Assessment	Repeat1	Fold06	1,485
Analysis	Repeat2	Fold06	13,368
Assessment	Repeat2	Fold06	1,485
Analysis	Repeat3	Fold06	13,368
Assessment	Repeat3	Fold06	1,485
Analysis	Repeat1	Fold07	13,368
Assessment	Repeat1	Fold07	1,485
Analysis	Repeat2	Fold07	13,368
Assessment	Repeat2	Fold07	1,485
Analysis	Repeat3	Fold07	13,368
Assessment	Repeat3	Fold07	1,485
Analysis	Repeat1	Fold08	13,368
Assessment	Repeat1	Fold08	1,485
Analysis	Repeat2	Fold08	13,368
Assessment	Repeat2	Fold08	1,485
Analysis	Repeat3	Fold08	13,368
Assessment	Repeat3	Fold08	1,485

Analysis	Repeat1	Fold09	13,368
Assessment	Repeat1	Fold09	1,485
Analysis	Repeat2	Fold09	13,368
Assessment	Repeat2	Fold09	1,485
Analysis	Repeat3	Fold09	13,368
Assessment	Repeat3	Fold09	1,485
Analysis	Repeat1	Fold10	13,368
Assessment	Repeat1	Fold10	1,485
Analysis	Repeat2	Fold10	13,368
Assessment	Repeat2	Fold10	1,485
Analysis	Repeat3	Fold10	13,368
Assessment	Repeat3	Fold10	1,485

- For some resamples, the number of rows in training (analysis) data is 13367 rows (9/10 X 14853) and in testing (assessment) data is 1486 rows (1/10 X 14853) as in resample 1,2,3 in the 3 repeats.
- In other resamples, the number of rows in training (analysis) data is 13,368 rows (9/10 X 14853) and in testing (assessment) data is 1485 rows (1/10 X 14853) as in resample 4,5,6,7,8,9, and 10 in the 3 repeats.

3.4.1.11. Plotting the Repeated 10-Fold Cross-Validation of gss Training Data

We can also plot which row was for the training data and which was for the testing data as a heat map within each resample and repeat by using the previously described functions.

However, here we will plot the resample number on the x-axis and facet by Repeat and using the nrow = 3 argument to make the 3 graphs in 3 rows.

```
tidy(folds) %>% ggplot(aes(x = Fold, y = Row, fill = Data))+
geom_tile()+ scale_fill_viridis_d()+ theme_classic()+
facet_wrap(vars(Repeat), nrow = 3, scales = "free")+
labs(title = "The assignment of different rows in 30 resamples of the general social survey training data\n to analysis or assessment data created by repeated 10-fold cross-validation")
```

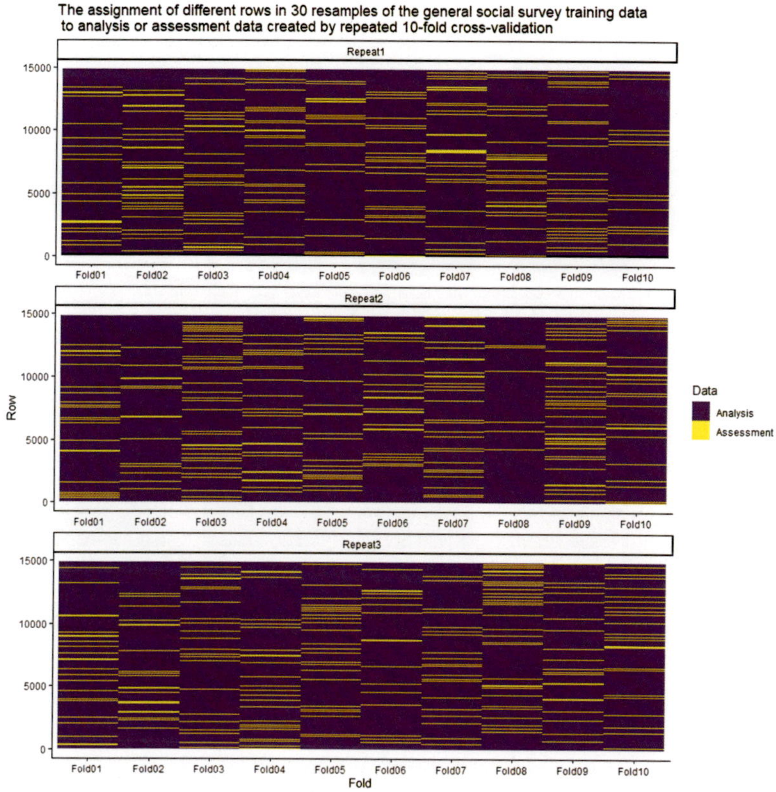

- The row numbers are different within the 3 repeats as seen by the different patterns.
- We can see that more clearly if we plot the repeat number on the x-axis and facet by fold so we will have 10 different graphs.

```
tidy(folds) %>% ggplot(aes(x = Repeat, y = Row, fill = Data))+
geom_tile()+ scale_fill_viridis_d()+ theme_classic()+
facet_wrap(vars(Fold), nrow = 2, scales = "free")+
labs(title = "The assignment of different rows in 30 resamples
of the gss training data \n to analysis or assessment data
created by repeated 10-fold cross-validation with repeat number
on x-axis")
```

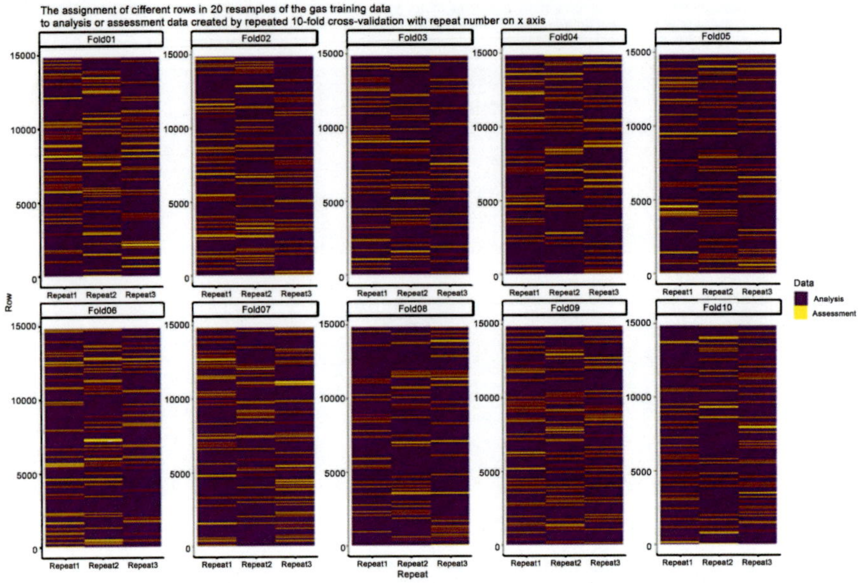

- Each resample or fold is repeated 3 times in 3 repeats but with a different pattern of analysis and assessment data.
- The heat map is overcrowded because we have 14853 rows in our training data. To get a less crowded plot, we can filter the data for the 1st 20 rows using the filter function with the argument Row <= 20 to get the row number equal to or less than 20 after the tidy function.

In addition, we add the argument color = "black" inside the geom_tile function to make the tiles with black borders and use the geom_text function to add text labels of row numbers to each tile as described previously.

```
tidy(folds) %>% filter(Row <= 20) %>%
ggplot(aes(x = Fold, y = Row, fill = Data))+
geom_tile(color = "black")+ scale_fill_viridis_d()+ theme_
classic()+
geom_text(aes(label = Row), color = "white")+
facet_wrap(vars(Repeat), nrow = 1, scales = "free")+
labs(title = "The assignment of 20 rows in 30 resamples of the
gss training data \n to analysis or assessment data created by
repeated 10-fold cross-validation")
```

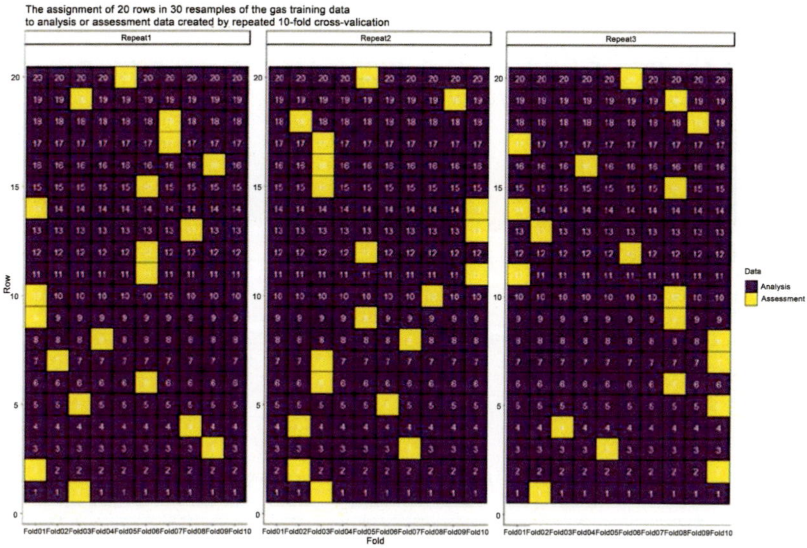

- There is no overlapping between the row numbers in the analysis and assessment data within each resample meaning that each row is either included in the analysis or assessment data within each resample.
- Any row is included only once in 1 assessment data across the 10 resamples. For example, row 20 is only included in assessment data in resample 5 in repeat 1 and repeat 2, in assessment data in resample 6 in repeat 3, and in analysis data in the other 9 resamples of the 3 repeats.
- For row number 1, it is only included in assessment data in resample 3 of repeats 1 and 2, in resample 2 of repeat 3, and in analysis data in the other 9 resamples of the 3 repeats, and so on.

3.4.1.12. Fit a Linear Model to 30 Resamples of gss Training Data

- To fit a linear model on the analysis data and test the model on the assessment data of 30 resamples of folds data, we use the fit_resamples function as before.

```
lm_res<- fit_resamples(linear_reg(mode = "regression",
engine = "lm"),
tvhours ~ age + marital+ rincome,
folds)
```

```
lm_res
## # Resampling results
## # 10-fold cross-validation repeated 3 times
## # A tibble: 30 × 5
## splits id id2 .metrics .notes
## <list> <chr> <chr> <list> <list>
## 1 <split [13367/1486]> Repeat1 Fold01 <tibble [2 × 4]> <tibble
[0 × 3]>
## 2 <split [13367/1486]> Repeat1 Fold02 <tibble [2 × 4]> <tibble
[0 × 3]>
## 3 <split [13367/1486]> Repeat1 Fold03 <tibble [2 × 4]> <tibble
[0 × 3]>
## 4 <split [13368/1485]> Repeat1 Fold04 <tibble [2 × 4]> <tibble
[0 × 3]>
## 5 <split [13368/1485]> Repeat1 Fold05 <tibble [2 × 4]> <tibble
[0 × 3]>
## 6 <split [13368/1485]> Repeat1 Fold06 <tibble [2 × 4]> <tibble
[0 × 3]>
## 7 <split [13368/1485]> Repeat1 Fold07 <tibble [2 × 4]> <tibble
[0 × 3]>
## 8 <split [13368/1485]> Repeat1 Fold08 <tibble [2 × 4]> <tibble
[0 × 3]>
## 9 <split [13368/1485]> Repeat1 Fold09 <tibble [2 × 4]> <tibble
[0 × 3]>
## 10 <split [13368/1485]> Repeat1 Fold10 <tibble [2 × 4]>
<tibble [0 × 3]>
## # i 20 more rows
```

The resulting object "lm_res" contains the results of applying this linear model on these 30 resamples of training data. It contains 5 columns:

- The splits column is a list of each combination of analysis and assessment data.
- The id column is an id column for the repeat number from 1 to 3.
- The id2 column is an id column for the resample number within each repeat from 1 to 10.
- The 1st 3 columns are the same as that of the folds data.
- The .metrics column is a list of performance metrics of applying the linear model to the corresponding assessment data (1486 or 1485

rows). Each performance metric is saved in 2 rows and 4 columns [2 X 4] tibble or data frame. These will be extracted in the next step.

- The .notes column is a list of notes or warnings when applying the linear model to each analysis data (13367 or 13368 rows). Each note is saved in 0 rows and 3 columns [0 X 3] tibble or data frame meaning that there are no notes when applying this model to each analysis data.

To extract the 30 performance metrics for each combination of analysis and assessment data, we use the collect_metrics function.

```
lm_res %>% collect_metrics() %>% flextable() %>% theme_box() %>%
set_caption(caption = "The mean RMSE and R squared of linear
model on 30 resamples of the general social survey training data
created by repeated 10-fold cross-validation")
```

Table 3.15. The Mean RMSE and R Squared of Linear Model on 30 Resamples of the General Social Survey Training Data Created by Repeated 10-Fold Cross-Validation

.metric	.estimator	mean	n	std_err	.config
rmse	standard	2.06933056	30	0.04508086	Preprocessor1_Model1
rsq	standard	0.04616868	30	0.00310049	Preprocessor1_Model1

- We have n = 30 because we have 30 resamples of training data.
- The mean RMSE = 2.07.
- The mean Rsq or R squared = 0.046 or 4.6%.
- To get the 30 performance metrics, we use the argument summarize = FALSE inside the collect_metrics function.

```
lm_res %>% collect_metrics(summarize = FALSE) %>% flextable()
%>%
theme_box() %>%
set_caption(caption = "The RMSE and R squared of linear model on
30 resamples of the general social survey training data created
by repeated 10-fold cross-validation")
```

Table 3.16. The RMSE and R Squared of Linear Model on 30 Resamples of the

General Social Survey Training Data Created by Repeated 10-Fold Cross-Validation

id	id2	.metric	.estimator	.estimate	.config
Repeat1	Fold01	rmse	standard	2.12147640	Preprocessor1_Model1
Repeat1	Fold01	rsq	standard	0.08229515	Preprocessor1_Model1
Repeat1	Fold02	rmse	standard	2.08111902	Preprocessor1_Model1
Repeat1	Fold02	rsq	standard	0.03078954	Preprocessor1_Model1
Repeat1	Fold03	rmse	standard	2.64122970	Preprocessor1_Model1
Repeat1	Fold03	rsq	standard	0.01442343	Preprocessor1_Model1
Repeat1	Fold04	rmse	standard	2.18893393	Preprocessor1_Model1
Repeat1	Fold04	rsq	standard	0.06007981	Preprocessor1_Model1
Repeat1	Fold05	rmse	standard	1.92721411	Preprocessor1_Model1
Repeat1	Fold05	rsq	standard	0.05786171	Preprocessor1_Model1
Repeat1	Fold06	rmse	standard	1.79859209	Preprocessor1_Model1
Repeat1	Fold06	rsq	standard	0.03540502	Preprocessor1_Model1
Repeat1	Fold07	rmse	standard	1.77102798	Preprocessor1_Model1
Repeat1	Fold07	rsq	standard	0.04776312	Preprocessor1_Model1
Repeat1	Fold08	rmse	standard	2.15657309	Preprocessor1_Model1
Repeat1	Fold08	rsq	standard	0.04071703	Preprocessor1_Model1
Repeat1	Fold09	rmse	standard	1.93902372	Preprocessor1_Model1

Repeat1	Fold09	rsq	stan-dard	0.06812393	Preprocessor1_Model1
Repeat1	Fold10	rmse	stan-dard	2.07830057	Preprocessor1_Model1
Repeat1	Fold10	rsq	stan-dard	0.03061169	Preprocessor1_Model1
Repeat2	Fold01	rmse	stan-dard	1.90980715	Preprocessor1_Model1
Repeat2	Fold01	rsq	stan-dard	0.03910331	Preprocessor1_Model1
Repeat2	Fold02	rmse	stan-dard	1.93788815	Preprocessor1_Model1
Repeat2	Fold02	rsq	stan-dard	0.07677985	Preprocessor1_Model1
Repeat2	Fold03	rmse	stan-dard	2.36341455	Preprocessor1_Model1
Repeat2	Fold03	rsq	stan-dard	0.04191996	Preprocessor1_Model1
Repeat2	Fold04	rmse	stan-dard	1.74399748	Preprocessor1_Model1
Repeat2	Fold04	rsq	stan-dard	0.03029876	Preprocessor1_Model1
Repeat2	Fold05	rmse	stan-dard	2.51636695	Preprocessor1_Model1
Repeat2	Fold05	rsq	stan-dard	0.06296713	Preprocessor1_Model1
Repeat2	Fold06	rmse	stan-dard	2.01712088	Preprocessor1_Model1
Repeat2	Fold06	rsq	stan-dard	0.02119370	Preprocessor1_Model1
Repeat2	Fold07	rmse	stan-dard	1.88340851	Preprocessor1_Model1
Repeat2	Fold07	rsq	stan-dard	0.06340450	Preprocessor1_Model1
Repeat2	Fold08	rmse	stan-dard	2.32043466	Preprocessor1_Model1
Repeat2	Fold08	rsq	stan-dard	0.05515961	Preprocessor1_Model1
Repeat2	Fold09	rmse	stan-dard	2.31248647	Preprocessor1_Model1

Repeat2	Fold09	rsq	stan-dard	0.03210411	Preprocessor1_Model1
Repeat2	Fold10	rmse	stan-dard	1.61530751	Preprocessor1_Model1
Repeat2	Fold10	rsq	stan-dard	0.04409751	Preprocessor1_Model1
Repeat3	Fold01	rmse	stan-dard	1.88582728	Preprocessor1_Model1
Repeat3	Fold01	rsq	stan-dard	0.03814342	Preprocessor1_Model1
Repeat3	Fold02	rmse	stan-dard	1.91650465	Preprocessor1_Model1
Repeat3	Fold02	rsq	stan-dard	0.03116886	Preprocessor1_Model1
Repeat3	Fold03	rmse	stan-dard	2.07414783	Preprocessor1_Model1
Repeat3	Fold03	rsq	stan-dard	0.05758690	Preprocessor1_Model1
Repeat3	Fold04	rmse	stan-dard	2.23150854	Preprocessor1_Model1
Repeat3	Fold04	rsq	stan-dard	0.06333958	Preprocessor1_Model1
Repeat3	Fold05	rmse	stan-dard	2.28745045	Preprocessor1_Model1
Repeat3	Fold05	rsq	stan-dard	0.01435596	Preprocessor1_Model1
Repeat3	Fold06	rmse	stan-dard	1.85986785	Preprocessor1_Model1
Repeat3	Fold06	rsq	stan-dard	0.05481145	Preprocessor1_Model1
Repeat3	Fold07	rmse	stan-dard	1.96662912	Preprocessor1_Model1
Repeat3	Fold07	rsq	stan-dard	0.04789504	Preprocessor1_Model1
Repeat3	Fold08	rmse	stan-dard	2.13740413	Preprocessor1_Model1
Repeat3	Fold08	rsq	stan-dard	0.04791547	Preprocessor1_Model1
Repeat3	Fold09	rmse	stan-dard	2.50897721	Preprocessor1_Model1

Repeat3	Fold09	rsq	stan-dard	0.04196819	Preprocessor1_Model1
Repeat3	Fold10	rmse	stan-dard	1.88787669	Preprocessor1_Model1
Repeat3	Fold10	rsq	stan-dard	0.05277665	Preprocessor1_Model1

- The resulting table has 60 rows because each resample has 2 rows for RMSE and R squared.
- To get the common summary statistics of RMSE and R squared across the 30 resamples of training data, we use the same above functions.

```
lm_res %>% collect_metrics(summarize = FALSE) %>% group_by(.
metric) %>%
get_summary_stats(.estimate, type = "common") %>%
flextable() %>% theme_box() %>%
set_caption(caption = "The common summary statistics of RMSE and
R squared across the 30 resamples of the general social survey
training data created by repeated 10-fold cross-validation")
```

Table 3.17. The Common Summary Statistics of RMSE and R Squared Across the 30 Resamples of the General Social Survey Training Data Created by Repeated 10-Fold Cross-Validation

.metric	vari-able	n	min	max	me-dian	iqr	mean	sd	se	ci
rmse	.esti-mate	30	1.615	2.641	2.046	0.328	2.069	0.247	0.045	0.092
rsq	.esti-mate	30	0.014	0.082	0.046	0.025	0.046	0.017	0.003	0.006

We see that:

- n = 30 because we have 30 resamples of training data.
- The minimum RMSE = 1.615 and maximum RMSE = 2.641.
- The minimum R squared = 0.014 or 1.4% and the maximum R squared = 0.082 or 8.2%.
- The mean RMSE and R squared value are the same as calculated by the collect_metrics function.

3.4.1.13. Plot the Performance Metrics of the Linear Model on 30 Resamples of gss Training Data

- We can also plot the different RMSE and R squared values for the 30 resamples using the following functions after the collect_metrics function:

  ++ The mutate function with the argument id3 = paste(id,id2, sep = "_") *to create a new id column "id3" by pasting together the 2 id columns "id" and "id2" with "_"* separator.

  ++ The ggplot function with the argument aes(x = id3, y = .estimate, color = .metric) to plot id3 on the x-axis, .estimate value on y-axis, and coloring by the .metric type (RMSE or Rsquared).

  ++ The geom_point function to plot a scatter plot of points.

  ++ The geom_line with the argument aes(group = .metric) to plot a separate line for each performance metric (RMSE or R squared).

  ++ The facet_wrap function with the arguments:

  +++ *vars(.metric) to plot a separate plot for each metric.*

  +++ *scales = "free" so each plot has its own x and y-axis values.*

  +++ *nrow = 2 to make the 2 plots in 2 rows.*

  ++ The labs function with the title argument to add a plot title, the x argument to add an x-axis title, the y argument to add a y-axis title, and the color argument to add a legend title.

  ++ The theme_classic function removes the grey background and the white grid lines of the default ggplot.

  ++ The theme function with the argument axis.text.x = element_text(angle = 60, hjust = 1) to make the text on the x-axis inclined with 60 angle and with 1 horizontal justification.

```
lm_res %>% collect_metrics(summarize = FALSE) %>%
mutate(id3 = paste(id,id2,sep = "_")) %>%
ggplot(aes(x = id3, y = .estimate, color = .metric))+
geom_point()+ geom_line(aes(group = .metric))+
facet_wrap(vars(.metric), scales = "free", nrow = 2)+
labs(title = "The RMSE and R squared of linear model on 30 different resamples of the gss training data \n created by repeated 10-fold cross-validation",
```

```
x = "Resample", y = "Performance metric",
color = "Performance metric")+
theme_classic()+
theme(axis.text.x = element_text(angle = 60, hjust = 1))
```

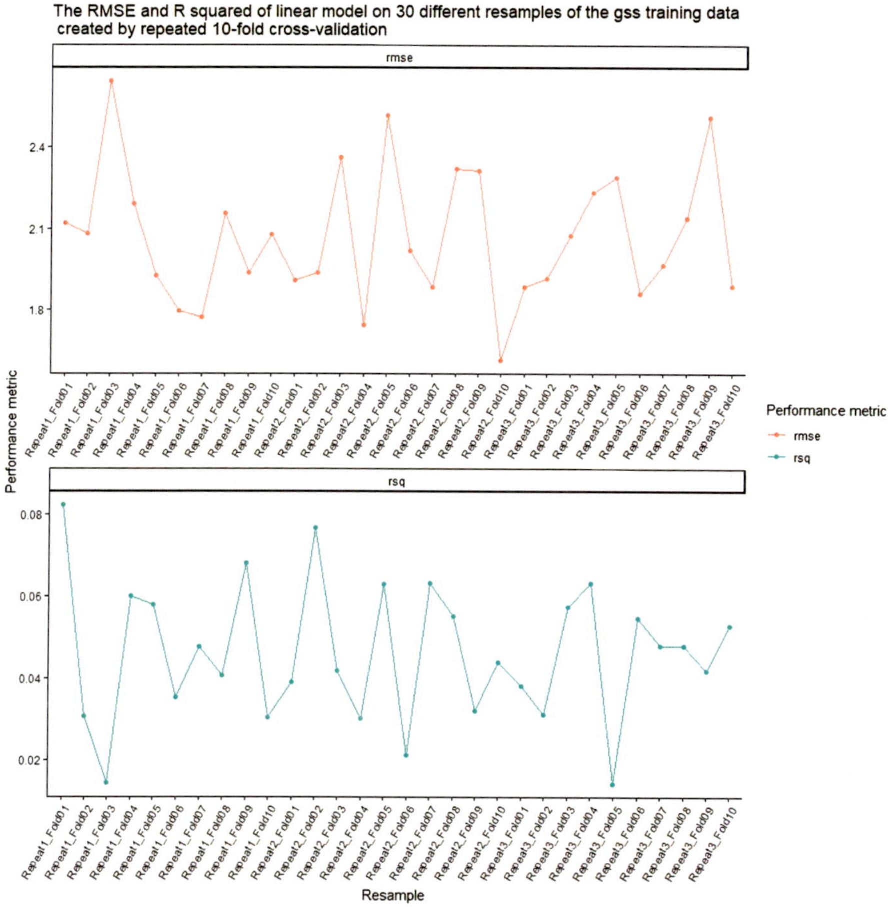

We see that:

- The lowest (best) RMSE value was for fold10 of repeat 2 (1.62).
- The highest (best) R squared was for fold01 of repeat 1 (0.082 or 8.2%).
- The highest (worst) RMSE value was for fold03 of repeat 1 (2.64).
- The lowest (worst) R squared was for fold03 of repeat 1 and fold05 of repeat 3 (0.0144 or 1.4% for both).

3.4.2. V-Fold Cross-Validation of BRFSS Training Data

3.4.2.1. 10-Fold Cross-Validation of BRFSS Training Data

- Similarly, we can split the training data into 10 folds using the v = 10 argument as described previously.
- However, before splitting the data, we convert the sex column to a factor because we will fit a classification tree model using sex as a categorical outcome.
- We will create another data frame "train_brfss2" that results from applying the mutate function on the train_brfss data using the argument sex = factor(sex) to convert the sex column to a factor column. The vfold_cv function will be applied to train_brfss2 data.
- We also use the set.seed function, before using the vfold_cv function, to make the splitting reproducible.

```
train_brfss2<-train_brfss %>% mutate(sex = factor(sex))
set.seed(123)
folds<-vfold_cv(train_brfss2, v = 10)
folds
## # 10-fold cross-validation
## # A tibble: 10 × 2
## splits id
## <list> <chr>
## 1 <split [151/17]> Fold01
## 2 <split [151/17]> Fold02
## 3 <split [151/17]> Fold03
## 4 <split [151/17]> Fold04
## 5 <split [151/17]> Fold05
## 6 <split [151/17]> Fold06
## 7 <split [151/17]> Fold07
## 8 <split [151/17]> Fold08
## 9 <split [152/16]> Fold09
## 10 <split [152/16]> Fold10
```

We see:

- We have 10 different rows. Each row corresponds to 1 resample of training data.

- Each row has a total rows of 168 which is the number of rows in training data. 151 + 17 = 152 + 16 = 168.
- Within each row, 9 of the 10 folds were grouped in the analysis data with 151 or 152 rows and the remaining fold was reserved as the assessment data with 17 or 16 rows.
- In each row, a separate fold of the 10 folds was reserved as the assessment data.
- The assessment data is about 0.1 of the total rows of training data (17 or 16 rows) because we have used the argument v = 10.

3.4.2.2. Exploring 10-Fold Cross-Validation of BRFSS Training Data

- We can use the tidy function on the folds object to detect which row is for training data and which row is for the testing data within each resample.

```
tidy(folds)
## # A tibble: 1,680 × 3
## Row Data Fold
## <int> <chr> <chr>
## 1 1 Analysis Fold01
## 2 1 Analysis Fold02
## 3 1 Analysis Fold03
## 4 1 Analysis Fold04
## 5 1 Analysis Fold05
## 6 1 Analysis Fold06
## 7 1 Analysis Fold07
## 8 1 Analysis Fold08
## 9 1 Analysis Fold10
## 10 2 Analysis Fold01
## # i 1,670 more rows
```

- The resulting data is 1680 rows because we have 10 resamples of training data with 168 rows. 168 × 10 = 1680.
- We have 3 columns:

++ The Row column which is the row number from 1 to 168.

++ The Data column which is a character column for the analysis data (training data) or assessment (testing) data.

```
++ The Fold column which is for the resample (fold) number from 1 to 10.
```

- For example, we see that row 1 is included in all resamples in the analysis (training) data except in resample 9 and so is included in resample 9 in the assessment (testing) data.
- By using the count function with Data and fold argument after the tidy function, we can see how many rows were for the training data and how many rows were for the testing data in each resample.
- We arrange the result by fold or resample number.

```
tidy(folds) %>% count(Data,Fold) %>% arrange(Fold) %>%
flextable() %>% theme_box() %>%
set_caption(caption = "The number of rows in the training and testing data of 10 resamples of the BRFSS data created by 10-fold cross-validation")
```

Table 3.18. The Number of Rows in the Training and Testing Data of 10 Resamples of the BRFSS Data Created by 10-Fold Cross-Validation

Data	Fold	n
Analysis	Fold01	151
Assessment	Fold01	17
Analysis	Fold02	151
Assessment	Fold02	17
Analysis	Fold03	151
Assessment	Fold03	17
Analysis	Fold04	151
Assessment	Fold04	17
Analysis	Fold05	151
Assessment	Fold05	17
Analysis	Fold06	151
Assessment	Fold06	17
Analysis	Fold07	151
Assessment	Fold07	17
Analysis	Fold08	151
Assessment	Fold08	17
Analysis	Fold09	152
Assessment	Fold09	16
Analysis	Fold10	152
Assessment	Fold10	16

- For some resamples, the number of rows in training (analysis) data is 151 rows (9/10 X 168) and in testing (assessment) data is 17 rows (1/10 X 168) as in resamples 1,2,3,4,5,6,7,8.

- In other resamples, the number of rows in training (analysis) data is 152 rows (9/10 X 168) and in testing (assessment) data is 16 rows (1/10 X 168) as in resamples 9 and 10.

3.4.2.3. Plotting 10-Fold Cross-Validation of BRFSS Training Data

We can also plot which row was for the training data and which was for the testing data as a heat map within each resample by using the previously described functions.

However, we will use nrow = 2 within the facet_wrap function to make all 10 graphs in 2 rows.

```
tidy(folds) %>% ggplot(aes(x = Data, y = Row, fill = Data))+
geom_tile()+ scale_fill_viridis_d()+ theme_classic()+
facet_wrap(vars(Fold), nrow = 2)+
labs(title = "The assignment of different rows in 10 resamples of
the BRFSS training data\n to analysis or assessment data created
by 10-fold cross-validation")
```

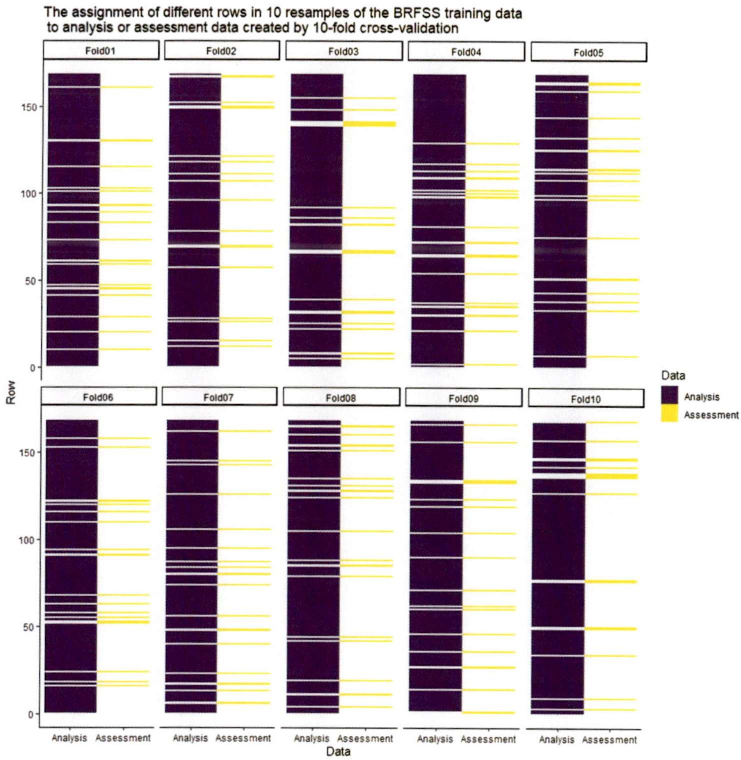

The heat map is overcrowded because we have 168 rows in our training data. To get a less crowded plot, we can filter the data for the 1st 20 rows using the filter function with the argument Row <= 20 to get the row number equal to or less than 20 after the tidy function.

In addition, we add the argument color = "black" inside the geom_tile function to make the tiles with black borders and use the geom_text function to add text labels to each tile as described previously.

```
tidy(folds) %>% filter(Row <= 20) %>%
ggplot(aes(x = Data, y = Row, fill = Data))+
geom_tile(color = "black")+ scale_fill_viridis_d()+ theme_classic()+
geom_text(aes(label = Row), color = "white")+
facet_wrap(vars(Fold), nrow = 2)+
labs(title = "The assignment of first 20 rows in 10 resamples of the BRFSS training data\n to analysis or assessment data created by 10-fold cross-validation")
```

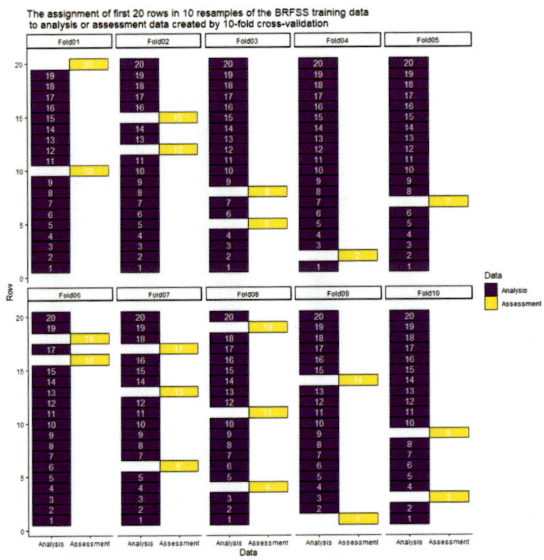

- There is no overlapping between the row numbers in the analysis and assessment data within each resample meaning that each row is either included in the analysis or assessment data within each resample.
- Any row is included only once in 1 assessment data across the 10 resamples. For example, row 20 is only included in assessment data in resample 1 and in analysis data in the other 9 resamples.

- For row number 1, it is only included in assessment data in resample 9 and in analysis data in the other 9 resamples, and so on.

3.4.2.4. Fit a Classification Tree Model to 10 Resamples of BRFSS Training Data

- To fit a classification tree model on the analysis data and test the model on the assessment data of 10 resamples of folds data, we use the fit_resamples function with the arguments:

  ++ decision_tree with the arguments: mode = "classification", engine = "rpart" which defines a decision tree model for predicting categorical outcomes using the rpart function discussed in Chapter 1.

  ++ sex ~ weight_lbs+ height_inch+income which is the model formula meaning that we want to predict sex (categorical outcome) using the respondent's weight, height, and reported income.

  ++ folds which are the 10 rows created above and each containing analysis data (151 or 152 rows) for fitting the model and assessment data (17 or 16 rows) for testing the model performance.

```
tree_res<- fit_resamples(decision_tree(mode = "classification",
engine = "rpart"),
sex ~ weight_lbs+ height_inch+income,
folds)
tree_res
## # Resampling results
## # 10-fold cross-validation
## # A tibble: 10 × 4
## splits id .metrics .notes
## <list> <chr> <list> <list>
## 1 <split [151/17]> Fold01 <tibble [2 × 4]> <tibble [0 × 3]>
## 2 <split [151/17]> Fold02 <tibble [2 × 4]> <tibble [0 × 3]>
## 3 <split [151/17]> Fold03 <tibble [2 × 4]> <tibble [0 × 3]>
## 4 <split [151/17]> Fold04 <tibble [2 × 4]> <tibble [0 × 3]>
## 5 <split [151/17]> Fold05 <tibble [2 × 4]> <tibble [0 × 3]>
## 6 <split [151/17]> Fold06 <tibble [2 × 4]> <tibble [0 × 3]>
## 7 <split [151/17]> Fold07 <tibble [2 × 4]> <tibble [0 × 3]>
```

```
## 8 <split [151/17]> Fold08 <tibble [2 × 4]> <tibble [0 × 3]>
## 9 <split [152/16]> Fold09 <tibble [2 × 4]> <tibble [0 × 3]>
## 10 <split [152/16]> Fold10 <tibble [2 × 4]> <tibble [0 × 3]>
```

The resulting object "tree_res" contains the results of applying this tree model on these 10 rows or resamples of training data. It contains 4 columns:

- The splits column is a list of each combination of analysis and assessment data.
- The id column is an id column for the resample number from 1 to 10.
- The 1st 2 columns are the same as that of the folds data.
- The .metrics column is a list of performance metrics of applying the tree model to the corresponding assessment data (17 or 16 rows). Each performance metric is saved in 2 rows and 4 columns [2 X 4] tibble or data frame. These will be extracted in the next step.
- The .notes column is a list of notes or warnings when applying the tree model to each analysis data (151 or 152 rows). Each note is saved in 0 rows and 3 columns [0 X 3] tibble or data frame meaning that there are no notes when applying this model to each analysis data.

To extract the 10 performance metrics for each combination of analysis and assessment data, we use the collect_metrics function.

```
tree_res %>% collect_metrics() %>% flextable() %>% theme_box()
%>%
set_caption(caption = "The mean accuracy and ROC AUC of tree
model on 10 different resamples of the BRFSS training data
created by 10-fold cross-validation")
```

Table 3.19. The Mean Accuracy and ROC AUC of Tree Model on 10 Different Resamples of the BRFSS Training Data Created by 10-Fold Cross-Validation

.metric	.estimator	mean	n	std_err	.config
accuracy	binary	0.8397059	10	0.01963999	Preprocessor1_Model1
roc_auc	binary	0.8682751	10	0.01504995	Preprocessor1_Model1

- The default behavior of the collect_metrics function is to summarize all performance metrics (n = 10) into their mean.

- The default calculated performance metrics for classification models are:

  ++ Accuracy with a mean value of 0.84 or 84%.

  ++ ROC AUC (Receiver-operating characteristic Area under the curve) with a mean value of 0.87.

- To get the 10 performance metrics, we use the argument summarize = FALSE inside the collect_metrics function.

```
tree_res %>% collect_metrics(summarize = FALSE) %>% flextable()
%>%
theme_box() %>%
set_caption(caption = "The accuracy and ROC AUC of tree model
on 10 different resamples of the BRFSS training data created by
10-fold cross-validation")
```

Table 3.20. The Accuracy and ROC AUC of Tree Model on 10 Different Resamples of the BRFSS Training Data Created by 10-Fold Cross-Validation

id	.metric	.estimator	.estimate	.config
Fold01	accuracy	binary	0.7647059	Preprocessor1_Model1
Fold01	roc_auc	binary	0.8106061	Preprocessor1_Model1
Fold02	accuracy	binary	0.7647059	Preprocessor1_Model1
Fold02	roc_auc	binary	0.7857143	Preprocessor1_Model1
Fold03	accuracy	binary	0.8823529	Preprocessor1_Model1
Fold03	roc_auc	binary	0.8863636	Preprocessor1_Model1
Fold04	accuracy	binary	0.8823529	Preprocessor1_Model1
Fold04	roc_auc	binary	0.9142857	Preprocessor1_Model1
Fold05	accuracy	binary	0.8235294	Preprocessor1_Model1
Fold05	roc_auc	binary	0.8750000	Preprocessor1_Model1
Fold06	accuracy	binary	0.8823529	Preprocessor1_Model1
Fold06	roc_auc	binary	0.8365385	Preprocessor1_Model1
Fold07	accuracy	binary	0.8823529	Preprocessor1_Model1
Fold07	roc_auc	binary	0.9469697	Preprocessor1_Model1
Fold08	accuracy	binary	0.7647059	Preprocessor1_Model1
Fold08	roc_auc	binary	0.8636364	Preprocessor1_Model1

Fold09	accuracy	binary	0.9375000	Preprocessor1_Model1
Fold09	roc_auc	binary	0.8909091	Preprocessor1_Model1
Fold10	accuracy	binary	0.8125000	Preprocessor1_Model1
Fold10	roc_auc	binary	0.8727273	Preprocessor1_Model1

- The resulting table has 20 rows because each resample has 2 rows for accuracy and ROC AUC.
- To get the common summary statistics of accuracy and ROC AUC across the 10 resamples of training data, we use the following functions after the collect_metrics function:

++ The group_by function with the .metric argument to split the 20 rows of data into 2 data with 10 rows each, one for accuracy and one for ROC AUC.

++ The get_summary_stats function with the arguments:

+++ .estimate to get the summary statistics of the .estimate column.

+++ type = "common" to get the common summary statistics of the .estimate column.

Then, we convert the result to a table as discussed in previous chapters.

```
tree_res %>% collect_metrics(summarize = FALSE) %>% group_by(.
metric) %>%
get_summary_stats(.estimate, type = "common") %>%
flextable() %>% theme_box() %>%
set_caption(caption = "The common summary statistics of accuracy
and ROC AUC across the 10 resamples of the BRFSS training data
created by 10-fold cross-validation")
```

Table 3.21. *The Common Summary Statistics of Accuracy and ROC AUC Across the 10 Resamples of the BRFSS Training Data Created by 10-Fold Cross-Validation*

.metric	variable	n	min	max	median	iqr	mean	sd	se	ci
accuracy	.estimate	10	0.765	0.938	0.853	0.106	0.840	0.062	0.020	0.044
roc_auc	.estimate	10	0.786	0.947	0.874	0.046	0.868	0.048	0.015	0.034

We see that:

- n = 10 because we have 10 resamples of training data.

- The minimum accuracy = 0.765 or 76.5% and the maximum accuracy = 0.938 or 93.8%.
- The minimum ROC AUC = 0.786 and the maximum ROC AUC = 0.947.
- The mean accuracy and ROC AUC value are the same as calculated by the collect_metrics function.

3.4.2.5. Plot the Performance Metrics of the Tree Model on 10 Resamples of BRFSS Training Data

- We can also plot the different accuracy and ROC AUC values for the 10 resamples using the following functions after the collect_metrics function:

  ++ The ggplot function with the argument aes(x = id, y = .estimate, color = .metric) to plot id on the x-axis, .estimate value on y-axis, and coloring by the .metric type (accuracy or ROC AUC).

  ++ The geom_point function to plot a scatter plot of points.

  ++ The geom_line with the argument aes(group = .metric) to plot a separate line for each performance metric (accuracy or ROC AUC).

  ++ The facet_wrap function with the arguments:

    +++ *vars(.metric) to plot a separate* plot *for each metric.*

    +++ *scales = "free" so each plot has its own x and y-axis values.*

    +++ *nrow = 2 to make the 2 plots in 2 rows.*

  ++ The labs function with the title argument to add a plot title, the x argument to add an x-axis title, the y argument to add a y-axis title, and the color argument to add a legend title.

  ++ The theme_classic function removes the grey background and the white grid lines of the default ggplot.

```
tree_res %>% collect_metrics(summarize = FALSE) %>%
ggplot(aes(x = id, y = .estimate, color = .metric))+
geom_point()+ geom_line(aes(group = .metric))+
facet_wrap(vars(.metric), scales = "free", nrow = 2)+
labs(title = "The accuracy and ROC AUC of tree model on 10
different resamples of the BRFSS training data\n created by 10-
fold cross-validation",
```

```
x = "Resample", y = "Performance metric",
color = "Performance metric")+
theme_classic()
```

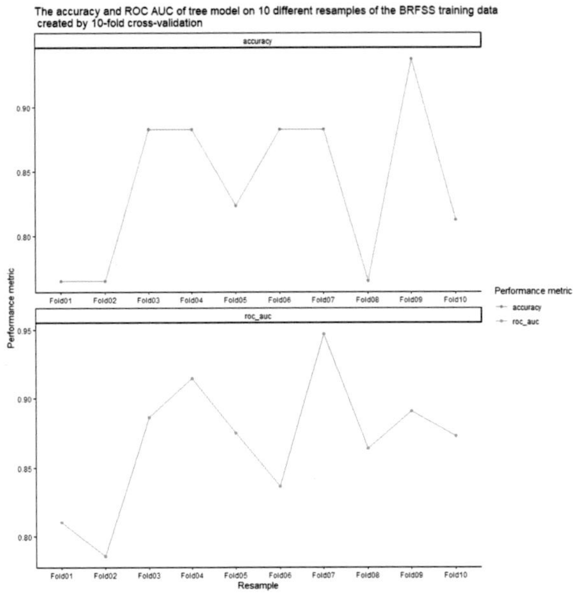

We see that:

- The highest (best) accuracy value was for fold09 or resample 9 (0.938 or 93.8%).
- The highest (best) ROC AUC was for fold07 or resample 7 (0.947).
- The lowest (worst) accuracy value was for fold01, fold02, and fold08 or resamples 1,2,8 (0.765 or 76.5%).
- The lowest (worst) ROC AUC value was for fold02 or resample 2 (0.786).

3.4.2.6. Repeated 10-Fold Cross-Validation of BRFSS Training Data

- To perform repeated 10-fold cross-validation, we can use the repeats argument inside the vfold_cv function.
- So we split the training data into 10 folds using the v = 10 argument and repeat this process 3 times using the repeats = 3 argument, so the result is 30 different resamples of training data. We split the train_ brfss2 data because this data contains the sex outcome as a factor column.
- We also use the set.seed function to make the splitting reproducible.

```
set.seed(123)
folds<-vfold_cv(train_brfss2, v = 10, repeats = 3)
folds
## # 10-fold cross-validation repeated 3 times
## # A tibble: 30 × 3
## splits id id2
## <list> <chr> <chr>
## 1 <split [151/17]> Repeat1 Fold01
## 2 <split [151/17]> Repeat1 Fold02
## 3 <split [151/17]> Repeat1 Fold03
## 4 <split [151/17]> Repeat1 Fold04
## 5 <split [151/17]> Repeat1 Fold05
## 6 <split [151/17]> Repeat1 Fold06
## 7 <split [151/17]> Repeat1 Fold07
## 8 <split [151/17]> Repeat1 Fold08
## 9 <split [152/16]> Repeat1 Fold09
## 10 <split [152/16]> Repeat1 Fold10
## # i 20 more rows
```

We see:

- We have 30 different rows. Each row corresponds to 1 resample of training data.
- Each row has 2 id values. Id for the repeat number (from 1 to 3) and id2 for the resample number (from 1 to 10) within that repeat.
- Each row has a total rows of 168 which is the number of rows in training data. 151 + 17 = 152 + 16 = 168.
- Within each row, 9 of the 10 folds were grouped in the analysis data with 151 or 152 rows, and the remaining fold was reserved as the assessment data with 17 or 16 rows respectively.
- In each row, a separate fold of the 10 folds was reserved as the assessment data.
- The assessment data is about 0.1 of the total rows of training data because we have used the argument v = 10.

3.4.2.7. Exploring the Repeated 10-Fold Cross-Validation of BRFSS Training Data

- We can use the tidy function on the folds object to detect which row is for training data and which row is for the testing data within each resample and repeat.

```
tidy(folds)
## # A tibble: 5,040 × 4
## Row Data Repeat Fold
## <int> <chr> <chr> <chr>
## 1 1 Analysis Repeat1 Fold01
## 2 1 Analysis Repeat1 Fold02
## 3 1 Analysis Repeat1 Fold03
## 4 1 Analysis Repeat1 Fold04
## 5 1 Analysis Repeat1 Fold05
## 6 1 Analysis Repeat1 Fold06
## 7 1 Analysis Repeat1 Fold07
## 8 1 Analysis Repeat1 Fold08
## 9 1 Analysis Repeat1 Fold10
## 10 1 Analysis Repeat2 Fold01
## # i 5,030 more rows
```

- The resulting data is 5040 rows because we have 30 resamples of training data with 168 rows. 168 × 30 = 5040.
- We have 4 columns:

  ++ The Row column which is the row number from 1 to 168.

  ++ The Data column which is a character column for the analysis data (training data) or assessment (testing) data.

  ++ The Repeat column for the repeat number of 1,2, or 3.

  ++ The Fold column which is for the resample (fold) number from 1 to 10.
- By using the count function with Data, Repeat, and fold argument after the tidy function, we can see how many rows were for the training data and how many rows were for the testing data in each resample.
- We arrange the result by fold and repeat number

```
tidy(folds) %>% count(Data,Repeat,Fold) %>% arrange(Fold,Repeat)
%>%
flextable() %>% theme_box() %>%
set_caption(caption = "The number of rows in the training and
testing data of 30 resamples of the BRFSS training data created
by repeated 10-fold cross-validation")
```

Table 3.22. The Number of Rows in the Training and Testing Data of 30 Resamples of the BRFSS Training Data Created by Repeated 10-Fold Cross-Validation

Data	Repeat	Fold	n
Analysis	Repeat1	Fold01	151
Assessment	Repeat1	Fold01	17
Analysis	Repeat2	Fold01	151
Assessment	Repeat2	Fold01	17
Analysis	Repeat3	Fold01	151
Assessment	Repeat3	Fold01	17
Analysis	Repeat1	Fold02	151
Assessment	Repeat1	Fold02	17
Analysis	Repeat2	Fold02	151
Assessment	Repeat2	Fold02	17
Analysis	Repeat3	Fold02	151
Assessment	Repeat3	Fold02	17
Analysis	Repeat1	Fold03	151
Assessment	Repeat1	Fold03	17
Analysis	Repeat2	Fold03	151
Assessment	Repeat2	Fold03	17
Analysis	Repeat3	Fold03	151
Assessment	Repeat3	Fold03	17
Analysis	Repeat1	Fold04	151
Assessment	Repeat1	Fold04	17
Analysis	Repeat2	Fold04	151
Assessment	Repeat2	Fold04	17
Analysis	Repeat3	Fold04	151
Assessment	Repeat3	Fold04	17
Analysis	Repeat1	Fold05	151
Assessment	Repeat1	Fold05	17
Analysis	Repeat2	Fold05	151

Assessment	Repeat2	Fold05	17
Analysis	Repeat3	Fold05	151
Assessment	Repeat3	Fold05	17
Analysis	Repeat1	Fold06	151
Assessment	Repeat1	Fold06	17
Analysis	Repeat2	Fold06	151
Assessment	Repeat2	Fold06	17
Analysis	Repeat3	Fold06	151
Assessment	Repeat3	Fold06	17
Analysis	Repeat1	Fold07	151
Assessment	Repeat1	Fold07	17
Analysis	Repeat2	Fold07	151
Assessment	Repeat2	Fold07	17
Analysis	Repeat3	Fold07	151
Assessment	Repeat3	Fold07	17
Analysis	Repeat1	Fold08	151
Assessment	Repeat1	Fold08	17
Analysis	Repeat2	Fold08	151
Assessment	Repeat2	Fold08	17
Analysis	Repeat3	Fold08	151
Assessment	Repeat3	Fold08	17
Analysis	Repeat1	Fold09	152
Assessment	Repeat1	Fold09	16
Analysis	Repeat2	Fold09	152
Assessment	Repeat2	Fold09	16
Analysis	Repeat3	Fold09	152
Assessment	Repeat3	Fold09	16
Analysis	Repeat1	Fold10	152
Assessment	Repeat1	Fold10	16
Analysis	Repeat2	Fold10	152
Assessment	Repeat2	Fold10	16
Analysis	Repeat3	Fold10	152
Assessment	Repeat3	Fold10	16

- For some resamples, the number of rows in training (analysis) data is 151 rows (9/10 X 168) and in testing (assessment) data is 17 rows (1/10 X 168) as in resamples 1,2,3,4,5,6,7,8 in the 3 repeats.

- In other resamples, the number of rows in training (analysis) data is 152 rows (9/10 X 168) and in testing (assessment) data is 16 rows (1/10 X 168) as in resamples 9 and 10 in the 3 repeats.

3.4.2.8. Plotting the Repeated 10-Fold Cross-Validation of BRFSS Training Data

We can also plot which row was for the training data and which was for the testing data as a heat map within each resample and repeat by using the previously described functions.

However, here we will plot the resample number on the x-axis and facet by Repeat and using the nrow = 3 argument to make the 3 graphs for 3 repeats in 3 rows.

```
tidy(folds) %>% ggplot(aes(x = Fold, y = Row, fill = Data))+
geom_tile()+ scale_fill_viridis_d()+ theme_classic()+
facet_wrap(vars(Repeat), nrow = 3, scales = "free")+
labs(title = "The assignment of different rows in 30 resamples of the BRFSS training data\n to analysis or assessment data created by repeated 10-fold cross-validation")
```

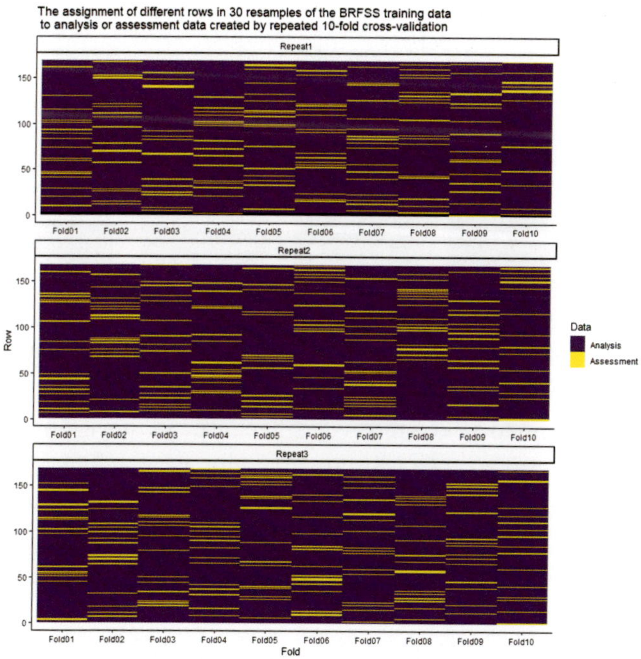

- The assignment of the same row numbers is different within the 3 repeats as seen by the different patterns of analysis and assessment data.
- We can see that more clearly if we plot the repeat number on the x-axis and facet by fold so we will have 10 different graphs.

```
tidy(folds) %>% ggplot(aes(x = Repeat, y = Row, fill = Data))+
geom_tile()+ scale_fill_viridis_d()+ theme_classic()+
facet_wrap(vars(Fold), nrow = 2, scales = "free")+
labs(title = "The assignment of different rows in 30 resamples of the BRFSS training data \n to analysis or assessment data created by repeated 10-fold cross-validation with repeat number on x-xias")
```

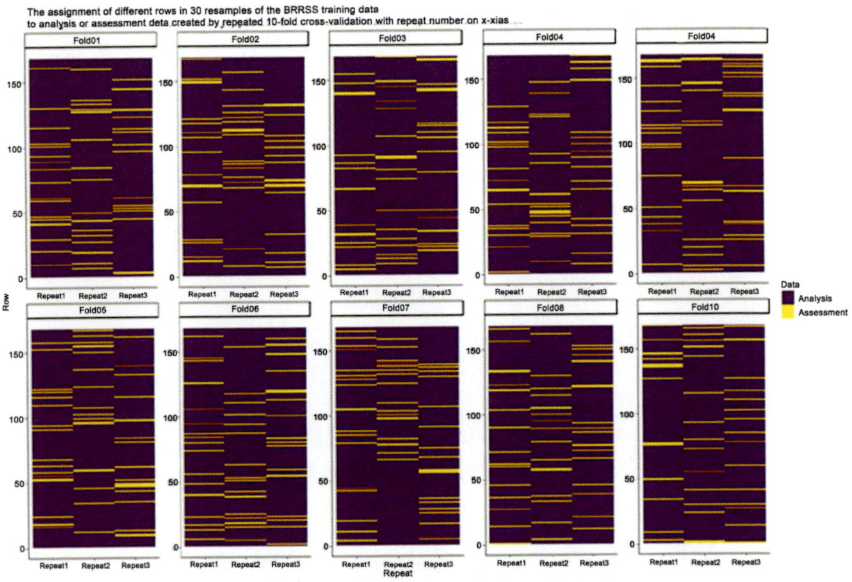

- Each resample or fold is repeated 3 times in 3 repeats but with a different pattern of analysis and assessment data.
- The heat map is overcrowded because we have 168 rows in our training data. To get a less crowded plot, we can filter the data for the 1st 20 rows using the filter function with the argument Row <= 20 to get the row number equal to or less than 20 after the tidy function.

In addition, we add the argument color = "black" inside the geom_tile function to make the tiles with black borders and use the geom_text function to add text labels of row numbers to each tile as described previously.

```
tidy(folds) %>% filter(Row <= 20) %>%
ggplot(aes(x = Fold, y = Row, fill = Data))+
geom_tile(color = "black")+ scale_fill_viridis_d()+ theme_
classic()+
geom_text(aes(label = Row), color = "white")+
facet_wrap(vars(Repeat), nrow = 1, scales = "free")+
labs(title = "The assignment of 20 rows in 30 resamples of the
BRFSS training data \n to analysis or assessment data created by
repeated 10-fold cross-validation")
```

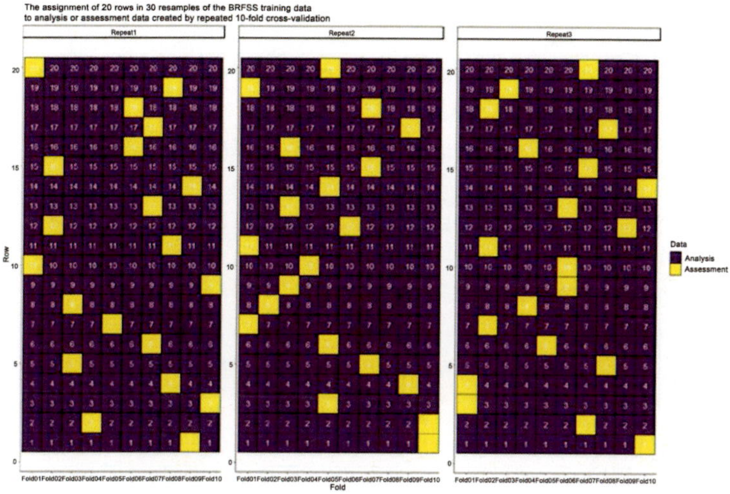

- There is no overlapping between the row numbers in the analysis and assessment data within each resample meaning that each row is either included in the analysis or assessment data within each resample.
- Any row is included only once in 1 assessment data across the 10 resamples of 1 repeat. For example, row 20 is only included in assessment data in resample 1 of repeat 1, resample 5 of repeat 2, and resample 7 of repeat 3.
- For row number 1, it is only included in assessment data in resample 9 of repeat 1 and in resample 10 of repeat 2 and 3, and so on.

3.4.2.9. Fit a Tree Model to 30 Resamples of BRFSS Training Data

- To fit a tree model on the analysis data and test the model on the assessment data of 30 resamples of folds data, we use the fit_resamples function as before.

```
tree_res<- fit_resamples(decision_tree(mode = "classification",
engine = "rpart"),
sex ~ weight_lbs+ height_inch+income,
folds)
tree_res
## # Resampling results
## # 10-fold cross-validation repeated 3 times
## # A tibble: 30 × 5
## splits id id2 .metrics .notes
## <list> <chr> <chr> <list> <list>
## 1 <split [151/17]> Repeat1 Fold01 <tibble [2 × 4]> <tibble
[0 × 3]>
## 2 <split [151/17]> Repeat1 Fold02 <tibble [2 × 4]> <tibble
[0 × 3]>
## 3 <split [151/17]> Repeat1 Fold03 <tibble [2 × 4]> <tibble
[0 × 3]>
## 4 <split [151/17]> Repeat1 Fold04 <tibble [2 × 4]> <tibble
[0 × 3]>
## 5 <split [151/17]> Repeat1 Fold05 <tibble [2 × 4]> <tibble
[0 × 3]>
## 6 <split [151/17]> Repeat1 Fold06 <tibble [2 × 4]> <tibble
[0 × 3]>
## 7 <split [151/17]> Repeat1 Fold07 <tibble [2 × 4]> <tibble
[0 × 3]>
## 8 <split [151/17]> Repeat1 Fold08 <tibble [2 × 4]> <tibble
[0 × 3]>
## 9 <split [152/16]> Repeat1 Fold09 <tibble [2 × 4]> <tibble
[0 × 3]>
## 10 <split [152/16]> Repeat1 Fold10 <tibble [2 × 4]> <tibble
[0 × 3]>
## # i 20 more rows
```

The resulting object "tree_res" contains the results of applying this tree model on these 30 resamples of training data. It contains 5 columns:

- The splits column is a list of each combination of analysis and assessment data.
- The id column is an id column for the repeat number from 1 to 3.
- The id2 column is an id column for the resample number from 1 to

10 within each repeat.

- The 1st 3 columns are the same as that of the folds data.
- The .metrics column is a list of performance metrics of applying the tree model to the corresponding assessment data (17 or 16 rows). Each performance metric is saved in 2 rows and 4 columns [2 X 4] tibble or data frame. These will be extracted in the next step.
- The .notes column is a list of notes or warnings when applying the tree model to each analysis data (151 or 152 rows). Each note is saved in 0 rows and 3 columns [0 X 3] tibble or data frame meaning that there are no notes when applying this model to each analysis data.

To extract the 30 performance metrics for each combination of analysis and assessment data, we use the collect_metrics function.

```
tree_res %>% collect_metrics() %>% flextable() %>% theme_box()
%>%
set_caption(caption = "The mean accuracy and ROC AUC of tree
model on 30 resamples of the BRFSS training data created by
repeated 10-fold cross-validation ")
```

Table 3.23. The Mean Accuracy and ROC AUC of Tree Model on 30 Resamples of the BRFSS Training Data Created by Repeated 10-Fold Cross-Validation

.metric	.estimator	mean	n	std_err	.config
accu-racy	binary	0.8334559	30	0.01702397	Preprocessor1_Model1
roc_auc	binary	0.8619701	30	0.01647774	Preprocessor1_Model1

- We have n = 30 because we have 30 resamples of training data.
- The mean accuracy = 0.833 or 83.3%.
- The mean ROC AUC = 0.862 or 86.2%.
- To get the 30 performance metrics, we use the argument summarize = FALSE inside the collect_metrics function.

```
tree_res %>% collect_metrics(summarize = FALSE) %>% flextable() %>%

theme_box() %>%

set_caption(caption = "The accuracy and ROC AUC of tree model on 30 resa-
mples of the BRFSS training data created by repeated 10-fold cross-validation")
```

Table 3.24. The Accuracy and ROC AUC of Tree Model on 30 Resamples of the BRFSS Training Data Created by Repeated 10-Fold Cross-Validation

id	id2	.metric	.estimator	.estimate	.config
Repeat1	Fold01	accuracy	binary	0.7647059	Preprocessor1_Model1
Repeat1	Fold01	roc_auc	binary	0.8106061	Preprocessor1_Model1
Repeat1	Fold02	accuracy	binary	0.7647059	Preprocessor1_Model1
Repeat1	Fold02	roc_auc	binary	0.7857143	Preprocessor1_Model1
Repeat1	Fold03	accuracy	binary	0.8823529	Preprocessor1_Model1
Repeat1	Fold03	roc_auc	binary	0.8863636	Preprocessor1_Model1
Repeat1	Fold04	accuracy	binary	0.8823529	Preprocessor1_Model1
Repeat1	Fold04	roc_auc	binary	0.9142857	Preprocessor1_Model1
Repeat1	Fold05	accuracy	binary	0.8235294	Preprocessor1_Model1
Repeat1	Fold05	roc_auc	binary	0.8750000	Preprocessor1_Model1
Repeat1	Fold06	accuracy	binary	0.8823529	Preprocessor1_Model1
Repeat1	Fold06	roc_auc	binary	0.8365385	Preprocessor1_Model1
Repeat1	Fold07	accuracy	binary	0.8823529	Preprocessor1_Model1
Repeat1	Fold07	roc_auc	binary	0.9469697	Preprocessor1_Model1
Repeat1	Fold08	accuracy	binary	0.7647059	Preprocessor1_Model1
Repeat1	Fold08	roc_auc	binary	0.8636364	Preprocessor1_Model1
Repeat1	Fold09	accuracy	binary	0.9375000	Preprocessor1_Model1
Repeat1	Fold09	roc_auc	binary	0.8909091	Preprocessor1_Model1
Repeat1	Fold10	accuracy	binary	0.8125000	Preprocessor1_Model1
Repeat1	Fold10	roc_auc	binary	0.8727273	Preprocessor1_Model1
Repeat2	Fold01	accuracy	binary	0.8235294	Preprocessor1_Model1
Repeat2	Fold01	roc_auc	binary	0.9545455	Preprocessor1_Model1
Repeat2	Fold02	accuracy	binary	0.8823529	Preprocessor1_Model1
Repeat2	Fold02	roc_auc	binary	0.9444444	Preprocessor1_Model1
Repeat2	Fold03	accuracy	binary	0.8823529	Preprocessor1_Model1
Repeat2	Fold03	roc_auc	binary	0.9000000	Preprocessor1_Model1
Repeat2	Fold04	accuracy	binary	0.7647059	Preprocessor1_Model1
Repeat2	Fold04	roc_auc	binary	0.7000000	Preprocessor1_Model1
Repeat2	Fold05	accuracy	binary	0.8235294	Preprocessor1_Model1
Repeat2	Fold05	roc_auc	binary	0.7500000	Preprocessor1_Model1
Repeat2	Fold06	accuracy	binary	0.5294118	Preprocessor1_Model1

Repeat2	Fold06	roc_auc	binary	0.5486111	Preprocessor1_Model1
Repeat2	Fold07	accuracy	binary	0.9411765	Preprocessor1_Model1
Repeat2	Fold07	roc_auc	binary	0.9375000	Preprocessor1_Model1
Repeat2	Fold08	accuracy	binary	0.8823529	Preprocessor1_Model1
Repeat2	Fold08	roc_auc	binary	0.8750000	Preprocessor1_Model1
Repeat2	Fold09	accuracy	binary	0.9375000	Preprocessor1_Model1
Repeat2	Fold09	roc_auc	binary	0.9166667	Preprocessor1_Model1
Repeat2	Fold10	accuracy	binary	0.9375000	Preprocessor1_Model1
Repeat2	Fold10	roc_auc	binary	0.9871795	Preprocessor1_Model1
Repeat3	Fold01	accuracy	binary	0.8823529	Preprocessor1_Model1
Repeat3	Fold01	roc_auc	binary	0.9621212	Preprocessor1_Model1
Repeat3	Fold02	accuracy	binary	0.8235294	Preprocessor1_Model1
Repeat3	Fold02	roc_auc	binary	0.8541667	Preprocessor1_Model1
Repeat3	Fold03	accuracy	binary	0.8823529	Preprocessor1_Model1
Repeat3	Fold03	roc_auc	binary	0.8750000	Preprocessor1_Model1
Repeat3	Fold04	accuracy	binary	0.9411765	Preprocessor1_Model1
Repeat3	Fold04	roc_auc	binary	0.9711538	Preprocessor1_Model1
Repeat3	Fold05	accuracy	binary	0.8823529	Preprocessor1_Model1
Repeat3	Fold05	roc_auc	binary	0.8714286	Preprocessor1_Model1
Repeat3	Fold06	accuracy	binary	0.8235294	Preprocessor1_Model1
Repeat3	Fold06	roc_auc	binary	0.7750000	Preprocessor1_Model1
Repeat3	Fold07	accuracy	binary	0.8235294	Preprocessor1_Model1
Repeat3	Fold07	roc_auc	binary	0.8819444	Preprocessor1_Model1
Repeat3	Fold08	accuracy	binary	0.7058824	Preprocessor1_Model1
Repeat3	Fold08	roc_auc	binary	0.7954545	Preprocessor1_Model1
Repeat3	Fold09	accuracy	binary	0.8125000	Preprocessor1_Model1
Repeat3	Fold09	roc_auc	binary	0.8636364	Preprocessor1_Model1
Repeat3	Fold10	accuracy	binary	0.6250000	Preprocessor1_Model1
Repeat3	Fold10	roc_auc	binary	0.8125000	Preprocessor1_Model1

- The resulting table has 60 rows because each resample has 2 rows for accuracy and ROC AUC.
- To get the common summary statistics of accuracy and ROC AUC across the 30 resamples of training data, we use the same above functions.

```
tree_res %>% collect_metrics(summarize = FALSE) %>% group_by(.
metric) %>%
get_summary_stats(.estimate, type = "common") %>%
flextable() %>% theme_box() %>%
set_caption(caption = "The common summary statistics of accuracy
and ROC AUC across the 30 resamples of the BRFSS training data
created by repeated 10-fold cross-validation")
```

Table 3.25. The Common Summary Statistics of Accuracy and ROC AUC Across the 30 Resamples of the BRFSS Training Data Created by Repeated 10-Fold Cross-Validation

.metric	variable	n	min	max	median	iqr	mean	sd	se	ci
accuracy	.estimate	30	0.529	0.941	0.853	0.070	0.833	0.093	0.017	0.035
roc_auc	.estimate	30	0.549	0.987	0.875	0.098	0.862	0.090	0.016	0.034

We see that:

- n = 30 because we have 30 resamples of training data.
- The minimum accuracy = 0.529 or 52.9% and the maximum accuracy = 0.941 or 94.1%.
- The minimum ROC AUC = 0.549 and the maximum ROC AUC = 0.987.
- The mean accuracy and ROC AUC value are the same as that calculated by the collect_metrics function.

3.4.2.10. Plot the Performance Metrics of the Tree Model on 30 Resamples of BRFSS Data

- We can plot the different accuracy and ROC AUC values for the 30 resamples using the following functions after the collect_metrics function:

  ++ The mutate function to create an id column (id3) by using the paste function with the arguments (id,id2, sep = "_") *to make a new id column by pasting the 2 id columns and separating them by the "_"* symbol.

  ++ The ggplot function with the argument aes(x = id3, y = .estimate, color = .metric) to plot id3 on the x-axis, .estimate value on the y-axis, and coloring by the .metric type (accuracy or ROC AUC).

++ The geom_point function to plot a scatter plot of points.

++ The geom_line with the argument aes(group = .metric) to plot a separate line for each performance metric (accuracy or ROC AUC).

++ The facet_wrap function with the arguments:

+++ *vars(.metric) to plot a separate plot for each metric.*

+++ *scales = "free" so each plot has its own x and y-axis values.*

+++ *nrow = 2 to make the 2 plots in 2 rows.*

++ The labs function with the title argument to add a plot title, the x argument to add an x-axis title, the y argument to add a y-axis title, and the color argument to add a legend title.

++ The theme_classic function removes the grey background and the white grid lines of the default plot created by the ggplot function.

++ The theme function with the argument axis.text.x = element_text(angle = 60, hjust = 1) to make the x-axis text inclined at 60 with 1 horizontal justification.

```
tree_res %>% collect_metrics(summarize = FALSE) %>%
mutate(id3 = paste(id, id2, sep = "_")) %>%
ggplot(aes(x = id3, y = .estimate, color = .metric))+
geom_point()+ geom_line(aes(group = .metric))+
facet_wrap(vars(.metric), scales = "free", nrow = 2)+
labs(title = "The accuracy and ROC AUC of tree model on 30
different resamples of the BRFSS training data",
x = "Resample", y = "Performance metric",
color = "Performance metric")+
theme_classic()+
theme(axis.text.x = element_text(angle = 60, hjust = 1))
```

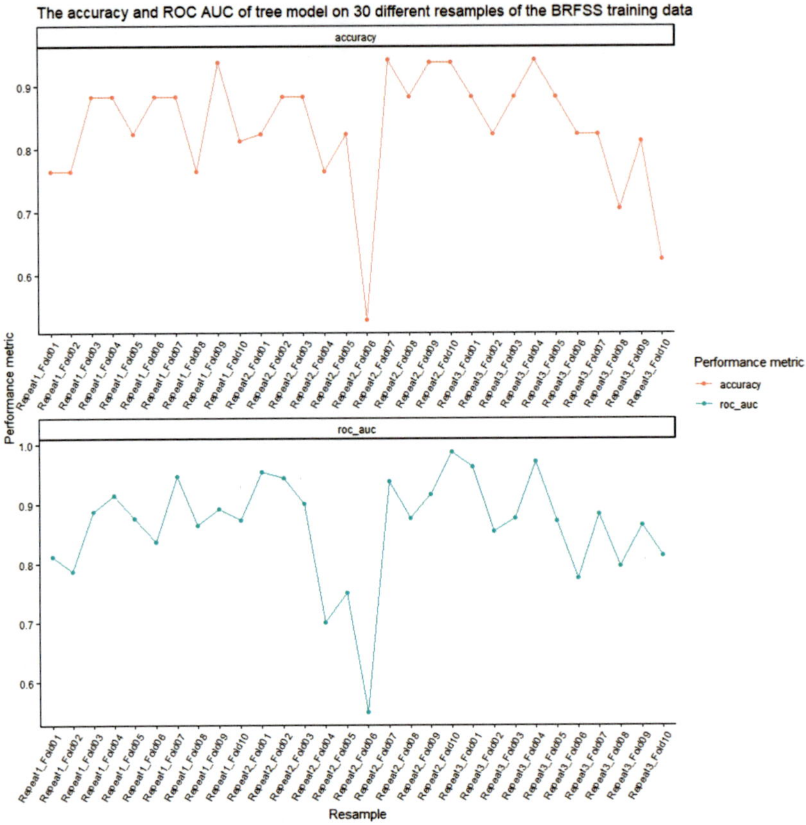

We see that:

- The highest (best) accuracy value was for fold07 of repeat 2 and fold04 of repeat 3 (0.941 or 94.1%).
- The highest (best) ROC AUC was for fold10 of repeat 2 (0.987).
- The lowest (worst) accuracy was for fold06 of repeat 2 (0.529 or 52.9%) which also has the lowest ROC AUC (0.549).

3.5. MONTE-CARLO CROSS-VALIDATION

In V-fold cross-validation, each observation or row is assigned to one assessment data, while Monte-Carlo cross-validation takes a random subset of your data for each assessment data, meaning each observation can be used in 0, 1, or many assessment data.

The analysis data is then made up of all the observations that weren't selected. Because each assessment data is sampled independently, you can repeat this as many times as you want.

3.5.1. Monte-Carlo Cross-Validation of gss Training Data

3.5.1.1. Producing 10 Resamples of gss Training Data

To apply Monte-Carlo cross-validation, we use the mc_cv function with the arguments:

- train_gss which is the training data.
- prop = 0.7 to make the analysis data 0.7 and assessment data 0.3 of total rows in training data.
- times = 10 to make 10 different resamples.
- We also use the set.seed function to make the splitting reproducible.

The resulting object is called "split_gss."

```
set.seed(123)
split_gss<-mc_cv(train_gss, prop = 0.7, times = 10)
split_gss
## # Monte Carlo cross-validation (0.7/0.3) with 10 resamples
## # A tibble: 10 × 2
## splits id
## <list> <chr>
## 1 <split [10397/4456]> Resample01
## 2 <split [10397/4456]> Resample02
## 3 <split [10397/4456]> Resample03
## 4 <split [10397/4456]> Resample04
## 5 <split [10397/4456]> Resample05
## 6 <split [10397/4456]> Resample06
## 7 <split [10397/4456]> Resample07
## 8 <split [10397/4456]> Resample08
## 9 <split [10397/4456]> Resample09
## 10 <split [10397/4456]> Resample10
```

We see:

- We have 10 different rows. Each row corresponds to 1 resample of training data.
- Each row has a total rows of 14853 which is the number of rows in training data. 10397 + 4456 = 14853.

- Within each row, 0.3 of the total rows were grouped in the assessment data with 4456 rows and the remaining 0.7 rows were grouped as the analysis data with 10397 rows.

3.5.1.2. Exploring 10 Resamples of gss Training Data Created by Monte-Carlo Cross-Validation

- We can use the tidy function on the split_gss object to detect which row is for analysis data and which row is for the assessment data within each resample.

```
tidy(split_gss)
## # A tibble: 148,530 × 3
## Row Data Resample
## <int> <chr> <chr>
## 1 1 Analysis Resample01
## 2 1 Analysis Resample03
## 3 1 Analysis Resample05
## 4 1 Analysis Resample09
## 5 1 Analysis Resample10
## 6 2 Analysis Resample01
## 7 2 Analysis Resample02
## 8 2 Analysis Resample03
## 9 2 Analysis Resample05
## 10 2 Analysis Resample07
## # i 148,520 more rows
```

- The resulting data is 148,530 rows because we have 10 resamples of training data with 14853 rows. $14853 \times 10 = 148530$.
- We have 3 columns:

++ The Row column which is the row number from 1 to 14853.

++ The Data column which is a character column for the analysis data (training data) or assessment (testing) data.

++ The Resample column which is for the resample number from 1 to 10.

- For example, we see that row 1 is included in the analysis (training) data in resamples 1,3,5,9,10 and so is included in the assessment (testing) data in resamples 2,4,6,7,8.

- By using the count function with the Data and Resample argument after the tidy function, we can see how many rows were for the training data and how many rows were for the testing data in each resample.
- We arrange the result by resample number

```
tidy(split_gss) %>% count(Data,Resample) %>% arrange(Resample)
%>%
flextable() %>% theme_box() %>%
set_caption(caption = "The number of rows in the training and testing data of 10 resamples of the general social survey data created by Monte-Carlo cross-validation repeated 10 times")
```

Table 3.26. The Number of Rows in the Training and Testing Data of 10 Resamples of the General Social Survey Data Created by Monte-Carlo Cross-Validation Repeated 10 Times

Data	**Resample**	**n**
Analysis	Resample01	10,397
Assessment	Resample01	4,456
Analysis	Resample02	10,397
Assessment	Resample02	4,456
Analysis	Resample03	10,397
Assessment	Resample03	4,456
Analysis	Resample04	10,397
Assessment	Resample04	4,456
Analysis	Resample05	10,397
Assessment	Resample05	4,456
Analysis	Resample06	10,397
Assessment	Resample06	4,456
Analysis	Resample07	10,397
Assessment	Resample07	4,456
Analysis	Resample08	10,397
Assessment	Resample08	4,456
Analysis	Resample09	10,397
Assessment	Resample09	4,456
Analysis	Resample10	10,397
Assessment	Resample10	4,456

- In all resamples, the number of rows in training (analysis) data is 10397 rows (7/10 X 14853), and in testing (assessment) data is 4456 rows (3/10 X 14853).

3.5.1.3. Plotting 10 Resamples of gss Training Data Created by Monte-Carlo Cross-Validation

We can also plot which row was for the training data and which was for the testing data as a heat map within each resample by using the previously described functions.

However, we will use nrow = 2 within the facet_wrap function to make all 10 graphs in 2 rows.

```
tidy(split_gss) %>% ggplot(aes(x = Data, y = Row, fill = Data))+
geom_tile()+ scale_fill_viridis_d()+ theme_classic()+
facet_wrap(vars(Resample), nrow = 2)+
labs(title = "The assignment of different rows in 10 resamples of the general social survey training data\n to analysis or assessment data created by Monte-Carlo cross-validation repeated 10 times")
```

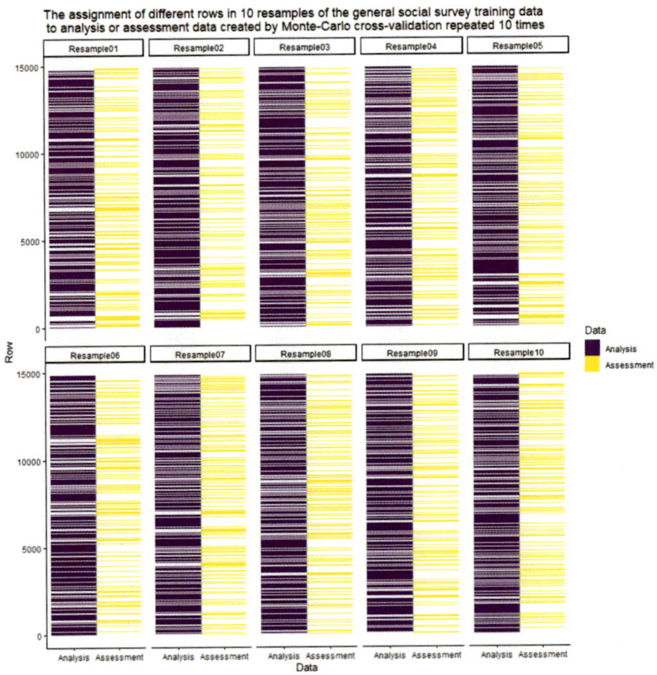

The heat map is overcrowded because we have 14853 rows in our training data. To get a less crowded plot, we can filter the data for the 1st 20 rows using the filter function with the argument Row <= 20 to get the row number equal to or less than 20 after the tidy function.

In addition, we add the argument color = "black" inside the geom_tile function to make the tiles with black borders and use the geom_text function to add text labels to each tile as described previously.

```
tidy(split_gss) %>% filter(Row <= 20) %>%
ggplot(aes(x = Data, y = Row, fill = Data))+
geom_tile(color = "black")+ scale_fill_viridis_d()+ theme_
classic()+
geom_text(aes(label = Row), color = "white")+
facet_wrap(vars(Resample), nrow = 2)+
labs(title = "The assignment of first 20 rows in 10 resamples
of the general social survey training data\n to analysis or
assessment data created by Monte-Carlo cross-validation repeated
10 times")
```

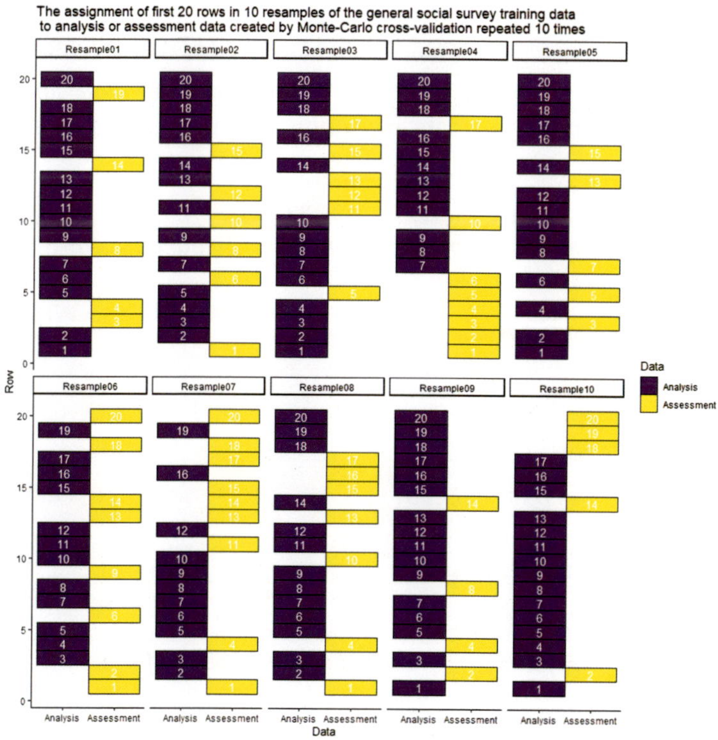

- There is no overlapping between the row numbers in the analysis and assessment data within each resample meaning that each row is either included in the analysis or assessment data within each resample.
- However, any row can be included in many assessment data across the 10 resamples. For example, row 20 is included in assessment data in resamples 6,7,10 and in analysis data in the other 7 resamples.
- For row number 1, it is included in assessment data in resamples 2,4,6,7,8 and in analysis data in the other 5 resamples, and so on.

3.5.1.4. Fit a Linear Model to 10 Resamples of gss Training Data Created by Monte-Carlo Cross-Validation

- To fit a linear model on the analysis data and test the model on the assessment data of 10 resamples of gss data, we use the fit_resamples function with the arguments:

  ++ linear_reg with the arguments mode = "regression" and engine = "lm" which defines a linear regression model for predicting numeric outcomes using the lm function discussed in Chapter 1.

  ++ tvhours ~ age + marital+ rincome which is the model formula meaning that we want to predict tv hours (numeric outcome) using the respondent's age, marital status, and reported income.

  ++ split_gss which are the 10 resamples created above, each containing analysis data for fitting the model and assessment data for testing the model performance.

```
lm_res<- fit_resamples(linear_reg(mode = "regression",
engine = "lm"),
tvhours ~ age + marital+ rincome,
split_gss)
lm_res
## # Resampling results
## # Monte Carlo cross-validation (0.7/0.3) with 10 resamples
## # A tibble: 10 × 4
## splits id .metrics .notes
## <list> <chr> <list> <list>
## 1 <split [10397/4456]> Resample01 <tibble [2 × 4]> <tibble
[0 × 3]>
## 2 <split [10397/4456]> Resample02 <tibble [2 × 4]> <tibble
```

```
[0 × 3]>
## 3 <split [10397/4456]> Resample03 <tibble [2 × 4]> <tibble
[0 × 3]>
## 4 <split [10397/4456]> Resample04 <tibble [2 × 4]> <tibble
[0 × 3]>
## 5 <split [10397/4456]> Resample05 <tibble [2 × 4]> <tibble
[0 × 3]>
## 6 <split [10397/4456]> Resample06 <tibble [2 × 4]> <tibble
[0 × 3]>
## 7 <split [10397/4456]> Resample07 <tibble [2 × 4]> <tibble
[0 × 3]>
## 8 <split [10397/4456]> Resample08 <tibble [2 × 4]> <tibble
[0 × 3]>
## 9 <split [10397/4456]> Resample09 <tibble [2 × 4]> <tibble
[0 × 3]>
## 10 <split [10397/4456]> Resample10 <tibble [2 × 4]> <tibble
[0 × 3]>
```

The resulting object "lm_res" contains the results of applying this linear model on these 10 rows or resamples of training data. It contains 4 columns:

- The splits column is a list of each combination of analysis and assessment data.
- The id column is an id column for the resample number from 1 to 10.
- The 1st 2 columns are the same as that of the split_gss data.
- The .metrics column is a list of performance metrics of applying the linear model to the corresponding assessment data (4456 rows). Each performance metric is saved in 2 rows and 4 columns [2 X 4] tibble or data frame. These will be extracted in the next step.
- The .notes column is a list of notes or warnings when applying the linear model to each analysis data (10397 rows). Each note is saved in 0 rows and 3 columns [0 X 3] tibble or data frame meaning that there are no notes when applying this model to each analysis data.

To extract the 10 performance metrics for each combination of analysis and assessment data, we use the collect_metrics function on the lm_res object.

```
lm_res %>% collect_metrics() %>% flextable() %>% theme_box() %>%
set_caption(caption = "The mean RMSE and R squared of linear
model on 10 resamples of the gss training data created by Monte-
Carlo cross-validation")
```

Table 3.27. The Mean RMSE and R Squared of Linear Model on 10 Resamples of the gss Training Data Created by Monte-Carlo Cross-Validation

.metric	.estimator	Mean	n	std_err	.config
rmse	standard	2.10786334	10	0.022138839	Preprocessor1_Model1
rsq	standard	0.04237136	10	0.001764618	Preprocessor1_Model1

- The default behavior of the collect_metrics function is to summarize all performance metrics (n = 10) into their mean.
- The default calculated performance metrics are:

++ *RMSE or root mean squared error with a mean value of 2.11.*

++ *Rsq or R squared with a mean value of 0.042 or 4.2%.*

- To get the 10 performance metrics, we use the argument summarize = FALSE inside the collect_metrics function.

```
lm_res %>% collect_metrics(summarize = FALSE) %>% flextable()
%>%
theme_box() %>%
set_caption(caption = "The RMSE and R squared of linear model
on 10 resamples of the gss training data created by Monte-Carlo
cross-validation")
```

Table 3.28. The RMSE and R Squared of Linear Model on 10 Resamples of the gss Training Data Created by Monte-Carlo Cross-Validation

id	.metric	.estimator	.estimate	.config
Resample01	rmse	standard	2.08267002	Preprocessor1_Model1
Resample01	rsq	standard	0.03586310	Preprocessor1_Model1
Resample02	rmse	standard	2.08770459	Preprocessor1_Model1
Resample02	rsq	standard	0.04194954	Preprocessor1_Model1
Resample03	rmse	standard	2.22432331	Preprocessor1_Model1
Resample03	rsq	standard	0.04450006	Preprocessor1_Model1
Resample04	rmse	standard	2.19876512	Preprocessor1_Model1
Resample04	rsq	standard	0.04002250	Preprocessor1_Model1

Resample05	rmse	standard	2.13094915	Preprocessor1_Model1
Resample05	rsq	standard	0.04105062	Preprocessor1_Model1
Resample06	rmse	standard	2.13198062	Preprocessor1_Model1
Resample06	rsq	standard	0.04527099	Preprocessor1_Model1
Resample07	rmse	standard	2.03227265	Preprocessor1_Model1
Resample07	rsq	standard	0.04072485	Preprocessor1_Model1
Resample08	rmse	standard	2.12927338	Preprocessor1_Model1
Resample08	rsq	standard	0.04296535	Preprocessor1_Model1
Resample09	rmse	standard	1.99920256	Preprocessor1_Model1
Resample09	rsq	standard	0.03587233	Preprocessor1_Model1
Resample10	rmse	standard	2.06149205	Preprocessor1_Model1
Resample10	rsq	standard	0.05549430	Preprocessor1_Model1

- The resulting table has 20 rows because each resample has 2 rows for RMSE and R squared.
- To get the common summary statistics of RMSE and R squared across the 10 resamples of training data, we use the following functions after the collect_metrics function:
  - ++ The group_by function with the .metric argument to split the 20 rows of data into 2 data with 10 rows each, one for RMSE and one for R squared.
  - ++ The get_summary_stats function with the arguments:

    +++ .estimate to get the summary statistics of the .estimate column.

    +++ type = "common" to get the common summary statistics of the .estimate column.

Then, we convert the result to a table as discussed in previous chapters.

```
lm_res %>% collect_metrics(summarize = FALSE) %>% group_by(.
metric) %>%
get_summary_stats(.estimate, type = "common") %>%
flextable() %>% theme_box() %>%
set_caption(caption = "The common summary statistics of RMSE
and R squared across the 10 resamples of the gss training data
created by Monte-Carlo cross-validation")
```

Table 3.29. The Common Summary Statistics of RMSE and R Squared Across the 10 Resamples of the gss Training Data Created by Monte-Carlo Cross-Validation

.metric	variable	n	min	max	median	iqr	mean	sd	se	ci
rmse	.estimate	10	1.999	2.224	2.108	0.065	2.108	0.070	0.022	0.050
rsq	.estimate	10	0.036	0.055	0.042	0.004	0.042	0.006	0.002	0.004

We see that:

- n = 10 because we have 10 resamples of training data.
- The minimum RMSE = 1.999 and maximum RMSE = 2.224.
- The minimum R squared = 0.036 or 3.6% and maximum R squared = 0.055 or 5.5%.
- The mean RMSE and R squared value are the same calculated by collect_metrics function.

3.5.1.5. Plot the Performance Metrics of the Linear Model on 10 resamples of gss Training Data Created by Monte-Carlo Cross-Validation

- We can also plot the different RMSE and R squared values for the 10 resamples using the following functions after the collect_metrics function:

  ++ The ggplot function with the argument aes(x = id, y = .estimate, color = .metric) to plot id on the x-axis, .estimate value on y-axis, and coloring by the .metric type (RMSE or Rsquared).

  ++ The geom_point function to plot a scatter plot of points.

  ++ The geom_line with the argument aes(group = .metric) to plot a separate line for each performance metric (RMSE or R squared).

  ++ The facet_wrap function with the arguments:

  – +++ vars(.metric) to plot a separate plot for each metric.

  – +++ scales = "free" so each plot has its own x and y-axis values.

  – +++ nrow = 2 to make the 2 plots in 2 rows.

  ++ The labs function with the title argument to add a plot title, the x argument to add an x-axis title, the y argument to add a y-axis title, and the color argument to add a legend title.

  `++ The theme_classic function removes the grey background and the white grid lines of the default ggplot.

++ The theme function using the argument axis.text.x = element_ text(angle = 60, hjust = 1) to make the x-axis text inclined at 60 angle with 1 horizontal justification.

```
lm_res %>% collect_metrics(summarize = FALSE) %>%
ggplot(aes(x = id, y = .estimate, color = .metric))+
geom_point()+ geom_line(aes(group = .metric))+
facet_wrap(vars(.metric), scales = "free", nrow = 2)+
labs(title = "The RMSE and R squared of linear model on 10
different resamples \nof the gss training data created by Monte-
Carlo cross-validation",
x = "Resample", y = "Performance metric",
color = "Performance metric")+
theme_classic()+
theme(axis.text.x = element_text(angle = 60, hjust = 1))
```

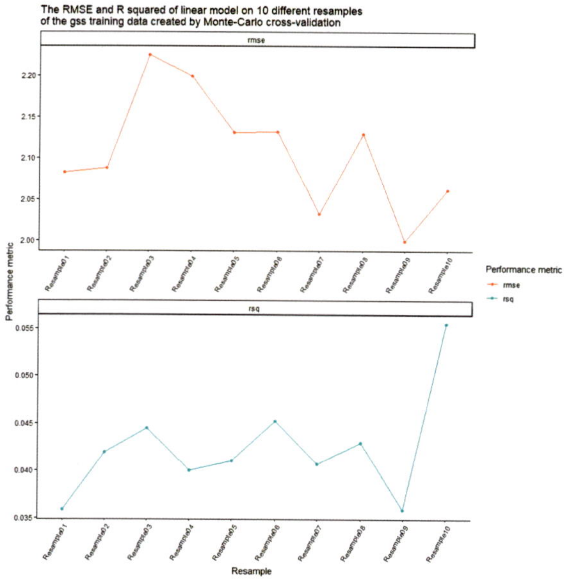

We see that:

- The lowest (best) RMSE value was for resample 9 (1.999).
- The highest (best) R squared was for resample 10 (0.055).
- The highest (worst) RMSE value was for resample 3 (2.224).
- The lowest (worst) R squared value was for resample 1 and 9 (0.036).

3.5.1.6. Producing 30 Resamples of gss Training Data

We can also use the mc_cv function as before but with the argument times = 30 to make 30 different resamples.

- We also use the set.seed function to make the splitting reproducible.

```
set.seed(123)
split_gss<-mc_cv(train_gss, prop = 0.7, times = 30)
split_gss
## # Monte Carlo cross-validation (0.7/0.3) with 30 resamples
## # A tibble: 30 × 2
## splits id
## <list> <chr>
## 1 <split [10397/4456]> Resample01
## 2 <split [10397/4456]> Resample02
## 3 <split [10397/4456]> Resample03
## 4 <split [10397/4456]> Resample04
## 5 <split [10397/4456]> Resample05
## 6 <split [10397/4456]> Resample06
## 7 <split [10397/4456]> Resample07
## 8 <split [10397/4456]> Resample08
## 9 <split [10397/4456]> Resample09
## 10 <split [10397/4456]> Resample10
## # i 20 more rows
```

We see:

- We have 30 different rows. Each row corresponds to 1 resample of training data.
- Each row has a total rows of 14853 which is the number of rows in training data. 10397 + 4456 = 14853.
- Within each row, 0.3 of total rows were grouped in the assessment data with 4456 rows and the remaining 0.7 rows was grouped as the analysis data with 10397 rows.

3.5.1.7. Exploring 30 Resamples of gss Training Data Created by Monte-Carlo Cross-Validation

- We can use the tidy function on the split_gss object to detect which row is for analysis data and which row is for the assessment data within each resample.

```
tidy(split_gss)
## # A tibble: 445,590 × 3
## Row Data Resample
## <int> <chr> <chr>
## 1 1 Analysis Resample01
## 2 1 Analysis Resample03
## 3 1 Analysis Resample05
## 4 1 Analysis Resample09
## 5 1 Analysis Resample10
## 6 1 Analysis Resample11
## 7 1 Analysis Resample13
## 8 1 Analysis Resample15
## 9 1 Analysis Resample16
## 10 1 Analysis Resample17
## # i 445,580 more rows
```

- The resulting data is 445,590 rows because we have 30 resamples of training data with 14853 rows. 14853 × 30 = 445,590.
- We have 3 columns:

  ++ The Row column which is the row number from 1 to 14853.

  ++ The Data column which is a character column for the analysis data (training data) or assessment (testing) data.

  ++ The Resample column which is for the resample number from 1 to 30.
- We can filter for row number 1 to see in which resample it was included in the assessment or analysis data using the filter function with the argument Row==1.

```
tidy(split_gss) %>% filter(Row==1) %>% flextable() %>% theme_
box() %>%
set_caption(caption = "The assignment of 1st row to analysis or
assessment data within 30 resamples of gss training data created
by Monte-Carlo cross-validation")
```

Table 3.30. The Assignment of 1st Row to Analysis or Assessment Data Within 30 Resamples of gss Training Data Created by Monte-Carlo Cross-Validation

Row	Data	Resample
1	Analysis	Resample01
1	Analysis	Resample03
1	Analysis	Resample05
1	Analysis	Resample09
1	Analysis	Resample10
1	Analysis	Resample11
1	Analysis	Resample13
1	Analysis	Resample15
1	Analysis	Resample16
1	Analysis	Resample17
1	Analysis	Resample18
1	Analysis	Resample21
1	Analysis	Resample23
1	Analysis	Resample24
1	Analysis	Resample25
1	Analysis	Resample26
1	Analysis	Resample27
1	Analysis	Resample28
1	Analysis	Resample29
1	Analysis	Resample30
1	Assessment	Resample02
1	Assessment	Resample04
1	Assessment	Resample06
1	Assessment	Resample07
1	Assessment	Resample08
1	Assessment	Resample12
1	Assessment	Resample14
1	Assessment	Resample19
1	Assessment	Resample20
1	Assessment	Resample22

- Row 1 is included in the analysis (training) data in resamples 1,3,5,9, 10,11,13,15,16,17,18,21,23,24,25,26,27,28,29,30 and so is included in the assessment (testing) data in resamples 2,4,6,7,8,12,14,19,20,22.

- By using the count function with Data and Resample argument after the tidy function, we can see how many rows were for the training data and how many rows for the testing data in each resample.
- We arrange the result by resample number.

```
tidy(split_gss) %>% count(Data,Resample) %>% arrange(Resample)
%>%
flextable() %>% theme_box() %>%
set_caption(caption = "The number of rows in the training and
testing data of 30 resamples of the general social survey data
created by Monte-Carlo cross-validation")
```

Table 3.31. The Number of rows in the Training and Testing Data of 30 Resamples of the General Social Survey Data Created by Monte-Carlo Cross-Validation

Data	Resample	n
Analysis	Resample01	10,397
Assessment	Resample01	4,456
Analysis	Resample02	10,397
Assessment	Resample02	4,456
Analysis	Resample03	10,397
Assessment	Resample03	4,456
Analysis	Resample04	10,397
Assessment	Resample04	4,456
Analysis	Resample05	10,397
Assessment	Resample05	4,456
Analysis	Resample06	10,397
Assessment	Resample06	4,456
Analysis	Resample07	10,397
Assessment	Resample07	4,456
Analysis	Resample08	10,397
Assessment	Resample08	4,456
Analysis	Resample09	10,397
Assessment	Resample09	4,456
Analysis	Resample10	10,397
Assessment	Resample10	4,456
Analysis	Resample11	10,397
Assessment	Resample11	4,456
Analysis	Resample12	10,397

Assessment	Resample12	4,456
Analysis	Resample13	10,397
Assessment	Resample13	4,456
Analysis	Resample14	10,397
Assessment	Resample14	4,456
Analysis	Resample15	10,397
Assessment	Resample15	4,456
Analysis	Resample16	10,397
Assessment	Resample16	4,456
Analysis	Resample17	10,397
Assessment	Resample17	4,456
Analysis	Resample18	10,397
Assessment	Resample18	4,456
Analysis	Resample19	10,397
Assessment	Resample19	4,456
Analysis	Resample20	10,397
Assessment	Resample20	4,456
Analysis	Resample21	10,397
Assessment	Resample21	4,456
Analysis	Resample22	10,397
Assessment	Resample22	4,456
Analysis	Resample23	10,397
Assessment	Resample23	4,456
Analysis	Resample24	10,397
Assessment	Resample24	4,456
Analysis	Resample25	10,397
Assessment	Resample25	4,456
Analysis	Resample26	10,397
Assessment	Resample26	4,456
Analysis	Resample27	10,397
Assessment	Resample27	4,456
Analysis	Resample28	10,397
Assessment	Resample28	4,456
Analysis	Resample29	10,397
Assessment	Resample29	4,456
Analysis	Resample30	10,397
Assessment	Resample30	4,456

- In all resamples, the number of rows in training (analysis) data is 10397 rows (7/10 X 14853) and in testing (assessment) data is 4456 rows (3/10 X 14853).

3.5.1.8. Plotting 30 Resamples of gss Training Data Created by Monte-Carlo Cross-Validation

We can also plot which row was for the training data and which was for the testing data as a heat map within each resample by using the previously described functions.

However, we will use nrow = 6 within facet_wrap function to make all 30 graphs in 6 rows.

```
tidy(split_gss) %>% ggplot(aes(x = Data, y = Row, fill = Data))+
geom_tile()+ scale_fill_viridis_d()+ theme_classic()+
facet_wrap(vars(Resample), nrow = 6)+
labs(title = "The assignment of different rows in 30 resamples of the gss training data\n to analysis or assessment data created by Monte-Carlo cross-validation")
```

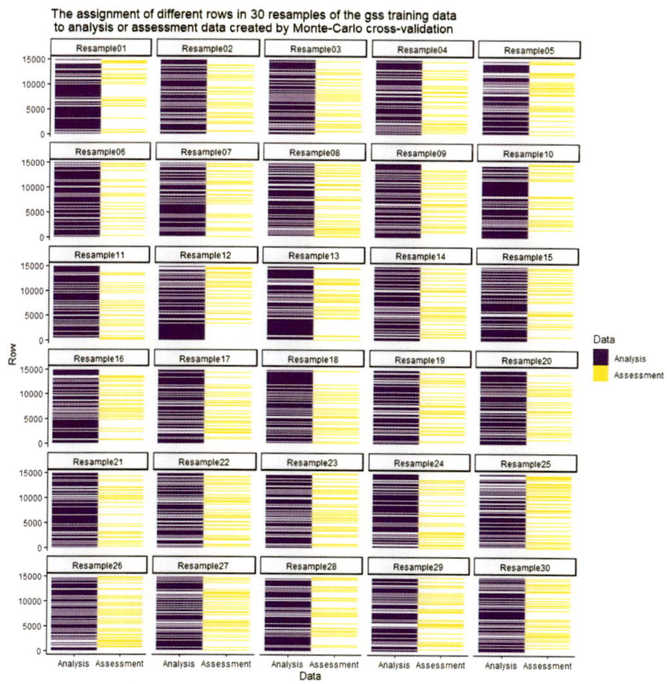

The heat map is overcrowded because we have 14853 rows in our training data. To get a less crowded plot, we can filter the data for the 1st 5 rows using the filter function with the argument Row <= 5 to get the row number equal to or less than 5 after the tidy function.

In addition, we add the argument color = "black" inside the geom_tile function to make the tiles with black borders and use the geom_text function to add text labels to each tile as described previously.

```
tidy(split_gss) %>% filter(Row <= 5) %>%
ggplot(aes(x = Data, y = Row, fill = Data))+
geom_tile(color = "black")+ scale_fill_viridis_d()+ theme_
classic()+
geom_text(aes(label = Row), color = "white")+
facet_wrap(vars(Resample), nrow = 6)+
labs(title = "The assignment of first 5 rows in 30 resamples of
the gss training data\n to analysis or assessment data created
by Monte-Carlo cross-validation")
```

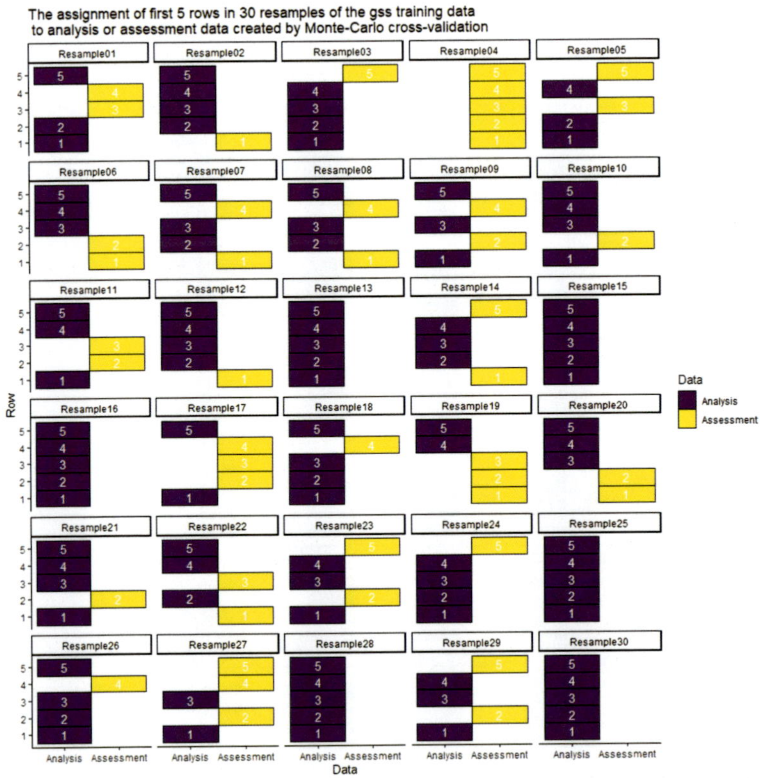

- There is no overlapping between the row numbers in the analysis and assessment data within each resample meaning that each row is either included in the analysis or assessment data within each resample.
- However, any row can be included in many assessment data across the 30 resamples. For example, the row 5 is included in assessment data in resamples 3,4,5,14,23,24,27,29 and in analysis data in other 22 resamples.
- For the row number 1, it is included in assessment data in resamples 2,4,6,7,8,12,14,19,20,22 and in analysis data in other 20 resamples, and so on.

3.5.1.9. Fit a Linear Model to 30 Resamples of gss Training Data Created by Monte-Carlo Cross-Validation

- To fit a linear model on the analysis data and test the model on the assessment data of 30 resamples of gss data, we use the fit_resamples function with the same above arguments.

```
lm_res<- fit_resamples(linear_reg(mode = "regression",
engine = "lm"),
tvhours ~ age + marital+ rincome,
split_gss)
lm_res
## # Resampling results
## # Monte Carlo cross-validation (0.7/0.3) with 30 resamples
## # A tibble: 30 × 4
## splits id .metrics .notes
## <list> <chr> <list> <list>
## 1 <split [10397/4456]> Resample01 <tibble [2 × 4]> <tibble
[0 × 3]>
## 2 <split [10397/4456]> Resample02 <tibble [2 × 4]> <tibble
[0 × 3]>
## 3 <split [10397/4456]> Resample03 <tibble [2 × 4]> <tibble
[0 × 3]>
## 4 <split [10397/4456]> Resample04 <tibble [2 × 4]> <tibble
[0 × 3]>
## 5 <split [10397/4456]> Resample05 <tibble [2 × 4]> <tibble
```

```
[0 × 3]>
## 6 <split [10397/4456]> Resample06 <tibble [2 × 4]> <tibble [0 × 3]>
## 7 <split [10397/4456]> Resample07 <tibble [2 × 4]> <tibble [0 × 3]>
## 8 <split [10397/4456]> Resample08 <tibble [2 × 4]> <tibble [0 × 3]>
## 9 <split [10397/4456]> Resample09 <tibble [2 × 4]> <tibble [0 × 3]>
## 10 <split [10397/4456]> Resample10 <tibble [2 × 4]> <tibble [0 × 3]>
## # i 20 more rows
```

The resulting object "lm_res" contains the results of applying this linear model on these 30 rows or resamples of training data. It contains the same 4 columns described previously.

To extract the 30 performance metrics for each combination of analysis and assessment data, we use the collect_metrics function on lm_res object.

```
lm_res %>% collect_metrics() %>% flextable() %>% theme_box() %>%
set_caption(caption = "The mean RMSE and R squared of linear model on 30 different resamples of the gss training data created by Monte-Carlo cross-validation")
```

Table 3.32. The Mean RMSE and R Squared of Linear Model on 30 Different Resamples of the gss Training Data Created by Monte-Carlo Cross-Validation

.metric	.estimator	mean	n	std_err	.config
rmse	standard	2.07678663	30	0.015203623	Preprocessor1_ Model1
rsq	standard	0.04441673	30	0.001198028	Preprocessor1_ Model1

- The default behavior of collect_metrics function is to summarize all performance metrics (n = 30) into their mean.
- The default calculated performance metrics are:

  ++ RMSE or root mean squared error with a mean value of 2.08.

  ++ Rsq or R squared with a mean value of 0.044 or 4.4%.
- To get the 30 performance metrics, we use the argument summarize = FALSE inside the collect_metrics function.

```
lm_res %>% collect_metrics(summarize = FALSE) %>% flextable()
%>%
theme_box() %>%
set_caption(caption = "The RMSE and R squared of linear model
on 30 different resamples \nof the gss training data created by
Monte-Carlo cross-validation")
```

Table 3.33. The RMSE and R Squared of Linear Model on 30 Different Resamples of the gss Training Data Created by Monte-Carlo Cross-Validation

id	.metric	.estimator	.estimate	.config
Resample01	rmse	standard	2.08267002	Preprocessor1_Model1
Resample01	rsq	standard	0.03586310	Preprocessor1_Model1
Resample02	rmse	standard	2.08770459	Preprocessor1_Model1
Resample02	rsq	standard	0.04194954	Preprocessor1_Model1
Resample03	rmse	standard	2.22432331	Preprocessor1_Model1
Resample03	rsq	standard	0.04450006	Preprocessor1_Model1
Resample04	rmse	standard	2.19876512	Preprocessor1_Model1
Resample04	rsq	standard	0.04002250	Preprocessor1_Model1
Resample05	rmse	standard	2.13094915	Preprocessor1_Model1
Resample05	rsq	standard	0.04105062	Preprocessor1_Model1
Resample06	rmse	standard	2.13198062	Preprocessor1_Model1
Resample06	rsq	standard	0.04527099	Preprocessor1_Model1
Resample07	rmse	standard	2.03227265	Preprocessor1_Model1
Resample07	rsq	standard	0.04072485	Preprocessor1_Model1
Resample08	rmse	standard	2.12927338	Preprocessor1_Model1
Resample08	rsq	standard	0.04296535	Preprocessor1_Model1
Resample09	rmse	standard	1.99920256	Preprocessor1_Model1
Resample09	rsq	standard	0.03587233	Preprocessor1_Model1
Resample10	rmse	standard	2.06149205	Preprocessor1_Model1
Resample10	rsq	standard	0.05549430	Preprocessor1_Model1
Resample11	rmse	standard	2.01721924	Preprocessor1_Model1
Resample11	rsq	standard	0.03271188	Preprocessor1_Model1
Resample12	rmse	standard	2.01343151	Preprocessor1_Model1
Resample12	rsq	standard	0.05004291	Preprocessor1_Model1
Resample13	rmse	standard	2.13451967	Preprocessor1_Model1
Resample13	rsq	standard	0.04120765	Preprocessor1_Model1
Resample14	rmse	standard	2.19193121	Preprocessor1_Model1
Resample14	rsq	standard	0.04158092	Preprocessor1_Model1
Resample15	rmse	standard	2.12358466	Preprocessor1_Model1
Resample15	rsq	standard	0.04706557	Preprocessor1_Model1
Resample16	rmse	standard	2.05631847	Preprocessor1_Model1
Resample16	rsq	standard	0.04208314	Preprocessor1_Model1

Resample17	rmse	standard	2.04658613	Preprocessor1_Model1
Resample17	rsq	standard	0.05774582	Preprocessor1_Model1
Resample18	rmse	standard	2.11577996	Preprocessor1_Model1
Resample18	rsq	standard	0.04022645	Preprocessor1_Model1
Resample19	rmse	standard	2.02130860	Preprocessor1_Model1
Resample19	rsq	standard	0.04495581	Preprocessor1_Model1
Resample20	rmse	standard	2.10294539	Preprocessor1_Model1
Resample20	rsq	standard	0.04451843	Preprocessor1_Model1
Resample21	rmse	standard	1.94907190	Preprocessor1_Model1
Resample21	rsq	standard	0.03605260	Preprocessor1_Model1
Resample22	rmse	standard	1.94919070	Preprocessor1_Model1
Resample22	rsq	standard	0.05112730	Preprocessor1_Model1
Resample23	rmse	standard	2.24975371	Preprocessor1_Model1
Resample23	rsq	standard	0.05108376	Preprocessor1_Model1
Resample24	rmse	standard	1.97777160	Preprocessor1_Model1
Resample24	rsq	standard	0.04206919	Preprocessor1_Model1
Resample25	rmse	standard	1.91735787	Preprocessor1_Model1
Resample25	rsq	standard	0.04856413	Preprocessor1_Model1
Resample26	rmse	standard	2.05439254	Preprocessor1_Model1
Resample26	rsq	standard	0.04275080	Preprocessor1_Model1
Resample27	rmse	standard	2.09155241	Preprocessor1_Model1
Resample27	rsq	standard	0.06105838	Preprocessor1_Model1
Resample28	rmse	standard	1.97081429	Preprocessor1_Model1
Resample28	rsq	standard	0.04429132	Preprocessor1_Model1
Resample29	rmse	standard	2.10029903	Preprocessor1_Model1
Resample29	rsq	standard	0.03893562	Preprocessor1_Model1
Resample30	rmse	standard	2.14113659	Preprocessor1_Model1
Resample30	rsq	standard	0.05071662	Preprocessor1_Model1

- The resulting table has 60 rows because each resample has 2 rows for RMSE and R squared.
- To get the common summary statistics of RMSE and R squared across the 30 resamples of training data, we use the following functions after the collect_metrics function:

  ++ The group_by function with the .metric argument to split the 60 rows of data into 2 data with 30 rows each, one for RMSE and one for R squared.

  ++ The get_summary_stats function with the arguments:

  – +++ .estimate to get the summary statistics of the .estimate column.

  – +++ type = "common" to get the common summary statistics of the .estimate column.

Then, we convert the result to a table as discussed in previous chapters.

```
lm_res %>% collect_metrics(summarize = FALSE) %>% group_by(.
metric) %>%
get_summary_stats(.estimate, type = "common") %>%
flextable() %>% theme_box() %>%
set_caption(caption = "The common summary statistics of RMSE
and R squared across the 30 resamples of the gss training data
created by Monte-Carlo cross-validation")
```

Table 3.34. The Common Summary Statistics of RMSE and R Squared Across the 30 Resamples of the gss Training Data Created by Monte-Carlo Cross-Validation

.metric	variable	n	min	max	median	iqr	mean	sd	se	ci
rmse	.estimate	30	1.917	2.250	2.085	0.112	2.077	0.083	0.015	0.031
rsq	.estimate	30	0.033	0.061	0.043	0.007	0.044	0.007	0.001	0.002

We see that:

- n = 30 because we have 30 resamples of training data.
- The minimum RMSE = 1.917 and maximum RMSE = 2.25.
- The minimum R squared = 0.033 or 3.3% and the maximum R squared = 0.061 or 6.1%.
- The mean RMSE and R squared value are the same as calculated by the collect_metrics function.

3.5.1.10. Plot the Performance Metrics of the Linear Model on 30 Resamples of gss Training Data Created by Monte-Carlo Cross-Validation

- We can also plot the different RMSE and R squared values for the 30 resamples using the same functions after the collect_metrics function.

```
lm_res %>% collect_metrics(summarize = FALSE) %>%
ggplot(aes(x = id, y = .estimate, color = .metric))+
geom_point()+ geom_line(aes(group = .metric))+
facet_wrap(vars(.metric), scales = "free", nrow = 2)+
```

```
labs(title = "The RMSE and R squared of linear model on 30 different resamples of the gss training data created by Monte-Carlo cross-validation",
x = "Resample", y = "Performance metric",
color = "Performance metric")+
theme_classic()+
theme(axis.text.x = element_text(angle = 60, hjust = 1))
```

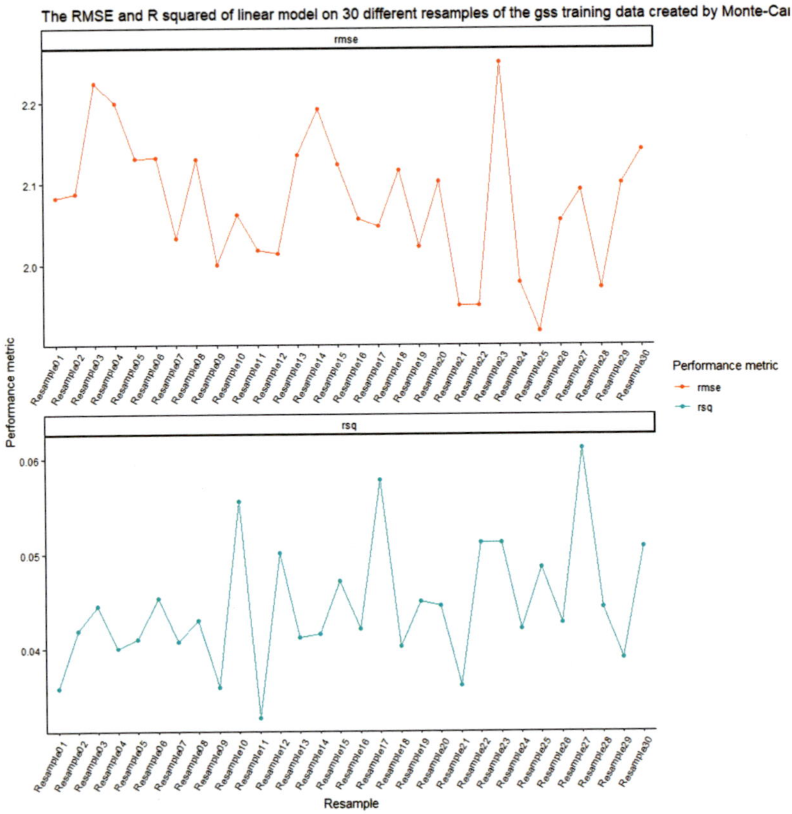

We see that:

- The lowest (best) RMSE value was for resample 25 (1.917).
- The highest (best) R squared was for resample 27 (0.061).
- The highest (worst) RMSE value was for resample 23 (2.25).
- The lowest (worst) R squared value was for resample 11 (0.033).

Generally, Monte-Carlo cross-validation produces more biased estimates than V-fold cross-validation. So, it is recommended to use 3 or more repeats of 10-fold cross-validation for model assessment.

3.5.2. Monte-Carlo Cross-Validation of BRFSS Data

3.5.2.1. Producing 30 Resamples of BRFSS Training Data

We can also use the mc_cv function as before but with the argument times = 30 to make 30 different resamples.

- We also use the set.seed function to make the splitting reproducible.
- We will use train_brfss2 training data because this is the data that contains the sex column as a factor.

```
set.seed(123)
split_brfss<-mc_cv(train_brfss2, prop = 0.7, times = 30)
split_brfss
## # Monte Carlo cross-validation (0.7/0.3) with 30 resamples
## # A tibble: 30 × 2
## splits id
## <list> <chr>
## 1 <split [117/51]> Resample01
## 2 <split [117/51]> Resample02
## 3 <split [117/51]> Resample03
## 4 <split [117/51]> Resample04
## 5 <split [117/51]> Resample05
## 6 <split [117/51]> Resample06
## 7 <split [117/51]> Resample07
## 8 <split [117/51]> Resample08
## 9 <split [117/51]> Resample09
## 10 <split [117/51]> Resample10
## # i 20 more rows
```

We see:

- We have 30 different rows. Each row corresponds to 1 resample of training data.
- Each row has a total rows of 168 which is the number of rows in training data. 117 + 51 = 168.
- Within each row, 0.3 of the total rows were grouped in the assessment data with 51 rows and the remaining 0.7 rows were grouped as the analysis data with 117 rows.

3.5.2.2. Exploring 30 Resamples of BRFSS Training Data Created by Monte-Carlo Cross-Validation

- We can use the tidy function on the split_brfss object to detect which row is for analysis data and which row is for the assessment data within each resample.

```
tidy(split_brfss)
## # A tibble: 5,040 × 3
## Row Data Resample
## <int> <chr> <chr>
## 1 1 Analysis Resample02
## 2 1 Analysis Resample05
## 3 1 Analysis Resample08
## 4 1 Analysis Resample09
## 5 1 Analysis Resample10
## 6 1 Analysis Resample11
## 7 1 Analysis Resample12
## 8 1 Analysis Resample18
## 9 1 Analysis Resample22
## 10 1 Analysis Resample23
## # i 5,030 more rows
```

- The resulting data is 5,040 rows because we have 30 resamples of training data with 168 rows. $168 \times 30 = 5040$.
- We have 3 columns:
  - ++ The Row column which is the row number from 1 to 168.
  - ++ The Data column which is a character column for the analysis data (training data) or assessment (testing) data.
  - ++ The Resample column which is for the resample number from 1 to 30.
- We can filter for row number 1 to see in which resample it was included in the assessment or analysis data using the filter function with the argument Row==1.

```
tidy(split_brfss) %>% filter(Row==1) %>% flextable() %>% theme_box() %>%
set_caption(caption = "The assignment of 1st row to analysis or assessment data within 30 resamples of BRFSS training data created by Monte-Carlo cross-validation")
```

Table 3.35. The Assignment of 1st Row to Analysis or Assessment Data Within 30 Resamples of BRFSS Training Data Created by Monte-Carlo Cross-Validation

Row	Data	Resample
1	Analysis	Resample02
1	Analysis	Resample05
1	Analysis	Resample08
1	Analysis	Resample09
1	Analysis	Resample10
1	Analysis	Resample11
1	Analysis	Resample12
1	Analysis	Resample18
1	Analysis	Resample22
1	Analysis	Resample23
1	Analysis	Resample24
1	Analysis	Resample26
1	Analysis	Resample27
1	Analysis	Resample28
1	Analysis	Resample29
1	Analysis	Resample30
1	Assessment	Resample01
1	Assessment	Resample03
1	Assessment	Resample04
1	Assessment	Resample06
1	Assessment	Resample07
1	Assessment	Resample13
1	Assessment	Resample14
1	Assessment	Resample15
1	Assessment	Resample16
1	Assessment	Resample17
1	Assessment	Resample19
1	Assessment	Resample20
1	Assessment	Resample21
1	Assessment	Resample25

- Row 1 is included in the analysis (training) data in resamples 2,5 ,8,9,10,11,12,18,22,23,24,26,27,28,29,30 and so is included in the assessment (testing) data in resamples 1,3,4,6,7,13,14,15,16,17,19 ,20,21,25.

- By using the count function with the Data and Resample argument after the tidy function, we can see how many rows were for the training data and how many rows were for the testing data in each resample.
- We arrange the result by resample number.

```
tidy(split_brfss) %>% count(Data,Resample) %>% arrange(Resample)
%>%
flextable() %>% theme_box() %>%
set_caption(caption = "The number of rows in the training and testing data of 30 resamples of the BRFSS training data created by Monte-Carlo cross-validation")
```

Table 3.36. The Number of Rows in the Training and Testing Data of 30 Resamples of the BRFSS Training Data Created by Monte-Carlo Cross-Validation

Data	Resample	n
Analysis	Resample01	117
Assessment	Resample01	51
Analysis	Resample02	117
Assessment	Resample02	51
Analysis	Resample03	117
Assessment	Resample03	51
Analysis	Resample04	117
Assessment	Resample04	51
Analysis	Resample05	117
Assessment	Resample05	51
Analysis	Resample06	117
Assessment	Resample06	51
Analysis	Resample07	117
Assessment	Resample07	51
Analysis	Resample08	117
Assessment	Resample08	51
Analysis	Resample09	117
Assessment	Resample09	51
Analysis	Resample10	117
Assessment	Resample10	51
Analysis	Resample11	117
Assessment	Resample11	51

Analysis	Resample12	117
Assessment	Resample12	51
Analysis	Resample13	117
Assessment	Resample13	51
Analysis	Resample14	117
Assessment	Resample14	51
Analysis	Resample15	117
Assessment	Resample15	51
Analysis	Resample16	117
Assessment	Resample16	51
Analysis	Resample17	117
Assessment	Resample17	51
Analysis	Resample18	117
Assessment	Resample18	51
Analysis	Resample19	117
Assessment	Resample19	51
Analysis	Resample20	117
Assessment	Resample20	51
Analysis	Resample21	117
Assessment	Resample21	51
Analysis	Resample22	117
Assessment	Resample22	51
Analysis	Resample23	117
Assessment	Resample23	51
Analysis	Resample24	117
Assessment	Resample24	51
Analysis	Resample25	117
Assessment	Resample25	51
Analysis	Resample26	117
Assessment	Resample26	51
Analysis	Resample27	117
Assessment	Resample27	51
Analysis	Resample28	117
Assessment	Resample28	51
Analysis	Resample29	117
Assessment	Resample29	51
Analysis	Resample30	117
Assessment	Resample30	51

- In all resamples, the number of rows in training (analysis) data is 117 rows (7/10 X 168), and in testing (assessment) data is 51 rows (3/10 X 168).

3.5.2.3. Plotting 30 Resamples of BRFSS Training Data Created by Monte-Carlo Cross-Validation

We can also plot which row was for the training data and which was for the testing data as a heat map within each resample by using the previously described functions.

However, we will use nrow = 6 within the facet_wrap function to make all 30 graphs in 6 rows.

```
tidy(split_brfss) %>% ggplot(aes(x = Data, y = Row, fill =
Data))+
geom_tile()+ scale_fill_viridis_d()+ theme_classic()+
facet_wrap(vars(Resample), nrow = 6)+
labs(title = "The assignment of different rows in 30 resamples of
the BRFSS training data\n to analysis or assessment data created
by Monte-Carlo cross-validation")
```

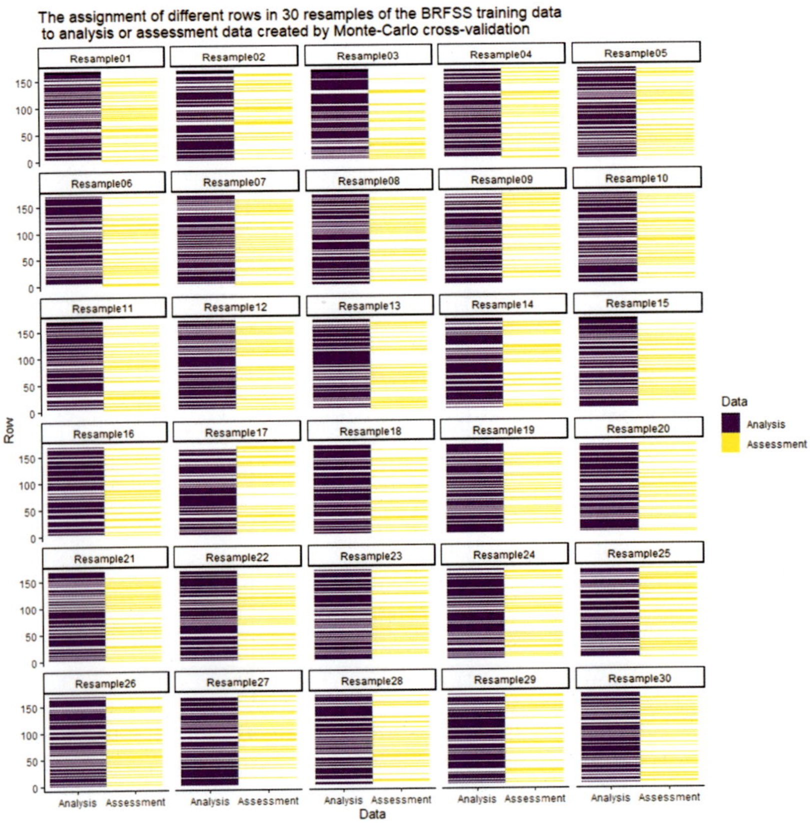

The heat map is overcrowded because we have 168 rows in our training data. To get a less crowded plot, we can filter the data for the 1st 5 rows using the filter function with the argument Row <= 5 to get the row number equal to or less than 5 after the tidy function.

In addition, we add the argument color = “black” inside the geom_tile function to make the tiles with black borders and use the geom_text function to add text labels to each tile as described previously.

```
tidy(split_brfss) %>% filter(Row <= 5) %>%
ggplot(aes(x = Data, y = Row, fill = Data))+
geom_tile(color = “black”)+ scale_fill_viridis_d()+ theme_classic()+
geom_text(aes(label = Row), color = “white”)+
facet_wrap(vars(Resample), nrow = 6)+
labs(title = “The assignment of first 5 rows in 30 resamples of the BRFSS training data\n to analysis or assessment data created by Monte-Carlo cross-validation”)
```

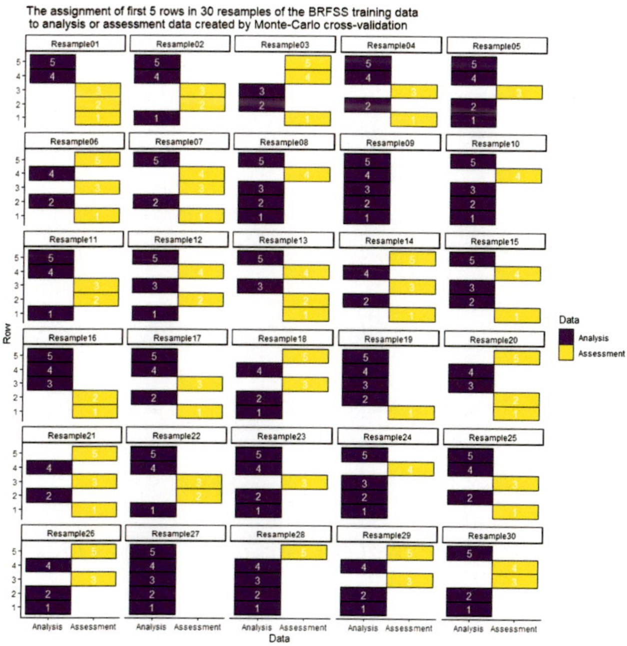

- There is no overlapping between the row numbers in the analysis and assessment data within each resample meaning that each row is either included in the analysis or assessment data within each resample.
- However, any row can be included in many assessment data across the 30 resamples. For example, row 5 is included in assessment data in resamples 3,6,14,18,20,21,26,28,29 and in analysis data in other resamples.

3.5.2.4. Fit a Tree Model to 30 Resamples of BRFSS Training Data Created by Monte-Carlo Cross-Validation

- To fit a decision tree model on the analysis data and test the model on the assessment data of 30 resamples of BRFSS data, we use the fit_resamples function with the same above arguments in section 3.4.2.9.

```
tree_res<- fit_resamples(decision_tree(mode = "classification",
engine = "rpart"),
sex ~ weight_lbs+ height_inch+income,
split_brfss)
tree_res
## # Resampling results
## # Monte Carlo cross-validation (0.7/0.3) with 30 resamples
## # A tibble: 30 × 4
## splits id .metrics .notes
## <list> <chr> <list> <list>
## 1 <split [117/51]> Resample01 <tibble [2 × 4]> <tibble [0 ×
3]>
## 2 <split [117/51]> Resample02 <tibble [2 × 4]> <tibble [0 ×
3]>
## 3 <split [117/51]> Resample03 <tibble [2 × 4]> <tibble [0 ×
3]>
## 4 <split [117/51]> Resample04 <tibble [2 × 4]> <tibble [0 ×
3]>
## 5 <split [117/51]> Resample05 <tibble [2 × 4]> <tibble [0 ×
3]>
## 6 <split [117/51]> Resample06 <tibble [2 × 4]> <tibble [0 ×
```

```
3]>
## 7 <split [117/51]> Resample07 <tibble [2 × 4]> <tibble [0 ×
3]>
## 8 <split [117/51]> Resample08 <tibble [2 × 4]> <tibble [0 ×
3]>
## 9 <split [117/51]> Resample09 <tibble [2 × 4]> <tibble [0 ×
3]>
## 10 <split [117/51]> Resample10 <tibble [2 × 4]> <tibble [0 ×
3]>
## # i 20 more rows
```

The resulting object "tree_res" contains the results of applying this tree model on these 30 rows or resamples of training data. It contains the same 4 columns described previously.

To extract the 30 performance metrics for each combination of analysis and assessment data, we use the collect_metrics function.

```
tree_res %>% collect_metrics() %>% flextable() %>% theme_box()
%>%
set_caption(caption = "The mean accuracy and ROC AUC of tree
model on 30 different resamples of the BRFSS training data
created by Monte-Carlo cross-validation")
```

Table 3.37. The Mean Accuracy and ROC AUC of Tree Model on 30 Different Resamples of the BRFSS Training Data Created by Monte-Carlo Cross-Validation

.metric	.estimator	mean	n	std_err	.config
accuracy	binary	0.8163399	30	0.01040456	Preprocessor1_Model1
roc_auc	binary	0.8510299	30	0.01146896	Preprocessor1_Model1

- We have n = 30 because we have 30 resamples of training data.
- The mean accuracy = 0.816 or 81.6%.
- The mean ROC AUC = 0.851 or 85.1%.
- To get the 30 performance metrics, we use the argument summarize = FALSE inside the collect_metrics function.

```
tree_res %>% collect_metrics(summarize = FALSE) %>% flextable()
%>%
```

```
theme_box() %>%
set_caption(caption = "The accuracy and ROC AUC of tree model on 30 different resamples of the BRFSS training data created by Monte-Carlo cross-validation")
```

Table 3.38. The Accuracy and ROC AUC of Tree Model on 30 Different Resamples of the BRFSS Training Data Created by Monte-Carlo Cross-Validation

id	.metric	.estimator	.estimate	.config
Resample01	accuracy	binary	0.8039216	Preprocessor1_Model1
Resample01	roc_auc	binary	0.8088235	Preprocessor1_Model1
Resample02	accuracy	binary	0.9019608	Preprocessor1_Model1
Resample02	roc_auc	binary	0.9004934	Preprocessor1_Model1
Resample03	accuracy	binary	0.6862745	Preprocessor1_Model1
Resample03	roc_auc	binary	0.8602484	Preprocessor1_Model1
Resample04	accuracy	binary	0.8627451	Preprocessor1_Model1
Resample04	roc_auc	binary	0.8720539	Preprocessor1_Model1
Resample05	accuracy	binary	0.8627451	Preprocessor1_Model1
Resample05	roc_auc	binary	0.9183502	Preprocessor1_Model1
Resample06	accuracy	binary	0.9019608	Preprocessor1_Model1
Resample06	roc_auc	binary	0.9169408	Preprocessor1_Model1
Resample07	accuracy	binary	0.7450980	Preprocessor1_Model1
Resample07	roc_auc	binary	0.8244514	Preprocessor1_Model1
Resample08	accuracy	binary	0.8431373	Preprocessor1_Model1

Resample08	roc_auc	binary	0.9082492	Preprocessor1_Model1
Resample09	accuracy	binary	0.8627451	Preprocessor1_Model1
Resample09	roc_auc	binary	0.8692434	Preprocessor1_Model1
Resample10	accuracy	binary	0.7450980	Preprocessor1_Model1
Resample10	roc_auc	binary	0.8325397	Preprocessor1_Model1
Resample11	accuracy	binary	0.8627451	Preprocessor1_Model1
Resample11	roc_auc	binary	0.8676471	Preprocessor1_Model1
Resample12	accuracy	binary	0.8627451	Preprocessor1_Model1
Resample12	roc_auc	binary	0.7717742	Preprocessor1_Model1
Resample13	accuracy	binary	0.8431373	Preprocessor1_Model1
Resample13	roc_auc	binary	0.8957680	Preprocessor1_Model1
Resample14	accuracy	binary	0.8627451	Preprocessor1_Model1
Resample14	roc_auc	binary	0.9129630	Preprocessor1_Model1
Resample15	accuracy	binary	0.8431373	Preprocessor1_Model1
Resample15	roc_auc	binary	0.9021382	Preprocessor1_Model1
Resample16	accuracy	binary	0.8039216	Preprocessor1_Model1
Resample16	roc_auc	binary	0.7962963	Preprocessor1_Model1
Resample17	accuracy	binary	0.8039216	Preprocessor1_Model1
Resample17	roc_auc	binary	0.8913043	Preprocessor1_Model1
Resample18	accuracy	binary	0.8039216	Preprocessor1_Model1

Resample18	roc_auc	binary	0.8503289	Preprocessor1_Model1
Resample19	accuracy	binary	0.8431373	Preprocessor1_Model1
Resample19	roc_auc	binary	0.8282828	Preprocessor1_Model1
Resample20	accuracy	binary	0.6862745	Preprocessor1_Model1
Resample20	roc_auc	binary	0.6088710	Preprocessor1_Model1
Resample21	accuracy	binary	0.7843137	Preprocessor1_Model1
Resample21	roc_auc	binary	0.8148148	Preprocessor1_Model1
Resample22	accuracy	binary	0.8823529	Preprocessor1_Model1
Resample22	roc_auc	binary	0.8935986	Preprocessor1_Model1
Resample23	accuracy	binary	0.8235294	Preprocessor1_Model1
Resample23	roc_auc	binary	0.8282258	Preprocessor1_Model1
Resample24	accuracy	binary	0.8039216	Preprocessor1_Model1
Resample24	roc_auc	binary	0.8804714	Preprocessor1_Model1
Resample25	accuracy	binary	0.7647059	Preprocessor1_Model1
Resample25	roc_auc	binary	0.7709677	Preprocessor1_Model1
Resample26	accuracy	binary	0.7647059	Preprocessor1_Model1
Resample26	roc_auc	binary	0.8440439	Preprocessor1_Model1
Resample27	accuracy	binary	0.7647059	Preprocessor1_Model1
Resample27	roc_auc	binary	0.8042763	Preprocessor1_Model1
Resample28	accuracy	binary	0.8823529	Preprocessor1_Model1

Resample28	roc_auc	binary	0.8935484	Preprocessor1_Model1
Resample29	accuracy	binary	0.7843137	Preprocessor1_Model1
Resample29	roc_auc	binary	0.8666667	Preprocessor1_Model1
Resample30	accuracy	binary	0.8039216	Preprocessor1_Model1
Resample30	roc_auc	binary	0.8975155	Preprocessor1_Model1

- The resulting table has 60 rows because each resample has 2 rows for accuracy and ROC AUC.
- To get the common summary statistics of accuracy and ROC AUC across the 30 resamples of training data, we use the same above functions.

```
tree_res %>% collect_metrics(summarize = FALSE) %>% group_by(.
metric) %>%
get_summary_stats(.estimate, type = "common") %>%
flextable() %>% theme_box() %>%
set_caption(caption = "The common summary statistics of accuracy
and ROC AUC across the 30 resamples of the BRFSS training data
created by Monte-Carlo cross-validation")
```

Table 3.39. The Common Summary Statistics of Accuracy and ROC AUC Across the 30 Resamples of the BRFSS Training Data Created by Monte-Carlo Cross-Validation

.metric	variable	n	min	max	median	iqr	mean	sd	se	ci
accuracy	.estimate	30	0.686	0.902	0.814	0.078	0.816	0.057	0.010	0.021
roc_auc	.estimate	30	0.609	0.918	0.867	0.070	0.851	0.063	0.011	0.023

We see that:

- n = 30 because we have 30 resamples of training data.
- The minimum accuracy = 0.686 or 68.6% and the maximum accuracy = 0.902 or 90.2%.
- The minimum ROC AUC = 0.609 and the maximum ROC AUC = 0.918.

- The mean accuracy and ROC AUC value are the same as that calculated by the collect_metrics function.

3.5.2.5. Plot the Performance Metrics of the Tree Model on 30 Resamples of BRFSS Data

We can plot the different accuracy and ROC AUC values for the 30 resamples using the following functions after the collect_metrics function:

- The ggplot function with the argument aes(x = id, y = .estimate, color = .metric) to plot id on the x-axis, .estimate value on y-axis, and coloring by the .metric type (accuracy or ROC AUC).
- The geom_point function to plot a scatter plot of points.
- The geom_line with the argument aes(group = .metric) plots a separate line for each performance metric (accuracy or ROC AUC).
- The facet_wrap function with the arguments:

  ++ vars(.metric) to plot a separate plot for each metric.

  ++ scales = "free" so each plot has its own x and y-axis values.

  ++ nrow = 2 to make the 2 plots in 2 rows.
- The labs function with the title argument to add a plot title, the x argument to add an x-axis title, the y argument to add a y-axis title, and the color argument to add a legend title.
- The theme_classic function removes the grey background and the white grid lines of the default plot created by the ggplot function.
- The theme function with the argument axis.text.x = element_text(angle = 60, hjust = 1) to make the x-axis text inclined at 60 with 1 horizontal justification.

```
tree_res %>% collect_metrics(summarize = FALSE) %>%
ggplot(aes(x = id, y = .estimate, color = .metric))+
geom_point()+ geom_line(aes(group = .metric))+
facet_wrap(vars(.metric), scales = "free", nrow = 2)+
labs(title = "The accuracy and ROC AUC of tree model on 30
different resamples of the BRFSS training data\n created by
Monte-Carlo cross-validation",
x = "Resample", y = "Performance metric",
color = "Performance metric")+
theme_classic()+
theme(axis.text.x = element_text(angle = 60, hjust = 1))
```

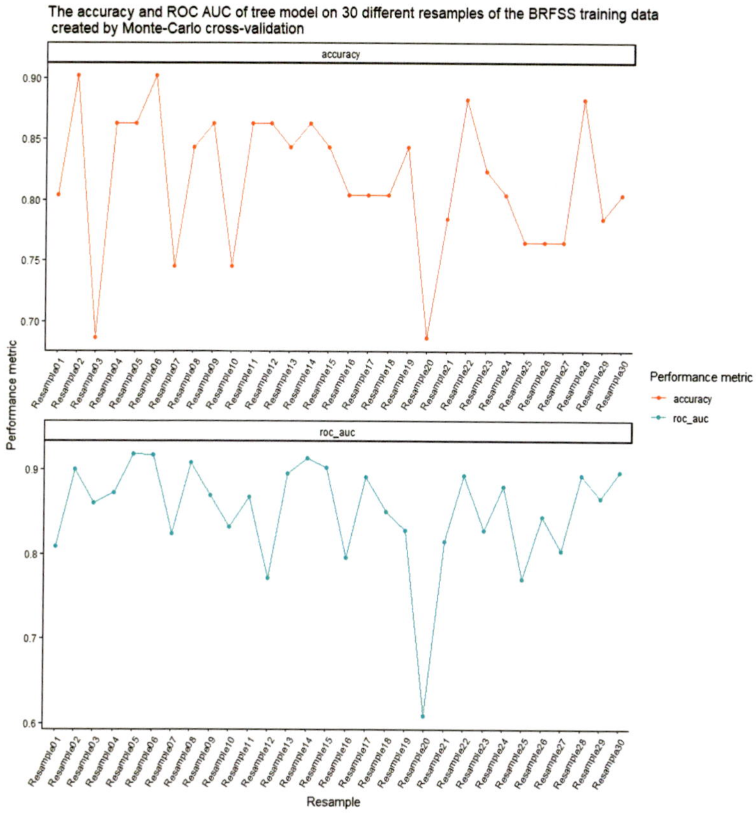

We see that:

- The highest (best) accuracy value was for resamples 2 and 6 (0.902 or 90.2% for both).
- The highest (best) ROC AUC was for resample 5 (0.918).
- The lowest (worst) accuracy was for resamples 3 and 20 (0.686 or 68.6% for both).
- The lowest (worst) ROC AUC was for resample 20 (0.609).

Generally, Monte-Carlo cross-validation produces more biased estimates than V-fold cross-validation. So, it is recommended to use 3 or more repeats of 10-fold cross-validation for model assessment.

3.6. BOOTSTRAP RESAMPLING

- A bootstrap resample is a sample of training data, but with the same size as training data, taken with replacement so that a single row might be sampled multiple times in the same resample.

- The assessment set is then made up of all the rows that weren't selected for the analysis set. Generally, bootstrap resampling produces pessimistic estimates of model accuracy and so not recommended.

3.6.1. Bootstrap Resampling of gss Training Data

3.6.1.1. Producing 30 Resamples of gss Training Data

We can use the bootstraps function but we can not control the proportion of data in the assessment and analysis data.

We use the bootstraps function with the arguments:

- train_gss which is the data we want to make bootstrap resamples from.
- times = 30 to make 30 different resamples.

We also use the set.seed function to make the splitting reproducible.

```
set.seed(123)
split_gss<-bootstraps(train_gss, times = 30)
split_gss
## # Bootstrap sampling
## # A tibble: 30 × 2
## splits id
## <list> <chr>
## 1 <split [14853/5475]> Bootstrap01
## 2 <split [14853/5489]> Bootstrap02
## 3 <split [14853/5425]> Bootstrap03
## 4 <split [14853/5494]> Bootstrap04
## 5 <split [14853/5476]> Bootstrap05
## 6 <split [14853/5456]> Bootstrap06
## 7 <split [14853/5514]> Bootstrap07
## 8 <split [14853/5528]> Bootstrap08
## 9 <split [14853/5451]> Bootstrap09
## 10 <split [14853/5433]> Bootstrap10
## # i 20 more rows
```

We see:

- We have 30 different rows. Each row corresponds to 1 resample of training data.
- Each row has total rows of 14853 rows (same rows of training data) and a different number of rows for the assessment and analysis data.
- For example, the 1st resample has 5475 rows in assessment data and so 14853–5475 = 9378 rows in the analysis data.
- In the 2nd resample, there are 5489 rows in assessment data, so 14853–5489 = 9364 rows in the analysis data, and so on.

3.6.1.2. Exploring 30 Resamples of gss Training Data Created by Bootstrap Resampling

- We can use the tidy function on the split_gss object to detect which row is for analysis data and which row is for the assessment data within each resample.

```
tidy(split_gss)
## # A tibble: 445,590 × 3
## Row Data Resample
## <int> <chr> <chr>
## 1 1 Analysis Bootstrap01
## 2 1 Analysis Bootstrap03
## 3 1 Analysis Bootstrap08
## 4 1 Analysis Bootstrap09
## 5 1 Analysis Bootstrap10
## 6 1 Analysis Bootstrap12
## 7 1 Analysis Bootstrap13
## 8 1 Analysis Bootstrap15
## 9 1 Analysis Bootstrap16
## 10 1 Analysis Bootstrap17
## # i 445,580 more rows
```

- The resulting data is 445,590 rows because we have 30 resamples of training data with 14853 rows. 14853 × 30 = 445,590.
- We have 3 columns:

  ++ The Row column which is the row number from 1 to 14853.

++ The Data column which is a character column for the analysis data (training data) or assessment (testing) data.

++ The Resample column which is for the resample number from 1 to 30.

We can filter for row number 1 to see in which resample it was included in the assessment or analysis data using the filter function with the argument Row==1.

```
tidy(split_gss) %>% filter(Row==1) %>% flextable() %>% theme_
box() %>%
set_caption(caption = "The assignment of 1st row to analysis or
assessment data within 30 resamples of gss training data created
by bootstrap sampling")
```

Table 3.40. The Assignment of 1st Row to Analysis or Assessment Data Within 30 Resamples of gss Training Data Created by Bootstrap Sampling

Row	Data	Resample
1	Analysis	Bootstrap01
1	Analysis	Bootstrap03
1	Analysis	Bootstrap08
1	Analysis	Bootstrap09
1	Analysis	Bootstrap10
1	Analysis	Bootstrap12
1	Analysis	Bootstrap13
1	Analysis	Bootstrap15
1	Analysis	Bootstrap16
1	Analysis	Bootstrap17
1	Analysis	Bootstrap19
1	Analysis	Bootstrap22
1	Analysis	Bootstrap23
1	Analysis	Bootstrap24
1	Analysis	Bootstrap25
1	Analysis	Bootstrap27
1	Assessment	Bootstrap02
1	Assessment	Bootstrap04
1	Assessment	Bootstrap05
1	Assessment	Bootstrap06

1	Assessment	Bootstrap07
1	Assessment	Bootstrap11
1	Assessment	Bootstrap14
1	Assessment	Bootstrap18
1	Assessment	Bootstrap20
1	Assessment	Bootstrap21
1	Assessment	Bootstrap26
1	Assessment	Bootstrap28
1	Assessment	Bootstrap29
1	Assessment	Bootstrap30

- Row 1 is included in the analysis (training) data in resamples 1,3 ,8,9,10,12,13,15,16,17,19,22,23,24,25,27 and so is included in the assessment (testing) data in resamples 2,4,5,6,7,11,14,18,20,21,26 ,28,29,30.
- By using the count function with the Data and Resample argument after the tidy function, we can see how many rows were for the training data and how many rows were for the testing data in each resample.
- We arrange the result by resample number.

```
tidy(split_gss) %>% count(Data,Resample) %>% arrange(Resample)
%>%
flextable() %>% theme_box() %>%
set_caption(caption = "The number of rows in the training and
testing data of 30 resamples of the general social survey data
created by bootstrap sampling")
```

Table 3.41. The Number of Rows in the Training and Testing Data of 30 Resamples of the General Social Survey Data Created by Bootstrap Sampling

Data	Resample	n
Analysis	Bootstrap01	9,378
Assessment	Bootstrap01	5,475
Analysis	Bootstrap02	9,364
Assessment	Bootstrap02	5,489
Analysis	Bootstrap03	9,428
Assessment	Bootstrap03	5,425
Analysis	Bootstrap04	9,359

Assessment	Bootstrap04	5,494
Analysis	Bootstrap05	9,377
Assessment	Bootstrap05	5,476
Analysis	Bootstrap06	9,397
Assessment	Bootstrap06	5,456
Analysis	Bootstrap07	9,339
Assessment	Bootstrap07	5,514
Analysis	Bootstrap08	9,325
Assessment	Bootstrap08	5,528
Analysis	Bootstrap09	9,402
Assessment	Bootstrap09	5,451
Analysis	Bootstrap10	9,420
Assessment	Bootstrap10	5,433
Analysis	Bootstrap11	9,345
Assessment	Bootstrap11	5,508
Analysis	Bootstrap12	9,398
Assessment	Bootstrap12	5,455
Analysis	Bootstrap13	9,371
Assessment	Bootstrap13	5,482
Analysis	Bootstrap14	9,364
Assessment	Bootstrap14	5,489
Analysis	Bootstrap15	9,426
Assessment	Bootstrap15	5,427
Analysis	Bootstrap16	9,408
Assessment	Bootstrap16	5,445
Analysis	Bootstrap17	9,414
Assessment	Bootstrap17	5,439
Analysis	Bootstrap18	9,426
Assessment	Bootstrap18	5,427
Analysis	Bootstrap19	9,416
Assessment	Bootstrap19	5,437
Analysis	Bootstrap20	9,402
Assessment	Bootstrap20	5,451
Analysis	Bootstrap21	9,351
Assessment	Bootstrap21	5,502
Analysis	Bootstrap22	9,332

Assessment	Bootstrap22	5,521
Analysis	Bootstrap23	9,357
Assessment	Bootstrap23	5,496
Analysis	Bootstrap24	9,387
Assessment	Bootstrap24	5,466
Analysis	Bootstrap25	9,438
Assessment	Bootstrap25	5,415
Analysis	Bootstrap26	9,339
Assessment	Bootstrap26	5,514
Analysis	Bootstrap27	9,350
Assessment	Bootstrap27	5,503
Analysis	Bootstrap28	9,422
Assessment	Bootstrap28	5,431
Analysis	Bootstrap29	9,379
Assessment	Bootstrap29	5,474
Analysis	Bootstrap30	9,342
Assessment	Bootstrap30	5,511

- In all resamples, the number of rows in total data is 14853 rows.
- Every resample has a different number of rows in the analysis and assessment data.
- In the 1st resample, the number of rows in analysis data is 9378 rows, and in assessment data is 5475.
- In the 2nd resample, the number of rows in the analysis data is 9364 rows, and in the assessment data is 5489.
- In the 3rd resample, the number of rows in analysis data is 9428 rows, and in assessment data is 5425, and so on.

3.6.1.3. Plotting 30 Resamples of gss Training Data Created by Bootstrap Resampling

We can also plot which row was for the training data and which was for the testing data as a heat map within each resample by using the previously described functions.

However, we will use nrow = 6 within the facet_wrap function to make all 30 graphs in 6 rows.

```
tidy(split_gss) %>% ggplot(aes(x = Data, y = Row, fill = Data))+
```

```
geom_tile()+ scale_fill_viridis_d()+ theme_classic()+
facet_wrap(vars(Resample), nrow = 6)+
labs(title = "The assignment of different rows in 30 resamples of
the gss training data\n to analysis or assessment data created
by bootstrap resampling")
```

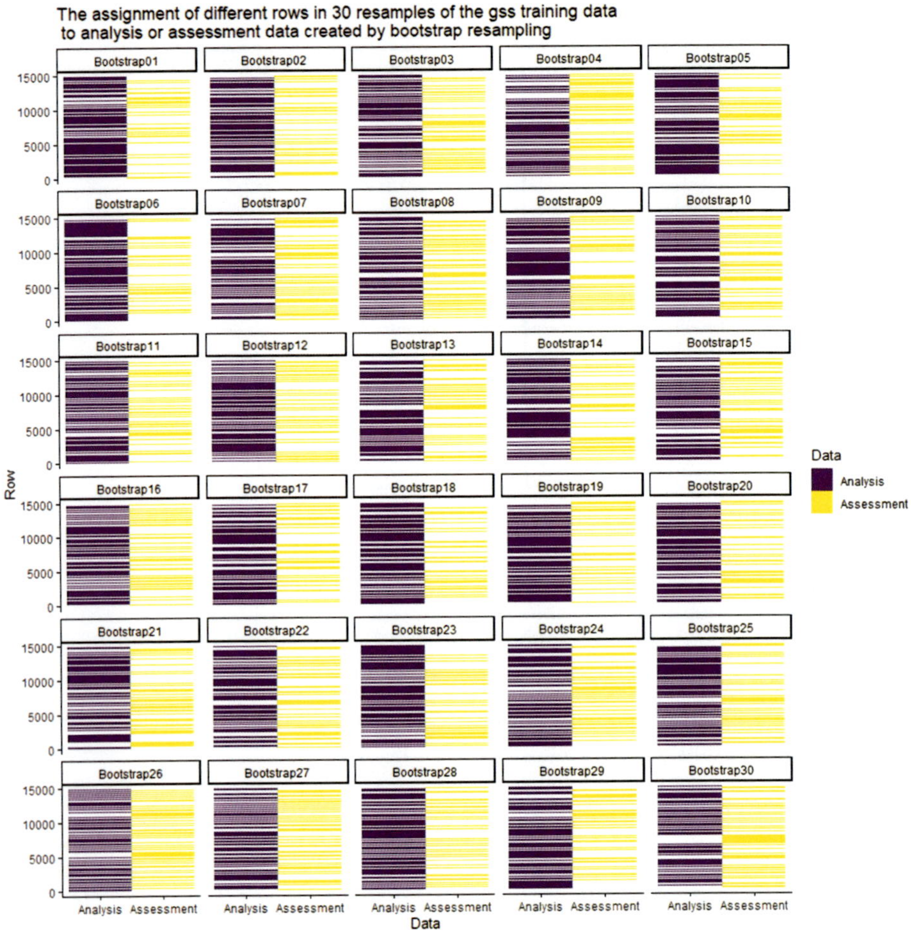

The heat map is overcrowded because we have 14853 rows in our training data. To get a less crowded plot, we can filter the data for the 1st 5 rows using the filter function with the argument Row <= 5 to get the row number equal to or less than 5 after the tidy function.

In addition, we add the argument color = "black" inside the geom_tile function to make the tiles with black borders and use the geom_text function to add text labels to each tile as described previously.

```
tidy(split_gss) %>% filter(Row <= 5) %>%
ggplot(aes(x = Data, y = Row, fill = Data))+
geom_tile(color = “black”)+ scale_fill_viridis_d()+ theme_
classic()+
geom_text(aes(label = Row), color = “white”)+
facet_wrap(vars(Resample), nrow = 6)+
labs(title = “The assignment of first 5 rows in 30 resamples of
the gss training data\n to analysis or assessment data created
by bootstrap resampling”)
```

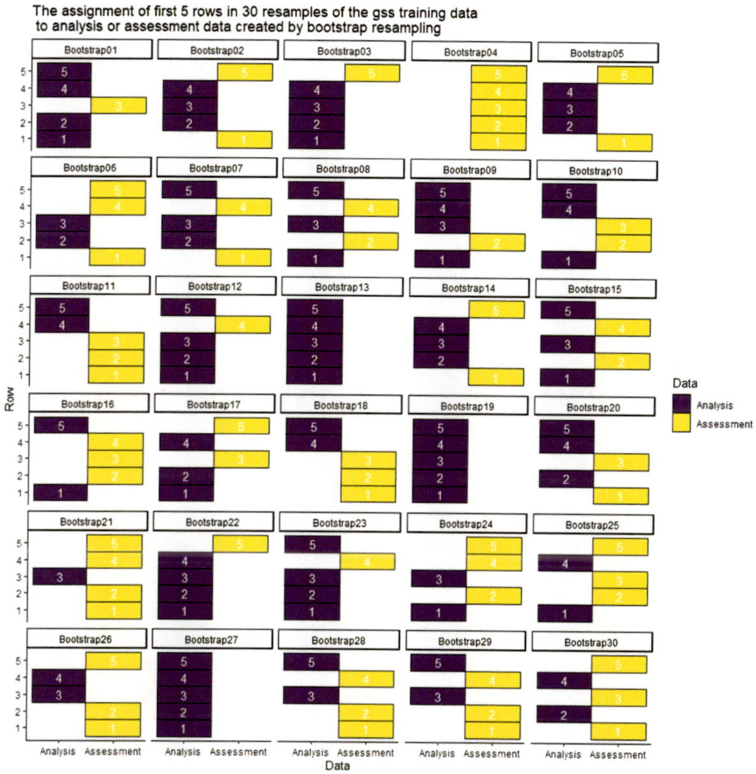

- There is no overlapping between the row numbers in the analysis and assessment data within each resample meaning that each row is either included in the analysis or assessment data within each resample.
- However, any row can be included in many assessment data across the 30 resamples. For example, row 5 is included in assessment data in resamples 2,3,4,5,6,14,17,21,23,22,24,25,26,30 and in analysis data in other resamples.

- For the row number 1, it is included in assessment data in resamples 2,4,5,6,7,11,14,18,20,21,26,28,29,30 and in analysis data in other resamples, and so on.

3.6.1.4. Fit a Linear Model to 30 Resamples of gss Training Data Created by Bootstrap Resampling

To fit a linear model on the analysis data and test the model on the assessment data of 30 resamples of gss data, we use the fit_resamples function with the same above arguments.

```
lm_res<- fit_resamples(linear_reg(mode = "regression",
engine = "lm"),
tvhours ~ age + marital+ rincome,
split_gss)
lm_res
## # Resampling results
## # Bootstrap sampling
## # A tibble: 30 × 4
## splits id .metrics .notes
## <list> <chr> <list> <list>
## 1 <split [14853/5475]> Bootstrap01 <tibble [2 × 4]> <tibble
[0 × 3]>
## 2 <split [14853/5489]> Bootstrap02 <tibble [2 × 4]> <tibble
[0 × 3]>
## 3 <split [14853/5425]> Bootstrap03 <tibble [2 × 4]> <tibble
[0 × 3]>
## 4 <split [14853/5494]> Bootstrap04 <tibble [2 × 4]> <tibble
[0 × 3]>
## 5 <split [14853/5476]> Bootstrap05 <tibble [2 × 4]> <tibble
[0 × 3]>
## 6 <split [14853/5456]> Bootstrap06 <tibble [2 × 4]> <tibble
[0 × 3]>
## 7 <split [14853/5514]> Bootstrap07 <tibble [2 × 4]> <tibble
[0 × 3]>
## 8 <split [14853/5528]> Bootstrap08 <tibble [2 × 4]> <tibble
[0 × 3]>
## 9 <split [14853/5451]> Bootstrap09 <tibble [2 × 4]> <tibble
```

```
[0 × 3]>
## 10 <split [14853/5433]> Bootstrap10 <tibble [2 × 4]> <tibble
[0 × 3]>
## # i 20 more rows
```

The resulting object "lm_res" contains the results of applying this linear model on these 30 rows or resamples of training data. It contains the same 4 columns described previously.

To extract the 30 performance metrics for each combination of analysis and assessment data, we use the collect_metrics function on the lm_res object.

```
lm_res %>% collect_metrics() %>% flextable() %>% theme_box() %>%
set_caption(caption = "The mean RMSE and R squared of linear
model on 30 different resamples of the gss training data created
by bootstrap resampling")
```

Table 3.42. The Mean RMSE and R Squared of Linear Model on 30 Different Resamples of the gss Training Data Created by Bootstrap Resampling

.metric	.estimator	mean	n	std_err	.config
rmse	standard	2.03161236	30	0.017999270	Preprocessor1_Model1
rsq	standard	0.04306977	30	0.001244463	Preprocessor1_Model1

- The default behavior of the collect_metrics function is to summarize all performance metrics (n = 30) into their mean.
- The default calculated performance metrics are:

  ++ RMSE or root mean squared error with a mean value of 2.03.

  ++ Rsq or R squared with a mean value of 0.043 or 4.3%.

- To get the 30 performance metrics, we use the argument summarize = FALSE inside the collect_metrics function.

```
lm_res %>% collect_metrics(summarize = FALSE) %>% flextable()
%>%
theme_box() %>%
set_caption(caption = "The RMSE and R squared of linear model
on 30 different resamples of the gss training data created by
bootstrap resampling")
```

Table 3.43. The RMSE and R Squared of Linear Model on 30 Different Resamples of the gss Training Data Created by Bootstrap Resampling

id	.metric	.estimator	.estimate	.config
Bootstrap01	rmse	standard	2.02258130	Preprocessor1_Model1
Bootstrap01	rsq	standard	0.03684989	Preprocessor1_Model1
Bootstrap02	rmse	standard	1.97860430	Preprocessor1_Model1
Bootstrap02	rsq	standard	0.03967312	Preprocessor1_Model1
Bootstrap03	rmse	standard	2.12868133	Preprocessor1_Model1
Bootstrap03	rsq	standard	0.04533577	Preprocessor1_Model1
Bootstrap04	rmse	standard	2.06675974	Preprocessor1_Model1
Bootstrap04	rsq	standard	0.04072081	Preprocessor1_Model1
Bootstrap05	rmse	standard	2.12698677	Preprocessor1_Model1
Bootstrap05	rsq	standard	0.03142727	Preprocessor1_Model1
Bootstrap06	rmse	standard	1.93369371	Preprocessor1_Model1
Bootstrap06	rsq	standard	0.03833225	Preprocessor1_Model1
Bootstrap07	rmse	standard	2.28385506	Preprocessor1_Model1
Bootstrap07	rsq	standard	0.04099340	Preprocessor1_Model1
Bootstrap08	rmse	standard	2.10619243	Preprocessor1_Model1
Bootstrap08	rsq	standard	0.04012732	Preprocessor1_Model1
Bootstrap09	rmse	standard	2.11152088	Preprocessor1_Model1
Bootstrap09	rsq	standard	0.05319314	Preprocessor1_Model1
Bootstrap10	rmse	standard	1.98910784	Preprocessor1_Model1
Bootstrap10	rsq	standard	0.03277756	Preprocessor1_Model1
Bootstrap11	rmse	standard	2.20115758	Preprocessor1_Model1
Bootstrap11	rsq	standard	0.04362039	Preprocessor1_Model1
Bootstrap12	rmse	standard	2.11372535	Preprocessor1_Model1
Bootstrap12	rsq	standard	0.03942784	Preprocessor1_Model1
Bootstrap13	rmse	standard	1.99238414	Preprocessor1_Model1
Bootstrap13	rsq	standard	0.04735793	Preprocessor1_Model1
Bootstrap14	rmse	standard	2.15293272	Preprocessor1_Model1
Bootstrap14	rsq	standard	0.05885152	Preprocessor1_Model1
Bootstrap15	rmse	standard	1.95843028	Preprocessor1_Model1
Bootstrap15	rsq	standard	0.04553474	Preprocessor1_Model1
Bootstrap16	rmse	standard	1.95034290	Preprocessor1_Model1
Bootstrap16	rsq	standard	0.03752766	Preprocessor1_Model1
Bootstrap17	rmse	standard	2.09686297	Preprocessor1_Model1
Bootstrap17	rsq	standard	0.04986956	Preprocessor1_Model1

Bootstrap18	rmse	standard	2.03262083	Preprocessor1_Model1
Bootstrap18	rsq	standard	0.04254728	Preprocessor1_Model1
Bootstrap19	rmse	standard	1.89127726	Preprocessor1_Model1
Bootstrap19	rsq	standard	0.03791871	Preprocessor1_Model1
Bootstrap20	rmse	standard	1.96049844	Preprocessor1_Model1
Bootstrap20	rsq	standard	0.04643221	Preprocessor1_Model1
Bootstrap21	rmse	standard	1.94086390	Preprocessor1_Model1
Bootstrap21	rsq	standard	0.03594852	Preprocessor1_Model1
Bootstrap22	rmse	standard	2.02984683	Preprocessor1_Model1
Bootstrap22	rsq	standard	0.04523399	Preprocessor1_Model1
Bootstrap23	rmse	standard	1.96791633	Preprocessor1_Model1
Bootstrap23	rsq	standard	0.04343987	Preprocessor1_Model1
Bootstrap24	rmse	standard	2.09485729	Preprocessor1_Model1
Bootstrap24	rsq	standard	0.04838527	Preprocessor1_Model1
Bootstrap25	rmse	standard	2.09991875	Preprocessor1_Model1
Bootstrap25	rsq	standard	0.04247386	Preprocessor1_Model1
Bootstrap26	rmse	standard	1.96792519	Preprocessor1_Model1
Bootstrap26	rsq	standard	0.04482190	Preprocessor1_Model1
Bootstrap27	rmse	standard	1.92357871	Preprocessor1_Model1
Bootstrap27	rsq	standard	0.03901239	Preprocessor1_Model1
Bootstrap28	rmse	standard	2.04677441	Preprocessor1_Model1
Bootstrap28	rsq	standard	0.05950044	Preprocessor1_Model1
Bootstrap29	rmse	standard	1.92138680	Preprocessor1_Model1
Bootstrap29	rsq	standard	0.03430604	Preprocessor1_Model1
Bootstrap30	rmse	standard	1.85708676	Preprocessor1_Model1
Bootstrap30	rsq	standard	0.05045249	Preprocessor1_Model1

- The resulting table has 60 rows because each resample has 2 rows for RMSE and R squared.

To get the common summary statistics of RMSE and R squared across the 30 resamples of training data, we use the following functions after the collect_metrics function:

- The group_by function with the .metric argument splits the 60 rows of data into 2 data with 30 rows each, one for RMSE and one for R squared.
- The get_summary_stats function with the arguments:

  ++ .estimate to get the summary statistics of the .estimate column.

++ type = "common" to get the common summary statistics of the .estimate column.

Then, we convert the result to a table as discussed in previous chapters.

```
lm_res %>% collect_metrics(summarize = FALSE) %>% group_by(.
metric) %>%
get_summary_stats(.estimate, type = "common") %>%
flextable() %>% theme_box() %>%
set_caption(caption = "The common summary statistics of RMSE
and R squared across the 30 resamples of the gss training data
created by bootstrap resampling")
```

Table 3.44. The Common Summary Statistics of RMSE and R Squared Across the 30 Resamples of the gss Training Data Created by Bootstrap Resampling

.metric	variable	n	min	max	median	iqr	mean	sd	se	ci
rmse	.estimate	30	1.857	2.284	2.026	0.146	2.032	0.099	0.018	0.037
rsq	.estimate	30	0.031	0.060	0.043	0.008	0.043	0.007	0.001	0.003

We see that:

- n = 30 because we have 30 resamples of training data.
- The minimum RMSE = 1.857 and maximum RMSE = 2.284.
- The minimum R squared = 0.031 or 3.1% and the maximum R squared = 0.060 or 6.0%.
- The mean RMSE and R squared value are the same as calculated by the collect_metrics function.

3.6.1.5. Plot the Performance Metrics of the Linear Model on 30 Resamples of gss Training Data Created by Bootstrap Resampling

- We can also plot the different RMSE and R squared values for the 30 resamples using the same functions after the collect_metrics function.

```
lm_res %>% collect_metrics(summarize = FALSE) %>%
ggplot(aes(x = id, y = .estimate, color = .metric))+
geom_point()+ geom_line(aes(group = .metric))+
```

```
facet_wrap(vars(.metric), scales = "free", nrow = 2)+
labs(title = "The RMSE and R squared of linear model on 30 different resamples \nof the gss training data created by bootstrap resampling",
x = "Resample", y = "Performance metric",
color = "Performance metric")+
theme_classic()+
theme(axis.text.x = element_text(angle = 60, hjust = 1))
```

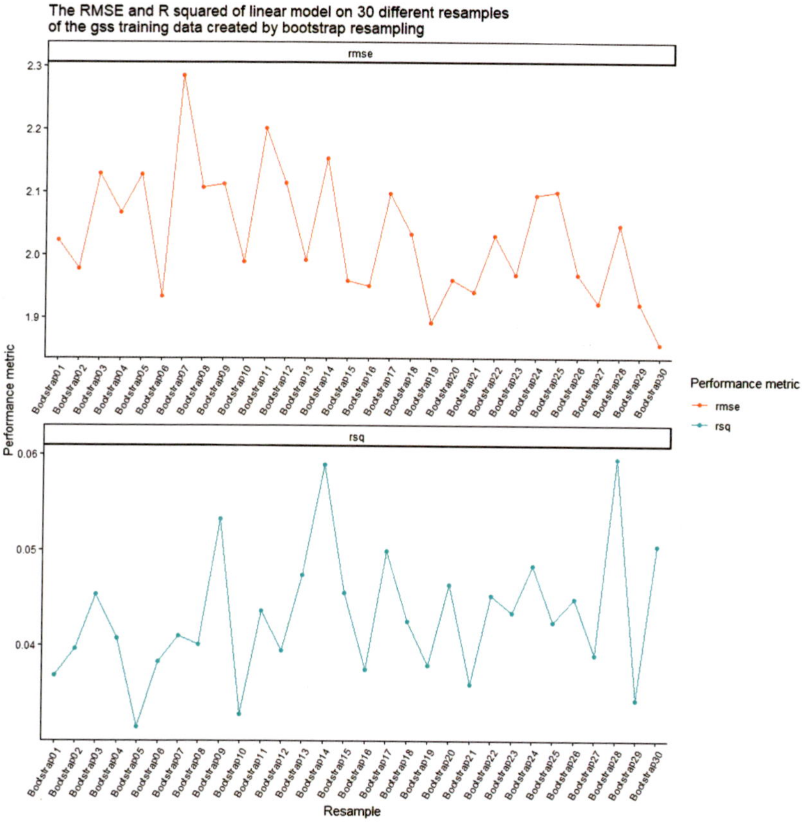

We see that:

- The lowest (best) RMSE value was for resample 30 (1.86).
- The highest (best) R squared was for resample 28 (0.0595).
- The highest (worst) RMSE value was for resample 7 (2.28).
- The lowest (worst) R squared value was for resample 5 (0.0314).

3.6.2. Bootstrap Resampling of BRFSS Training Data

3.6.2.1. Producing 30 Resamples of BRFSS Training Data

We can also use the bootstraps function as before with the argument times = 30 to make 30 different resamples.

- We also use the set.seed function to make the splitting reproducible.
- We will use train_brfss2 training data because this is the data that contains the sex column as a factor.

```
set.seed(123)
split_brfss<-bootstraps(train_brfss2, times = 30)
split_brfss
## # Bootstrap sampling
## # A tibble: 30 × 2
## splits id
## <list> <chr>
## 1 <split [168/63]> Bootstrap01
## 2 <split [168/62]> Bootstrap02
## 3 <split [168/61]> Bootstrap03
## 4 <split [168/61]> Bootstrap04
## 5 <split [168/60]> Bootstrap05
## 6 <split [168/58]> Bootstrap06
## 7 <split [168/63]> Bootstrap07
## 8 <split [168/60]> Bootstrap08
## 9 <split [168/71]> Bootstrap09
## 10 <split [168/60]> Bootstrap10
## # i 20 more rows
```

We see that:

- We have 30 different rows. Each row corresponds to 1 resample of training data.
- Each row has total rows of 168 rows (same rows of training data) and different number rows for the assessment and analysis data.
- For example, the 1st resample has 63 rows in assessment data and so 168 – 63 = 105 rows in the analysis data.
- In the 2nd resample, there are 62 rows in assessment data and so 168 – 62 = 106 rows in the analysis data, and so on.

3.6.2.2. Exploring 30 Resamples of BRFSS Training Data Created by Bootstrap Resampling

- We can use the tidy function on the split_brfss object to detect which row is for analysis data and which row is for the assessment data within each resample.

```
tidy(split_brfss)
## # A tibble: 5,040 × 3
## Row Data Resample
## <int> <chr> <chr>
## 1 1 Analysis Bootstrap01
## 2 1 Analysis Bootstrap07
## 3 1 Analysis Bootstrap08
## 4 1 Analysis Bootstrap12
## 5 1 Analysis Bootstrap13
## 6 1 Analysis Bootstrap15
## 7 1 Analysis Bootstrap16
## 8 1 Analysis Bootstrap18
## 9 1 Analysis Bootstrap19
## 10 1 Analysis Bootstrap20
## # i 5,030 more rows
```

- The resulting data is 5,040 rows because we have 30 resamples of training data with 168 rows. 168 × 30 = 5040.
- We have 3 columns:

  ++ The Row column which is the row number from 1 to 168.

  ++ The Data column which is a character column for the analysis data (training data) or assessment (testing) data.

  ++ The Resample column which is for the resample number from 1 to 30.
- We can filter for row number 1 to see in which resample it was included in the assessment or analysis data using the filter function with the argument Row==1.

```
tidy(split_brfss) %>% filter(Row==1) %>% flextable() %>% theme_
box() %>%
```

```
set_caption(caption = "The assignment of 1st row to analysis or assessment data within 30 resamples of BRFSS training data created by bootstrap resampling")
```

Table 3.45. The Assignment of 1st Row to Analysis or Assessment Data Within 30 Resamples of BRFSS Training Data Created by Bootstrap Resampling

Row	Data	Resample
1	Analysis	Bootstrap01
1	Analysis	Bootstrap07
1	Analysis	Bootstrap08
1	Analysis	Bootstrap12
1	Analysis	Bootstrap13
1	Analysis	Bootstrap15
1	Analysis	Bootstrap16
1	Analysis	Bootstrap18
1	Analysis	Bootstrap19
1	Analysis	Bootstrap20
1	Analysis	Bootstrap21
1	Analysis	Bootstrap24
1	Analysis	Bootstrap25
1	Analysis	Bootstrap26
1	Analysis	Bootstrap27
1	Analysis	Bootstrap28
1	Analysis	Bootstrap29
1	Assessment	Bootstrap02
1	Assessment	Bootstrap03
1	Assessment	Bootstrap04
1	Assessment	Bootstrap05
1	Assessment	Bootstrap06
1	Assessment	Bootstrap09
1	Assessment	Bootstrap10
1	Assessment	Bootstrap11
1	Assessment	Bootstrap14
1	Assessment	Bootstrap17
1	Assessment	Bootstrap22
1	Assessment	Bootstrap23
1	Assessment	Bootstrap30

- Row 1 is included in the analysis (training) data in resamples 1,7,8, 12,13,15,16,18,19,20,21,24,25,26,27,28,29 and so is included in the assessment (testing) data in resamples 2,3,4,5,6,9,10,11,14,17,22,2 3,30.
- By using the count function with the Data and Resample argument after the tidy function, we can see how many rows were for the training data and how many rows were for the testing data in each resample.
- We arrange the result by resample number.

```
tidy(split_brfss) %>% count(Data,Resample) %>% arrange(Resample)
%>%
flextable() %>% theme_box() %>%
set_caption(caption = "The number of rows in the training
and testing data of 30 resamples of the BRFSS data created by
bootstrap resampling")
```

Table 3.46. The Number of Rows in the Training and Testing Data of 30 Resamples of the BRFSS Data Created by Bootstrap Resampling

Data	Resample	n
Analysis	Bootstrap01	105
Assessment	Bootstrap01	63
Analysis	Bootstrap02	106
Assessment	Bootstrap02	62
Analysis	Bootstrap03	107
Assessment	Bootstrap03	61
Analysis	Bootstrap04	107
Assessment	Bootstrap04	61
Analysis	Bootstrap05	108
Assessment	Bootstrap05	60
Analysis	Bootstrap06	110
Assessment	Bootstrap06	58
Analysis	Bootstrap07	105
Assessment	Bootstrap07	63
Analysis	Bootstrap08	108
Assessment	Bootstrap08	60
Analysis	Bootstrap09	97

Assessment	Bootstrap09	71
Analysis	Bootstrap10	108
Assessment	Bootstrap10	60
Analysis	Bootstrap11	104
Assessment	Bootstrap11	64
Analysis	Bootstrap12	109
Assessment	Bootstrap12	59
Analysis	Bootstrap13	105
Assessment	Bootstrap13	63
Analysis	Bootstrap14	108
Assessment	Bootstrap14	60
Analysis	Bootstrap15	112
Assessment	Bootstrap15	56
Analysis	Bootstrap16	108
Assessment	Bootstrap16	60
Analysis	Bootstrap17	101
Assessment	Bootstrap17	67
Analysis	Bootstrap18	105
Assessment	Bootstrap18	63
Analysis	Bootstrap19	104
Assessment	Bootstrap19	64
Analysis	Bootstrap20	107
Assessment	Bootstrap20	61
Analysis	Bootstrap21	111
Assessment	Bootstrap21	57
Analysis	Bootstrap22	114
Assessment	Bootstrap22	54
Analysis	Bootstrap23	109
Assessment	Bootstrap23	59
Analysis	Bootstrap24	104
Assessment	Bootstrap24	64
Analysis	Bootstrap25	106
Assessment	Bootstrap25	62
Analysis	Bootstrap26	112
Assessment	Bootstrap26	56
Analysis	Bootstrap27	107

Assessment	Bootstrap27	61
Analysis	Bootstrap28	109
Assessment	Bootstrap28	59
Analysis	Bootstrap29	105
Assessment	Bootstrap29	63
Analysis	Bootstrap30	103
Assessment	Bootstrap30	65

- In all resamples, the number of rows in total data is 168 rows.
- Every resample has different number of rows in the analysis and assessment data.
- In the 1st resample, the number of rows in analysis data is 105 rows and in assessment data is 63.
- In the 2nd resample, the number of rows in analysis data is 106 rows and in assessment data is 62.
- In the 3rd resample, the number of rows in analysis data is 107 rows and in assessment data is 61, and so on.

3.6.2.3. Plotting 30 Resamples of BRFSS Training Data Created by Bootstrap Resampling

We can also plot which row was for the training data and which was for the testing data as a heat map within each resample by using the previously described functions.

However, we will use nrow = 6 within facet_wrap function to make all 30 graphs in 6 rows.

```
tidy(split_brfss) %>% ggplot(aes(x = Data, y = Row, fill =
Data))+
geom_tile()+ scale_fill_viridis_d()+ theme_classic()+
facet_wrap(vars(Resample), nrow = 6)+
labs(title = "The assignment of different rows in 30 resamples of
the BRFSS training data\n to analysis or assessment data created
by bootstrap resampling")
```

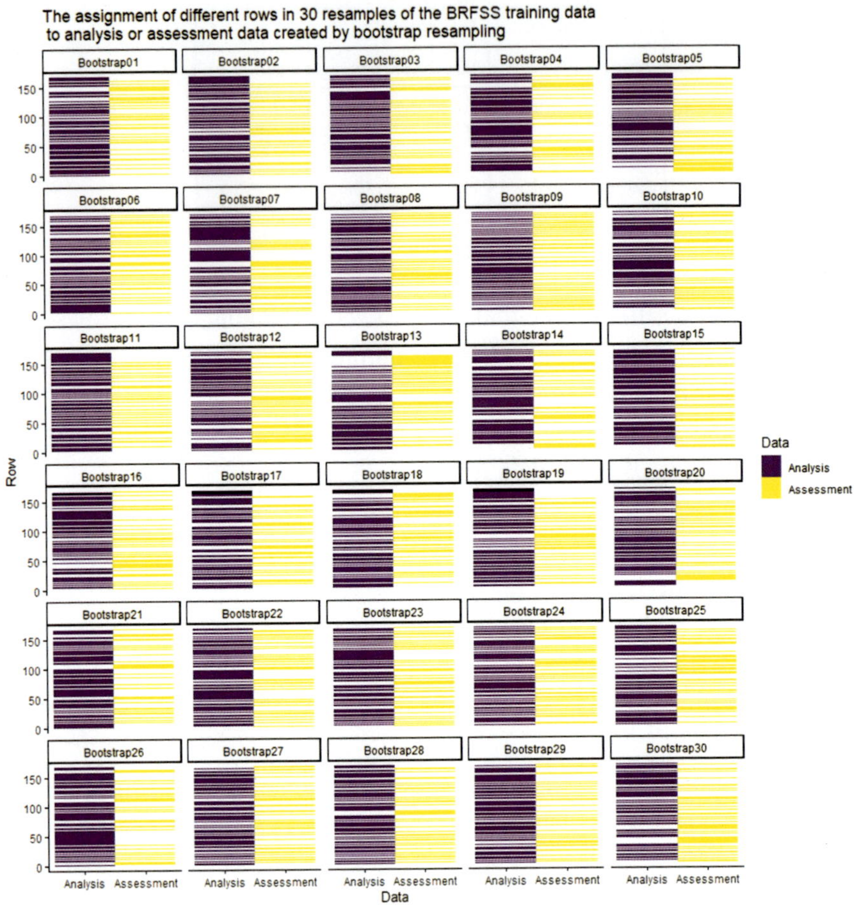

The heat map is overcrowded because we have 168 rows in our training data. To get a less crowded plot, we can filter the data for the 1st 5 rows using the filter function with the argument Row <= 5 to get the row number equal to or less than 5 after the tidy function.

In addition, we add the argument color = "black" inside the geom_tile function to make the tiles with black borders and use the geom_text function to add text labels to each tile as described previously.

```
tidy(split_brfss) %>% filter(Row <= 5) %>%
ggplot(aes(x = Data, y = Row, fill = Data))+
geom_tile(color = "black")+ scale_fill_viridis_d()+ theme_
classic()+
geom_text(aes(label = Row), color = "white")+
```

```
facet_wrap(vars(Resample), nrow = 6)+
labs(title = "The assignment of first 5 rows in 30 resamples of the BRFSS training data\n to analysis or assessment data created by bootstrap resampling")
```

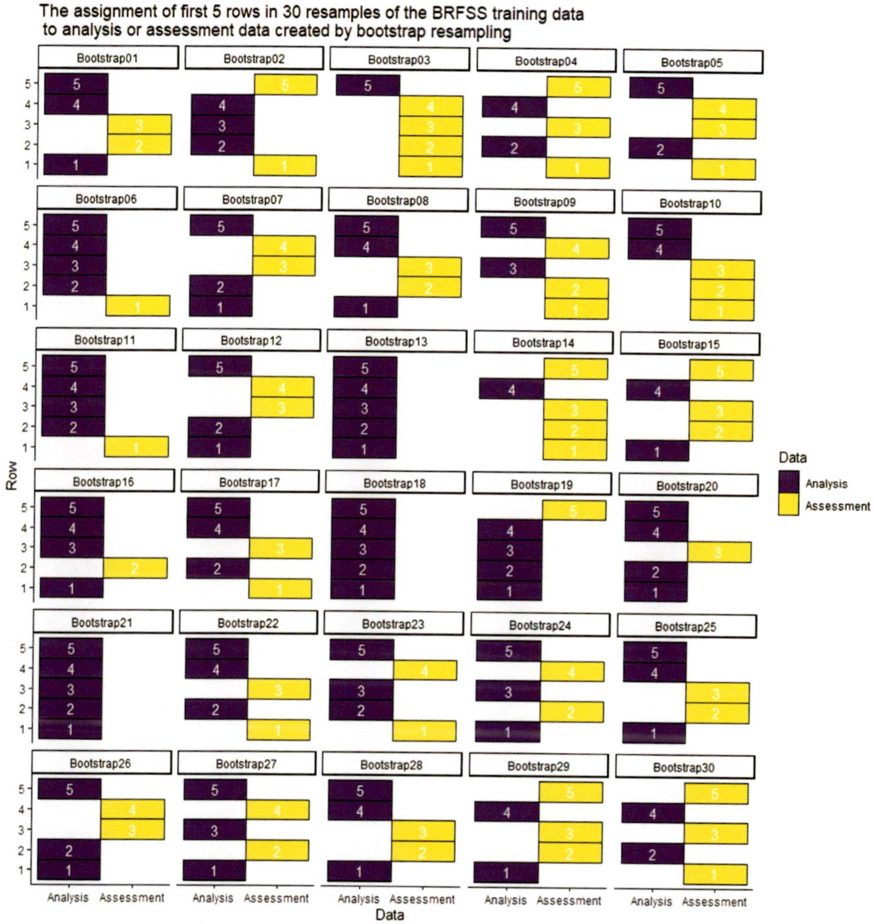

- There is no overlapping between the row numbers in the analysis and assessment data within each resample meaning that each row is either included in the analysis or assessment data within each resample.
- However, any row can be included in many assessment data across the 30 resamples. For example, the row 5 is included in assessment data in resamples 2,4,14,15,19,29,30 and in analysis data in other resamples.

3.6.2.4. Fit a Tree Model to 30 Resamples of BRFSS Training Data Created by Bootstrap Resampling

- To fit a decision tree model on the analysis data and test the model on the assessment data of 30 resamples of BRFSS data, we use the fit_resamples function with the same above arguments in section 3.4.2.9.

```
tree_res<- fit_resamples(decision_tree(mode = "classification",
engine = "rpart"),
sex ~ weight_lbs+ height_inch+income,
split_brfss)
tree_res
## # Resampling results
## # Bootstrap sampling
## # A tibble: 30 × 4
## splits id .metrics .notes
## <list> <chr> <list> <list>
## 1 <split [168/63]> Bootstrap01 <tibble [2 × 4]> <tibble [0 ×
3]>
## 2 <split [168/62]> Bootstrap02 <tibble [2 × 4]> <tibble [0 ×
3]>
## 3 <split [168/61]> Bootstrap03 <tibble [2 × 4]> <tibble [0 ×
3]>
## 4 <split [168/61]> Bootstrap04 <tibble [2 × 4]> <tibble [0 ×
3]>
## 5 <split [168/60]> Bootstrap05 <tibble [2 × 4]> <tibble [0 ×
3]>
## 6 <split [168/58]> Bootstrap06 <tibble [2 × 4]> <tibble [0 ×
3]>
## 7 <split [168/63]> Bootstrap07 <tibble [2 × 4]> <tibble [0 ×
3]>
## 8 <split [168/60]> Bootstrap08 <tibble [2 × 4]> <tibble [0 ×
3]>
## 9 <split [168/71]> Bootstrap09 <tibble [2 × 4]> <tibble [0 ×
3]>
## 10 <split [168/60]> Bootstrap10 <tibble [2 × 4]> <tibble [0
× 3]>
```

```
## # i 20 more rows
```

The resulting object "tree_res" contains the results of applying this tree model on these 30 rows or resamples of training data. It contains the same 4 columns described previously.

To extract the 30 performance metrics for each combination of analysis and assessment data, we use the collect_metrics function.

```
tree_res %>% collect_metrics() %>% flextable() %>% theme_box()
%>%
set_caption(caption = "The mean accuracy and ROC AUC of tree
model on 30 different resamples of the BRFSS training data
created by bootstrap resampling")
```

Table 3.47. The Mean Accuracy and ROC AUC of Tree Model on 30 Different Resamples of the BRFSS Training Data Created by Bootstrap Resampling

.metric	.estimator	mean	n	std_err	.config
accuracy	binary	0.7950424	30	0.008799319	Preprocessor1_Model1
roc_auc	binary	0.8375388	30	0.007280063	Preprocessor1_Model1

- We have n = 30 because we have 30 resamples of training data.
- The mean accuracy = 0.795 or 79.5%.
- The mean ROC AUC = 0.838 or 83.8%.
- To get the 30 performance metrics, we use the argument summarize = FALSE inside the collect_metrics function.

```
tree_res %>% collect_metrics(summarize = FALSE) %>% flextable()
%>%
theme_box() %>%
set_caption(caption = "The accuracy and ROC AUC of tree model
on 30 different resamples of the BRFSS training data created by
bootstrap resampling")
```

Table 3.48. The Accuracy and ROC AUC of Tree Model on 30 Different Resamples of the BRFSS Training Data Created by Bootstrap Resampling

id	.metric	.estimator	.estimate	.config
Bootstrap01	accuracy	binary	0.8571429	Preprocessor1_Model1

Bootstrap01	roc_auc	binary	0.8494565	Preprocessor1_Model1
Bootstrap02	accuracy	binary	0.8064516	Preprocessor1_Model1
Bootstrap02	roc_auc	binary	0.8969298	Preprocessor1_Model1
Bootstrap03	accuracy	binary	0.8524590	Preprocessor1_Model1
Bootstrap03	roc_auc	binary	0.8310023	Preprocessor1_Model1
Bootstrap04	accuracy	binary	0.8688525	Preprocessor1_Model1
Bootstrap04	roc_auc	binary	0.8094966	Preprocessor1_Model1
Bootstrap05	accuracy	binary	0.7500000	Preprocessor1_Model1
Bootstrap05	roc_auc	binary	0.8645833	Preprocessor1_Model1
Bootstrap06	accuracy	binary	0.7068966	Preprocessor1_Model1
Bootstrap06	roc_auc	binary	0.8188131	Preprocessor1_Model1
Bootstrap07	accuracy	binary	0.8571429	Preprocessor1_Model1
Bootstrap07	roc_auc	binary	0.8840812	Preprocessor1_Model1
Bootstrap08	accuracy	binary	0.8333333	Preprocessor1_Model1
Bootstrap08	roc_auc	binary	0.8400000	Preprocessor1_Model1
Bootstrap09	accuracy	binary	0.7887324	Preprocessor1_Model1
Bootstrap09	roc_auc	binary	0.8559113	Preprocessor1_Model1
Bootstrap10	accuracy	binary	0.8333333	Preprocessor1_Model1
Bootstrap10	roc_auc	binary	0.8303694	Preprocessor1_Model1
Bootstrap11	accuracy	binary	0.6875000	Preprocessor1_Model1
Bootstrap11	roc_auc	binary	0.8479167	Preprocessor1_Model1
Bootstrap12	accuracy	binary	0.7288136	Preprocessor1_Model1
Bootstrap12	roc_auc	binary	0.8652941	Preprocessor1_Model1
Bootstrap13	accuracy	binary	0.7777778	Preprocessor1_Model1
Bootstrap13	roc_auc	binary	0.8279915	Preprocessor1_Model1
Bootstrap14	accuracy	binary	0.7833333	Preprocessor1_Model1
Bootstrap14	roc_auc	binary	0.8868750	Preprocessor1_Model1
Bootstrap15	accuracy	binary	0.8214286	Preprocessor1_Model1
Bootstrap15	roc_auc	binary	0.7909677	Preprocessor1_Model1
Bootstrap16	accuracy	binary	0.7333333	Preprocessor1_Model1
Bootstrap16	roc_auc	binary	0.8110048	Preprocessor1_Model1
Bootstrap17	accuracy	binary	0.8358209	Preprocessor1_Model1
Bootstrap17	roc_auc	binary	0.8528571	Preprocessor1_Model1
Bootstrap18	accuracy	binary	0.7777778	Preprocessor1_Model1
Bootstrap18	roc_auc	binary	0.8442105	Preprocessor1_Model1
Bootstrap19	accuracy	binary	0.8125000	Preprocessor1_Model1
Bootstrap19	roc_auc	binary	0.8215385	Preprocessor1_Model1

Bootstrap20	accuracy	binary	0.7868852	Preprocessor1_Model1
Bootstrap20	roc_auc	binary	0.7837529	Preprocessor1_Model1
Bootstrap21	accuracy	binary	0.7894737	Preprocessor1_Model1
Bootstrap21	roc_auc	binary	0.7804054	Preprocessor1_Model1
Bootstrap22	accuracy	binary	0.7592593	Preprocessor1_Model1
Bootstrap22	roc_auc	binary	0.8856908	Preprocessor1_Model1
Bootstrap23	accuracy	binary	0.8305085	Preprocessor1_Model1
Bootstrap23	roc_auc	binary	0.8654762	Preprocessor1_Model1
Bootstrap24	accuracy	binary	0.7656250	Preprocessor1_Model1
Bootstrap24	roc_auc	binary	0.7051962	Preprocessor1_Model1
Bootstrap25	accuracy	binary	0.8709677	Preprocessor1_Model1
Bootstrap25	roc_auc	binary	0.8653409	Preprocessor1_Model1
Bootstrap26	accuracy	binary	0.8392857	Preprocessor1_Model1
Bootstrap26	roc_auc	binary	0.8673469	Preprocessor1_Model1
Bootstrap27	accuracy	binary	0.8032787	Preprocessor1_Model1
Bootstrap27	roc_auc	binary	0.8085586	Preprocessor1_Model1
Bootstrap28	accuracy	binary	0.7627119	Preprocessor1_Model1
Bootstrap28	roc_auc	binary	0.8291667	Preprocessor1_Model1
Bootstrap29	accuracy	binary	0.7460317	Preprocessor1_Model1
Bootstrap29	roc_auc	binary	0.8270975	Preprocessor1_Model1
Bootstrap30	accuracy	binary	0.7846154	Preprocessor1_Model1
Bootstrap30	roc_auc	binary	0.8788314	Preprocessor1_Model1

- The resulting table has 60 rows because each resample has 2 rows for accuracy and ROC AUC.
- To get the common summary statistics of accuracy and ROC AUC across the 30 resamples of training data, we use the same above functions.

```
tree_res %>% collect_metrics(summarize = FALSE) %>% group_by(.
metric) %>%
get_summary_stats(.estimate, type = "common") %>%
flextable() %>% theme_box() %>%
set_caption(caption = "The common summary statistics of accuracy
and ROC AUC across the 30 resamples of the BRFSS training data
created by bootstrap resampling")
```

Table 3.49. The Common Summary Statistics of Accuracy and ROC AUC Across the 30 Resamples of the BRFSS Training Data Created by Bootstrap Resampling

.metric	variable	n	min	max	median	iqr	mean	sd	se	ci
accuracy	.estimate	30	0.688	0.871	0.789	0.070	0.795	0.048	0.009	0.018
roc_auc	.estimate	30	0.705	0.897	0.842	0.046	0.838	0.040	0.007	0.015

We see that:

- n = 30 because we have 30 resamples of training data.
- The minimum accuracy = 0.688 or 68.8% and the maximum accuracy = 0.871 or 87.1%.
- The minimum ROC AUC = 0.705 and the maximum ROC AUC = 0.897.
- The mean accuracy and ROC AUC value are the same as that calculated by the collect_metrics function.

3.6.2.5. Plot the Performance Metrics of the Tree Model on 30 Resamples of BRFSS Data

We can plot the different accuracy and ROC AUC values for the 30 resamples using the following functions after the collect_metrics function:

- The ggplot function with the argument aes(x = id, y = .estimate, color = .metric) to plot id on x-axis, .estimate value on y-axis, and coloring by the .metric type (accuracy or ROC AUC).
- The geom_point function to plot a scatter plot of points.
- The geom_line with the argument aes(group = .metric) to plot a separate line for each performance metric (accuracy or ROC AUC).
- The facet_wrap function with the arguments:

  ++ vars(.metric) to plot a separate plot for each metric.

  ++ scales = "free" so each plot has its own x and y-axis values.

  ++ nrow = 2 to make the 2 plots in 2 rows.
- The labs function with the title argument to add a plot title, the x argument to add an x-axis title, the y argument to add a y-axis title, and the color argument to add a legend title.
- The theme_classic function to remove the grey background and the white grid lines of the default plot created using ggplot function.

- The theme function with the argument axis.text.x = element_text(angle = 60, hjust = 1) to make the x-axis text inclined at 60 with 1 horizontal justification.

```
tree_res %>% collect_metrics(summarize = FALSE) %>%
ggplot(aes(x = id, y = .estimate, color = .metric))+
geom_point()+ geom_line(aes(group = .metric))+
facet_wrap(vars(.metric), scales = "free", nrow = 2)+
labs(title = "The accuracy and ROC AUC of tree model on 30 different resamples of the BRFSS training data\n created by bootstrap resampling",
x = "Resample", y = "Performance metric",
color = "Performance metric")+
theme_classic()+
theme(axis.text.x = element_text(angle = 60, hjust = 1))
```

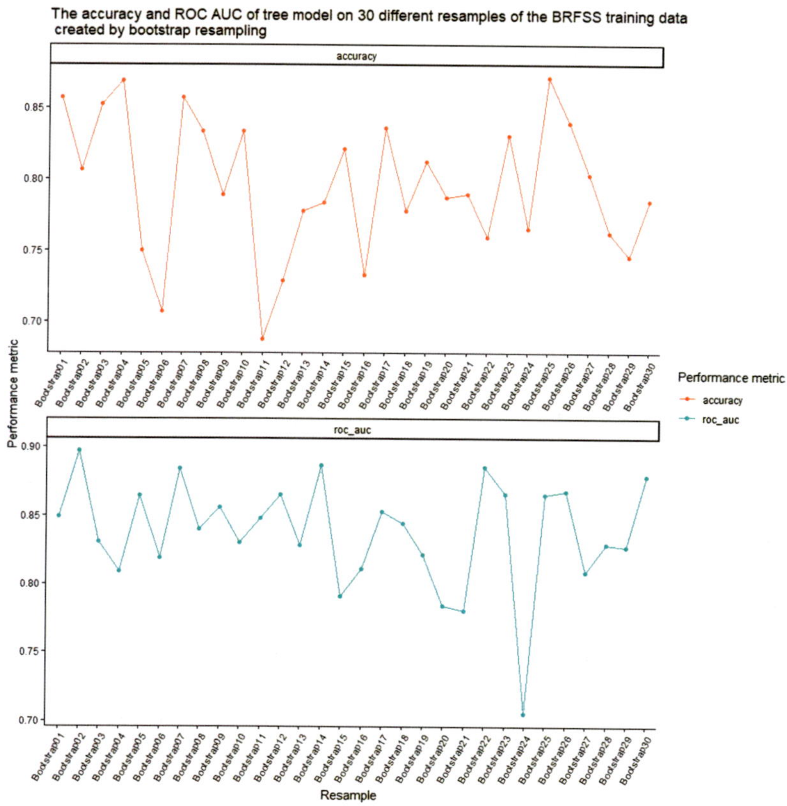

We see that:

- The highest (best) accuracy value was for resample 25 (0.871 or 87.1%).
- The highest (best) ROC AUC was for resample 2 (0.897).
- The lowest (worst) accuracy was for resample 11 (0.688 or 68.8%).

The lowest (worst) ROC AUC was for resample 24 (0.705).

Bibliography

1. Arthur, S. (1959). Some studies in machine learning using the game of checkers. *IBM Journal*, *3*(3), 210–229. http://ieeexplore.ieee.org/xpl/freeabs_all.jsp?arnumber=5389202 (accessed on 4th October 2024).
2. Firke, S. (2021). *janitor: Simple tools for examining and cleaning dirty data* (Version 2.1.0) [R package]. https://CRAN.R-project.org/package=janitor (accessed on 4th October 2024).
3. Gohel, D. (2022). *flextable: Functions for tabular reporting* (Version 0.7.0) [R package]. https://CRAN.R-project.org/package=flextable (accessed on 4th October 2024).
4. Grolemund, G., & Wickham, H. (2011). Dates and times made easy with lubridate. *Journal of Statistical Software*, *40*(3), 1-25. https://www.jstatsoft.org/v40/i03/ (accessed on 4th October 2024).
5. Kassambara, A. (2019). *datarium: Data bank for statistical analysis and visualization* (Version 0.1.0) [R package]. https://CRAN.R-project.org/package=datarium (accessed on 4th October 2024).
6. Kassambara, A. (2022). *rstatix: Pipe-friendly framework for basic statistical tests* (Version 0.7.1) [R package]. https://CRAN.R-project.org/package=rstatix (accessed on 4th October 2024).
7. Kuhn, M., Vaughan, D., & Hvitfeldt, E. (2023). *yardstick: Tidy characterizations of model performance* (Version 1.2.0) [R package]. https://CRAN.R-project.org/package=yardstick (accessed on 4th October 2024).
8. Kuhn, M., Wickham, H., & others. (2020). Tidymodels: A collection of packages for modeling and machine learning using tidyverse principles. https://www.tidymodels.org (accessed on 4th October 2024).

9. Mitchell, T. (1997). *Machine learning*. McGraw Hill.

10. R Core Team. (2022). *R: A language and environment for statistical computing*. R Foundation for Statistical Computing. https://www.R-project.org/ (accessed on 4th October 2024).

11. Therneau, T., & Atkinson, B. (2022). *rpart: Recursive partitioning and regression trees* (Version 4.1.16) [R package]. https://CRAN.R-project.org/package=rpart (accessed on 4th October 2024).

12. Tierney, N., Cook, D., McBain, M., & Fay, C. (2021). *Naniar: Data structures, summaries, and visualisations for missing data* (Version 0.6.1) [R package]. https://CRAN.R-project.org/package=naniar (accessed on 4th October 2024).

13. Wickham, H. (2020). *Modelr: Modelling functions that work with the pipe* (Version 0.1.8) [R package]. https://CRAN.R-project.org/package=modelr (accessed on 4th October 2024).

14. Wickham, H., Averick, M., Bryan, J., Chang, W., McGowan, L., François, R., Grolemund, G., Hayes, A., Henry, L., Hester, J., Kuhn, M., Pedersen, T. L., Miller, E., Bache, S. M., Müller, K., Ooms, J., Robinson, D., Seidel, D. P., Spinu, V., Takahashi, K., Vaughan, D., Wilke, C., Woo, K., & Yutani, H. (2019). Welcome to the tidyverse. *Journal of Open Source Software*, *4*(43), 1686. https://doi.org/10.21105/joss.01686 (accessed on 4th October 2024).

INDEX

D

E

F

G

H

S

T